ESSAYS ON EPHESIANS

Essays on Ephesians

Ernest Best

T&T CLARK
EDINBURGH

T&T CLARK LTD
59 GEORGE STREET
EDINBURGH EH2 2LQ
SCOTLAND

First published 1997

ISBN 0 567 08566 X

British Library Cataloguing-in-Publication Data
A catalogue record for this book is available from the British Library

Typeset by Fakenham Photosetting Limited, Fakenham, Norfolk
Printed and bound in Great Britain by MPG Books Ltd, Bodmin, Cornwall

To my Wife

Contents

Introduction

All these essays were written while I was preparing my commentary on Ephesians for the International Critical Commentary series (T. & T. Clark, Edinburgh, 1997). They explore some areas in greater depth than was possible in the commentary if it was to be kept within reasonable length in one volume. They appear as originally published with only the most necessary corrections. In respect of one major critical question my views changed during the time these articles were being written while I was working on the commentary. Like most scholars I began from the position that the author of Ephesians had used Colossians; as my work progressed I was forced to reject this and instead envisage the authors of Ephesians and Colossians as members of a continuing Pauline school and as mutually influencing one another. I have not however gone back and altered the earlier articles to conform with this position.

Most of these essays were written to honour other scholars and are not always readily accessible; I hope their collection here will then be of assistance to those studying Ephesians and preserve them from unnecessary journeys to, and search in, libraries. Three articles have not been reproduced. (i) 'Recipients and title of the Letter to the Ephesians: Why and When the Designation "Ephesians"?' *ANRW* II 25.4, pp. 3246–79. In this I explored the reasons why a letter lacking a destination came to acquire Ephesus as such; the results of my investigation were largely negative. (ii) My article on the relationship of Ephesians and Colossians, 'Who Used Whom', has not yet appeared in *New Testament Studies.* (iii) My article on Eph. 1.3, 'Fashions in Exegesis: Ephesians 1:3', originally published in the Festschrift for Anthony Tyrell Hanson, *Scripture: Meaning and Method* (ed. B. T. Thompson, Hull University Press, 1987, pp. 79–91) has already been reprinted in my collection *Interpreting Christ* (T. & T. Clark, Edinburgh, 1993, pp. 160–77).

I am grateful to those publishers and editors who have permitted the reprinting of the present essays.

Acknowledgements

Thanks are due to the following for permission to reproduce the essays in this volume:

Cambridge University Press in respect of 'Ephesians i.1', *Text and Interpretation: Studies in the New Testament presented to Matthew Black*, ed. E. Best and R. McL. Wilson (Cambridge, 1979), pp. 29–41. SPCK in respect of 'Ephesians 1.1 Again', *Paul and Paulinism, Essays in honour of C. K. Barrett*, ed. M. D. Hooker and S. G. Wilson (London, 1982), pp. 273–9.

Sheffield Academic Press in respect of 'Paul's Apostolic Authority—?', *Journal for the Study of the New Testament* 27 (1986), pp. 3–25; 'Dead in Trespasses and Sins (Eph. 2.1)', *Journal for the Study of the New Testament* 13 (1981), pp. 9–25, an issue in honour of Anthony T. Hanson; 'The Use of Credal and Liturgical Material in Ephesians', *Worship, Theology and Ministry in the Early Church. Essays in Honor of Ralph Martin*, ed. Michael J. Wilkins and Terence Paige (Sheffield, 1992), pp. 53–69; 'Ephesians 2.11–22; A Christian View of Judaism', *Text as Pretext. Essays in Honour of Robert Davidson*, ed. Robert P. Carroll (Sheffield, 1992), pp. 47–60.

Oxford University Press and *The Journal of Theological Studies* in respect of 'The Revelation to Evangelize the Gentiles', *JTS* xxxv (1984), pp. 1–30.

Union Theological Seminary in Virginia and *Interpretation* in respect of 'Ephesians: Two Types of Existence', *Interpretation* (January, 1993), pp. 39–51, an issue in honor of Paul J. Achtemeier.

Irish Biblical Studies in respect of 'Ephesians 4.28: Thieves in the Church', 14 (1992), pp. 2–9; 'Ministry in Ephesians', 15 (1993), pp. 146–66; 'The Haustafel in Ephesians (Eph. 5.22–6.9)', 16 (1994), pp. 146–60.

Abbreviations

AB	Anchor Bible
AE	Author of Ephesians
An(Anal)Bib	Analecta biblica
ANRW	*Aufstieg und Niedergang der römischen Welt* (ed. H. Temporini and W. Haase), Berlin
AT(h)ANT	Abhandlung zur Theologie des alten und neuen Testaments
BETL	Bibliotheca ephemeridum theologicarum lovaniensium
Bib	*Biblica*
BZ	*Biblische Zeitschrift*
CBQ	*Catholic Biblical Quarterly*
CGT	Cambridge Greek Testament
DBS	*Dictionnaire de la Bible, Supplément*
EKK	Evangelisch-Katholischer Kommentar
EvT	*Evangelische Theologie*
ExpT	*Expository Times*
FRLANT	Forschungen zur Religion und Literatur des alten und neuen Testaments
FS	Festschrift
GCS	Griechische christliche Schriftsteller
HTR	*Harvard Theological Review*
ICC	International Critical Commentary
Int	*Interpretation*
IrishBS	*Irish Biblical Studies*
JAC	*Jahrbuch für Antike und Christentum*

JBL	*Journal of Biblical Literature*
JSJ	*Journal for the Study of Judaism*
JSNT	*Journal for the Study of the New Testament*
JSNTSup	*JSNT* Supplement Series
JTS	*Journal of Theological Studies*
KEK	Kritisch-Exegetischer Kommentar
LAB	Liber Antiquitatum Biblicarum (Pseudo-Philo)
LCL	Loeb Classical Library
NEB	New English Bible
NICNT	New International Commentary on the New Testament
NIDNTT	*The New International Dictionary of New Testament Theology*
NRSV	New Revised Standard Version
NT	*Novum Testamentum*
NTS	*New Testament Studies*
RAC	*Reallexikon für Antike und Christentum*
RB	*Revue biblique*
REB	Revised English Bible
RevExp	*Review and Expositor*
RHR	*Revue de l'histoire des religions*
RivB(Bib)	*Rivista biblica*
RSV	Revised Standard Version
SBFLA	*Studii biblici franciscani liber annuus*
SBLDS	SBL Dissertation Series
SBLMS	SBL Monograph Series
SBS	Stuttgarter Bibelstudien
SBT	Studies in Biblical Theology
SE	Studia Evangelica
SJT	*Scottish Journal of Theology*
SNTSMS	Society for New Testament Studies Monograph Series
StTh	*Studia theologica*
SUNT	Studien zur Umwelt des neuen Testament
Suppl. *NT*	Supplement to *Novum Testamentum*
TDNT	ET of *TWNT*
THNT	Theologischer Handkommentar zum neuen Testament
TLZ	*Theologische Literaturzeitung*

TU	Texte und Untersuchungen
TWNT	*Theologisches Wörterbuch zum Neuen Testament* (ed. G. Kittel and G. Friedrich)
TZ	*Theologische Zeitschrift*
VoxEv	*Vox Evangelica*
WD	*Wort und Dienst*
WMANT	Wissenschaftliche Monographien zum alten und neuen Testament
WUNT	Wissenschaftliche Unterzuchungen zum neuen Testament
ZNW	*Zeitschrift für die neutestamentliche Wissenschaft*

1

Ephesians 1.1

1. The disputed reading in Eph. 1.1 forms a fascinating study in textual criticism. In the vast majority of cases the debate about disputed readings remains within the area of the immediate text but any decision in relation to Eph. 1.1 interrelates with decisions which have to be made about the authorship of the letter and about its purpose, nature and content. In this study all we can hope to do is to determine the proper approach and isolate the factors which affect a final decision. It is not proposed to review the history of the discussion and reference will be made only to the major suggestions which have appeared. J. Schmid has given us an excellent review of the main positions up to about 1927 with comprehensive lists of those who had adhered to each.[1]

In respect of the letter itself there seem to be certain results which have been generally acceptable to commentators. We may describe these as the 'constants' of the discussion. Four 'constants' appear relevant to our problem:

---

[1] J. Schmid, *Der Epheserbrief des Apostels Paulus* (Biblische Studien, volume XXII, Heft 3/4, Freiburg im Breisgau, 1928). More recent reviews will be found in E. Percy, *Die Probleme der Kolosser – und Epheserbriefe* (Lund, 1946), pp. 449–66; N. A. Dahl, 'Adresse und Proömium des Epheserbriefes', *TZ* 7 (1951), pp. 241–64; P. Dacquino, 'I destinatari della lettera agli Efesini', *RivB*, 6 (1958), pp. 102–10; A. van Roon, *The Authenticity of Ephesians* (Suppl. *NT* 39), pp. 72–85; A. Lindemann, 'Bemerkungen zu den Adressaten und zum Anlass des Epheserbriefes', *ZNW* 67 (1976), pp. 235–51.

(a) Paul is not or has not been personally known to the readers though they do know about him (1.15; 3.2, 4.20f).[2]

(b) The letter is not written to an individual Christian community but to a wider group (lack of personal details, etc.).

(c) It is not written to the universal church but to a limited group of communities (1.15ff; 6.21f).

(d) The letter is addressed largely, if not entirely, to Gentile Christians (2.1ff, 11ff; 3.1f; 4.17)

Amongst the relevant 'variables', i.e. matters upon which scholarly opinion has not solidified, are the authorship, intention and nature of the letter (a genuine letter or a meditation, prayer, treatise, sermon made into a letter?). A variable which takes us beyond the letter itself is its possible identification with the letter mentioned in Col. 4.16 ('to the Laodiceans'). Different decisions in relation to the variables render certain solutions to the problem more or less attractive.

2. The manuscript evidence is easily set out.

P: τοῖς ἁγίοις οὖσιν καὶ πιστοῖς 𝔓⁴⁶
B: τοῖς ἁγίοις τοῖς οὖσιν καὶ πιστοῖς ℵ* B* 424ᶜ 1739
A: τοῖς ἁγίοις τοῖς (om D) οὖσιν ἐν Ἐφέσῳ καὶ πιστοῖς *rell*

These are the only readings which require serious consideration; others, e.g. that with πᾶσιν τοῖς οὖσιν, can be safely eliminated. We shall refer to the three primary texts above as respectively the P, B and A text forms.

3. Patristic evidence.

3.1. It is clear that Origen neither read the reference to Ephesians in his text nor had a lacuna for he expounds the B text and has had to think up an explanation in order to escape its grammatical difficulties.[3] Basil[4] indicates that many if not all of the older manuscripts lack the reference 'in Ephesus'; in distinguishing between texts in this way he implies that some do

---

[2] It may also be true that the actual writer of Ephesians, if he was not Paul, did not personally know those to whom he wrote.

[3] For Origen's discussion see especially J. A. F. Gregg, 'The Commentary of Origen upon the Epistle to the Ephesians', *JTS* 3 (1902), pp. 233–44, 398–420, 551–76 at p. 235.

[4] *Adv. Eunom.* ii.19.

have the words. The construction of Marcion's text from the references in Tertullian[5] is not undisputed. It is generally held that Tertullian's accusations relate to the superscription to the letter and not to the text itself; in that case Marcion cannot have had the A text; this would also imply that Tertullian did not have 'in Ephesus' in his text. It is however just possible that Tertullian accuses Marcion of differing from the true church's reading of the text. It is also unclear whether Marcion had a manuscript with 'to the Laodiceans' implying that he knew the letter under this name, or whether he altered an existing text 'to the Ephesians' into 'to the Laodiceans' and if so why he altered it. Was he dependent on tradition or, less probably, did he carry through an early piece of historical critical analysis and, observing that it was inappropriate for Paul to have written a letter in which he said he had not known the Ephesians personally when in fact he had visited them, made a guess on the basis of Col. 4.16?

3.2. As well as the question of reading there is, as a discussion of Tertullian shows, the question of the superscription. All the manuscripts, including those in the B and P tradition, have the title 'To the Ephesians'. How far back does this go? As soon as, or very shortly after a collection of Paul's letters was made, some identification would have been necessary for the individual letters in the collection. The problem here is not that of the use of the letter but its use as a letter to the Ephesians. Church Fathers whether or not they read 'in Ephesus' certainly knew the letter as 'to the Ephesians' (e.g. Irenaeus,[6] Clement of Alexandria,[7] Origen,[8] Tertullian,[9] Canon Muratori[10]). The much earlier letter of Ignatius to the Ephesians is important. Are there signs of the dependence of its address on our Ephesians, suggesting that Ignatius knew our Ephesians as addressed to the Ephesians and was playing on this knowledge

---

[5] *Adv. Marc.* 5.11.12; 17.1.

[6] *Adv. Haer.* 5.2.2; 8.1; 14.3; 24.4.

[7] *Strom.* 4.8 (64.1 = *GCS* 2, p. 277); *Paed.* 1.5 (18.3 = *GCS* 1, p. 100).

[8] See n. 3 above.

[9] See n. 5 above.

[10] The evidence of Canon Muratori is not important if it dates from the fourth century, cf. A. C. Sundberg, 'Canon Muratori: A Fourth Century List', *HTR* 66 (1973), pp. 1–41.

in writing to them? With a greater recognition today of the influence of the liturgical tradition on early writing there is probably less reason to see Ignatius as dependent on Ephesians than both as dependent on that tradition.[11] We can probably then not trace back the recognition of the letter as 'to the Ephesians' earlier than Irenaeus, but that is not to say it was not so recognised earlier.

4. We now consider those solutions which accept one or other of the existing text forms.

4.1. The A text as the original reading. If this solution is accepted then because of (a) it is much easier to assume that Paul did not write the letter.[12] The A text has certain inherent difficulties. (i) The place name is awkwardly situated in that it appears to be especially associated with ἁγίοις and ἐν Χριστῷ Ἰησοῦ by implication with πιστοῖς. In Col. 1.2, where we also have a double address, 'saints and faithful brothers', the geographical designation clearly applies to both halves of the address as does the final phrase 'in Christ'. In 1 Cor. 1.2 the problem does not arise since those outside Corinth who are additionally addressed are introduced with a σύν phrase (cf. 2 Cor. 1.1; Phil. 1.1). (ii) (b) is not satisfied. (iii) If the account in Acts of Paul's visit to Ephesus reflects genuine tradition then the lack of personal reference to members of the community in Ephesus is surprising; (a) cannot be satisfied. (iv) If 'in Ephesus' was later omitted we should expect the scribe who did so to have also omitted τοῖς οὖσιν, for the B form of the text is very difficult to construe (see 4.2).

Assuming the A form of the text is original we require to account for the appearance of the B and P forms. The omission of 'in Ephesus' cannot be attributed to any of the ordinary scribal failures in sight or hearing but must have been deliberate. (i) A scribe observing that the writer of the letter had not visited the

---

[11] Against the view that Ignatius knew our letter as addressed to the Ephesians is his statement that there are many letters of Paul in which he mentions the Ephesians (Ign. *Eph.* 12.2); a reference to our letter would have enabled him to make his point more strikingly.

[12] E. K. Simpson, *New International Commentary on the NT* (Grand Rapids, Mich., 1972), is one of the few who accept this reading and Pauline authorship.

church to which he was writing and knowing that Paul had evangelized Ephesus may have thought it better to erase the reference to Ephesus than the attribution to Paul. This presupposes non-Pauline authorship. (ii) Ephesus as the destination of such an important letter may have been felt inappropriate in view of a subsequent failure on the part of the Ephesians to live up to the terms of the letter; such a failure might be deduced from Rev. 2.4f and the scribe believed he was fulfilling Rev. 2.5. (iii) It might have been felt that a letter dealing with a general subject and lacking personal reference should not be addressed to a particular congregation. (This argument has also been advanced to account for the G text of Romans.)

4.2. The B text as original. Such an assumption leaves a very difficult phrase to construe.

4.21. Origen[13] relates τοῖς οὖσιν to the singular participle with the article in the divine name as given in Exod. 3.14 and links this again with 1 Cor. 1.28f. The saints are those who have been called out of non-existence into real existence because of their participation in the one to whom real existence belongs. This is very far-fetched and lacks any parallel in NT thought: καὶ πιστοῖς comes in very oddly after it.

4.22. A number of commentators[14] translate 'to the saints who are (also) faithful in Christ Jesus'. It is doubtful if the Greek can easily be made to have this meaning.[15] It is also difficult to see what it means; almost by definition the saints are those who are faithful in Christ Jesus. πιστοί in this interpretation must be given the meaning 'faithful' rather than 'believers'.[16]

4.23. To avoid the difficulties of 4.22, attempts have been made to distinguish between the ἅγιοι and the πιστοί. G. B. Caird[17]

---

[13] See n. 3 above.

[14] Most recently E. J. Goodspeed, *The Meaning of Ephesians* (Chicago, Ill., 1933), p. 18; M. Barth (AB Commentary 34, volume 1, Garden City, New York, 1974).

[15] Cf. G. Zuntz, *The Text of the Epistles* (London, 1953), p. 228, n. 1.

[16] Whether πιστοί should be translated 'faithful' or 'believers' is another of the variables; supporting evidence for either translation can be adduced.

[17] G. B. Caird, *Paul's Letters from Prison* (Oxford, 1976), ad loc.; cf. J. C. Kirby, *Ephesians, Baptism and Pentecost* (London, 1968), pp. 170f; F. W. Beare, *Interpreters' Bible* x (New York/Nashville, 1953), pp. 601f; W. G. Kümmel, *Introduction*, ET, 2nd edition (London, 1975), p. 355.

has revived the attempt to refer the former to Jewish Christians and the latter to Gentile believers; presumably he would translate 'to those who are Jewish Christians and those who are also believers incorporate in Christ Jesus'.[18] He argues that οἱ ἅγιοι is sometimes used by Paul to refer to the Jewish Christians of Jerusalem (Rom. 15.25–31) and that it is used in this letter at 2.19 to refer to Jewish Christians. But where Paul uses the term in this way its meaning is clear from the context, and this meaning is not undisputed at 2.19;[19] certainly in other parts of the letter (1.18; 3.8; 3.18; 4.12; 5.3) it refers to both Jewish and Gentile saints. It does not possess the exclusively Jewish Christian reference in any of the addresses of the other Pauline letters. This translation at 1.1 might be easier to accept if the letter was not by Paul since it would then be unnecessary to argue for a variation in his normal usage of the word. This rendering conflicts with (d).

4.24. Lake and Cadbury[20] suggest understanding ποῖς οὖσιν as 'local', arguing that it has this sense in Acts 5.17; 13.1; 14.13; 28.17, and translating 'to the local saints and believers in Jesus Christ'. Even if the participle of εἶναι can have this meaning in the passages in Acts[21] it is in each instance geographically anchored by the context; in Eph. 1.1 it is impossible to know to what 'local' refers, and so it becomes meaningless. It is moreover not clear why only the ἅγιοι and not also the πιστοί are described as 'local'.

4.25. E. Mayser gives evidence to show that the participle of εἶναι with the article is often used almost redundantly in a kind of officialese (*Kanzleisprache*).[22] It is interesting at this point to go back and reread Origen who describes some phrase as redundant: εἰ μὴ παρέλκει προσκείμενον τὸ τοῖς ἁγίοις τοῖς

---

[18] He does not offer an actual translation.

[19] Some take it to refer to angels, cf. Gnilka, *Der Epheserbrief*, (Herders theologischer Kommentar zum NT, x, 2, Freiburg/Basel/Wien, 1971).

[20] Lake and Cadbury, *The Beginnings of Christianity*, edited by F. Jackson and K. Lake volume iv (London, 1942), p. 56; see also A. T. Robertson, *Grammar*, 3rd edition (New York, 1919), p. 1107.

[21] Lake and Cadbury are supported by N. Turner in J. H. Moulton, *Grammar*, 3, p. 152.

[22] E. Mayser, *Grammatik der griechischen Papyri aus der Ptolemäerzeit*, 2. 1, pp. 347f.

οὖσι. Which words does he suppose to be redundant? Reading deep meaning into redundant words accords with his exegetical methods. Since he goes on to comment on τοῖς οὖσι it must be this phrase which he regards as redundant. Lightfoot[23] indeed suggested that we should read τοῖς ἁγίοις τὸ τοῖς οὖσι in Origen (the text of Cramer's *Catenae* is often uncertain); Gregg,[24] following J. A. Robinson, reads τῷ τοῖς ἁγίοις τὸ τοῖς οὖσι which is preferable. The difficulty still remains why the redundant phrase should be attached only to ἁγίοις and not also to πιστοῖς, yet a redundant phrase in Ephesians would not be out of keeping with the style.

4.26. It can be seen that the real difficulty commentators have with the B text is its meaning. If we begin with it then it is quite easy to explain the appearance of the P text: a scribe may have allowed his eye to stray and missed the second τοῖς due to the three successive οις, or else noticing the difficulty of understanding the B text he thought he could render it clearer with an emendation. The A text will have appeared because οὖσιν (or its singular equivalent) is normally followed by a place name in the Pauline addresses. This would account for the peculiar position of the geographical name in the A text, but it does not account for the appearance of Ephesus rather than some other place.

4.27. That difficulty exists for all views except 4.1. If the letter was first given the superscription 'To the Ephesians' it is easy to see why the name later entered the text. But how did it obtain this superscription? If we assume that it appeared at or about the time the letters were collected it is also reasonable to assume that this collection was made at a place where both Paul's acquaintanceship with Ephesus was unknown, and also Acts was unknown since the latter depicts a long visit of Paul to Ephesus. In such circumstances the attribution might have been a deduction from 2 Tim. 4.12 combined with Eph. 6.21f; this implies that 2 Timothy was recognized as a Pauline letter when the deduction was made; it would therefore have been included in the collection (yet it is generally held that the Pastorals were

---

[23] Lightfoot, *Biblical Essays* (London, 1893), p. 378, n. 1.
[24] See n. 3, above.

not part of the earliest *Corpus Paulinum*). Various other suggestions have been made for the attribution 'To the Ephesians' or 'in Ephesus'. A nameless circular letter was found at Ephesus or the original letter was preserved at Ephesus and so 'Ephesus' was attached to it; the Ephesian church imagined itself an important church which should have a letter of its own and so appropriated a nameless letter; the circular letter had been distributed from Ephesus and so received that the name;[25] when the Pauline letters were collected at Ephesus, Ephesians was written as a general letter to introduce them;[26] a copy of a circular letter for churches in Asia but not intended for Ephesus was sent to Ephesus as the main church of the area and so eventually received its name. Schlier[27] suggests very tentatively that a copy of a circular letter was sent to Ephesus and therefore had the superscription 'To the Ephesians' on the outside to ensure its delivery; this presupposes the modern practice of redirecting an old letter in a fresh envelope with a new address; in those days the letter would have been taken by messenger and such an outside address would have been unnecessary. Kirby[28] believes the letter was written by one of the leaders of the church at Ephesus; a copy came to Corinth; there it required identification and the reference to Ephesus was inserted. The number and variety of suggestions and the inability of any one of them to gain general acceptance indicates the difficulty of the problem.

4.3. The P text as original.[29] This has never been seriously investigated.[30] It would be easier to accept if οὖσιν preceded ἁγίοις or followed the whole phrase, but as it stands it is still possible to translate it either as 'to those who are saints and believers in Christ Jesus' (treating οὖσιν as redundant 'officialese';

[25] Cf. Schmid, *Der Epheserbrief des Apostels Paulus,*, p. 128.

[26] Cf. Goodspeed, *The Meaning of Ephesians*, pp. 10f.

[27] H. Schlier, *Der Brief an die Epheser* (Düsseldorf, 1971), p. 32.

[28] Kirby, *Ephesians, Baptism and Pentecost*, pp. 170f.

[29] Since no special relation exists between $\mathfrak{P}^{46}$ and D (cf. Zuntz, *The Text of the Epistles*, pp. 41f) their combined evidence for this reading increases its probability.

[30] So far as I am aware it has only been seriously suggested by J. Belser, *Der Epheserbrief des Apostels Paulus* (Freiburg, 1908), and he based his suggestion on the reading of D (he could not have known $\mathfrak{P}^{46}$) and P. Benoit, *DBS*, VII, pp. 195–211, who says that this reading has been too little considered.

see 4.25)[31] or as 'to the local [see 4.24] saints and believers'. The former translation though it fits in with the
verbose style of Ephesians conflicts with (c) since it suggests an
unrestricted readership. The second provides a possible way of
avoiding the great difficulty of the idea of a circular letter (see
5.1 and 5.2) if we suppose that Tychicus carried the letter round
a number of churches; his presence within a particular community as he read the letter provided the necessary local anchorage
(see 4.24). The lack of precise identification of the readership
implied in either of these renderings is supported by the final
blessing. In the other letter of the Pauline corpus this is
invariably of the form 'the grace of the Lord Jesus (Christ) be
with you (your spirits) (all)', and the recipients are addressed in
the second person without qualification. The concluding grace
in Eph. 6.23f is not only much more elaborate but it is also
couched in the third person and contains a qualification in
6.24 where grace is said to be 'with all who love the Lord
Jesus Christ'. The use of the third person would harmonize
with both suggested renderings, but the qualification would
fit better with the first. The letter and the grace are only intended for those who acknowledge themselves as saints and
believers.

If either of these suggestions is possible how did the A and B
texts ever appear? It is almost impossible to imagine a scribe
creating the B text out of the P in order to make it simpler; nor
is there any way in which it could have been created acciden-
tally. It is therefore necessary to assume that the A text appeared
first. Codex Claromontanus may provide the missing link. If
οὖσιν was understood by any scribe as 'local' it would be natural
to add a place name directly after it to define it even without
τοῖς preceding it; then the normal form of the Pauline address
would force the introduction of τοῖς and the A text would come
into existence. The B text would appear because some scribes
remembered that MSS existed without a geographical designation. This suggestion does, at least, account for all the textual
evidence.

[31] Blass-Debrunner, *Grammatik*, § 413. 3* consider this impossible unless
accompanied by a qualifying phrase; this qualification could be 'in Christ
Jesus'.

5. We now turn to conjectural readings. All such readings have an initial disadvantage in that they add an extra stage to the development of the text. ·

5.1. The text contained a deliberate lacuna after τοῖς οὖσιν. This is a conjectural reading since no extant MS has such a lacuna. The lacuna was to be filled in by Tychicus as he read the letter to each particular church when he visited it or it was to be filled in by each church itself as the letter was passed from church to church, or else a number of copies were sent, each with a lacuna, and each church left to fill in its own name.

There are considerable difficulties with such a conjectural reading. (i) Roller's detailed examination of ancient letter writing suggests there is no evidence for the existence of letters in the contemporary world with such lacunae.[32] (ii) ἐν would always have been present;[33] no MS evidence exists for it except in connection with Ephesus (or, possibly, Laodicea). (iii) If the gap was to be filled up by each church why should copies without it continue to exist, for each church would make its own copy with its own name in it. (iv) Why should no memory of other churches, with the possible exception of Laodicea, remain in the manuscript evidence? (v) Why could Paul not have listed all the churches in the address instead of leaving a blank? He writes to the churches of Galatia. Could he not have written then to the churches of Asia or to those of the Lycus Valley or wherever the area was in which the alleged churches lay? 1 Peter is a round letter to the churches in a number of districts and each of the districts is listed (see 1.1). (vi) Why should strong evidence exist for the reading Ephesus since this was a church to which the letter was not addressed and therefore this name would not have been inserted in the lacuna? (This problem is less serious if the letter was not by Paul himself.) (vii) The alleged gap comes at the wrong point (see 4.1(i)).

The B text would arise quite easily from the conjectural text

---

[32] Cf. O. Roller, *Das Formular der paulinischen Briefe* (BWANT ɪv, 6 Stuttgart, 1933), pp. 199–212, 520–5. Only Zuntz, *The Text of the Epistles,* p. 228, n.1, disagrees, but the evidence he produces is slender and dubious. (The reference he gives to *Mus. Helv.* should be 5 (1948), 218ff.)

[33] Cf. Dahl, 'Adresse und Proömium des Epheserbriefes', pp. 243f.

once a scribe forgot to leave the lacuna. The P form would presumably have been derived from the B form by the process suggested in 4.2. It is the appearance of the A form which it is difficult to envisage (see 4.2).

5.2. A number of identical letters were sent to different churches each carrying an individual name. This practice can be paralleled in the ancient world.[34] Yet this solution has also great difficulties. (i) The failure of any place name other than Ephesus to survive in the manuscript tradition since (unlike 5.1) the theory requires their presence; (ii) the existence of strong manuscript tradition relating the letter to Ephesus when many of the details of the letter itself are inappropriate to such a reference; (iii) the recognized simpler method in use among Christians of addressing churches as a group; (iv) the appearance of the name at the wrong point (see 4.2(i)).

It is exceedingly difficult to see how any of the known text forms arose out of this conjectural reading. Since Ephesus cannot have been one of the original churches which was addressed the A text can only have appeared through the deliberate alteration of an existing name into that of Ephesus. The B text could only have appeared through the deliberate omission of the name of a church; this does not explain why the name of the church was omitted and a difficult sentence to construe created.

5.3. The original reading was ἐν Λαοδικείᾳ. If we were sure that this was the text Marcion read then we should have considered it in §4 and not here. Marcion may have been making a guess but if he was not then he probably had only the superscription 'To the Laodiceans' and nothing in the text. The most popular form of their theory is that put forward by Harnack.[35] Since it has been frequently discussed we do not need to outline it, but shall briefly indicate its difficulties. (i) The letter referred to in Col. 4.16 appears to be a letter directed to one congregation and not a general letter like our Ephesians. (ii) Colossians contains much personal detail; why should a letter to neighbouring Laodicea be

---

[34] Cf. Roller, *Das Formular der paulinischen Briefe*, pp. 207ff, 603f. This solution is accepted by Dahl, 'Adresse und Proömium des Epheserbriefes'.

[35] A. von Harnack, 'Die Adresse des Epheserbriefes', SBA Hist.-philos. Kl., 1910, pp. 696–709.

devoid of this? Epaphras gave Paul full information about
Colossae; why did he not also give him full information about
Laodicea? (iii) It seems more probable that Marcion was
making a honest guess than that he was acting on information
he possessed. (iv) The difficulty of Harnack's hypothesis is
increased if we suppose that Paul is not the author of Ephesians.
(v) A good case can also be made out for identifying the letter
of Col. 4.16 with that to Philemon.[36]

It is not easy to see how the present text forms evolved from
this supposed original reading. It may be that Ephesus was
substituted for Laodicea on the grounds that the church in
Laodicea proved a failure and its name deserved to be wiped
out (Rev. 3.14–22) but this does not explain the substitution of
Ephesus which itself is not too well spoken of in Rev. 2.1–7. We
have then to suppose conditions in which the B text would arise
and from it the P text. This involves a lengthy process. Alternatively the B text may have been created directly from the
original text by the omission of 'in Laodicea'. We have seen the
difficulty of this in 4.1 and it is a difficulty for all texts which
originally possessed a name. The introduction of 'in Ephesus'
would be a separate stage. Again this would be a lengthy
process. In either case the P text would have been evolved from
the B text.

5.4. The original place name was Colossae. Ochel[37] has suggested that Ephesians is a generalized Colossians intended to be
used in a wider area and to replace Colossians, and originally
put out as a letter to Colossae. Unfortunately canonical Colossians did not disappear and since two so similar letters
addressed to the same church were unacceptable some scribe
omitted the reference to Colossae. This clearly accounts for the
relation between Colossians and Ephesians and for the more
general nature of Ephesians. It is more acceptable if it is
assumed Paul was not the author of Ephesians. But it has
difficulties. (i) The complex situation which must be supposed

---

[36] Cf. Goodspeed, *The Meaning of Ephesians*, pp. 6f.

[37] W. Ochel, *Die Annahme einer Bearbeitung des Kolosserbriefes im Epheserbrief in
einer Analyse des Epheserbriefes untersucht* (Diss. Marburg, 1934). Unfortunately I
have not yet been able to consult this and depend on others for information
about it.

for the production of Ephesians is only a hypothesis. (ii) The relation between Ephesians and Colossians can be accounted for in other ways. (iii) The omission of ἐν Κολοσσαῖς left the difficult text with τοῖς οὖσιν. (iv) The theory does not account adequately for the insertion of 'in Ephesus'.

5.5. Schmid[38] conjectured τοῖς ἁγίοις καὶ πιστοῖς ἐν Χριστῷ Ἰησοῦ. This permits an understanding of the letter as a general letter, yet it could still have been written to a limited readership for 2 Peter and Jude are simpler in their general addresses yet have limited readership. The A text appeared because the latter was circulated from Ephesus and 'to the Ephesians', at first used as a superscription, eventually entered the text. Its awkward position allowed it to be recognized as an insertion. The inconsistency between the letter as it existed and a letter to Ephesus, which Paul had not visited, was then observed and the reference to Ephesus omitted.[39] Hence the B text. This conjecture involves a long and complicated process of textual development. It does not satisfactorily explain the reference to the peculiar position of the place name. If 2 Peter and Jude are taken as parallels to the type of universal letter addressed to a limited readership then this might suggest Ephesians comes from a date nearer to that of these other two letters. It does not satisfactorily explain why the name Ephesus was introduced.

5.6. A. van Roon[40] conjectures an original τοῖς ἁγίοις τοῖς οὖσιν ἐν Ἱεραπόλει καὶ ἐν Λαοδικείᾳ, πιστοῖς ἐν Χριστῷ Ἰησοῦ. This conflicts with none of the constants. He supports this by associating Col. 2.1 and 4.13 so that 2.16 refers to the Christians of Hierapolis and the ἀγών of 2.1a has the same reference as the prayers of Eph. 1.16, 17–23 and 3.16ff. When the two place names were omitted (to create an ecumenical

---

[38] J. Schmid, *Der Epheserbrief des Apostels Paulus*, pp. 125ff; cf. M. Goguel, 'Esquisse d'une solution nouvelle du problème de l'épître aux Éphésiens', *RHR* III (1935), pp. 254ff, and 112 (1936), pp. 73ff at p. 254, n. 1; Dacquino, 'I destinatari della lettera agli Efesini'. This also seems to be the reading adopted by Kirby, *Ephesians, Baptism and Pentecost*, p. 170, as original, though, curiously, he assumes that the 'saints' are Jewish Christians and the 'faithful' are Gentile Christians (cf. Caird, *Paul's Letters from Prison*, see 4.24).

[39] Kirby, *Ephesians, Baptism and Pentecost*, p. 170, believes the reference to Ephesus was removed when the letter came back from Corinth (see 4.28) to Ephesus.

[40] van Roon, *The Authenticity of Ephesians*, pp. 80ff.

letter) the καί which united them was retained; this explains its position in the B text. However it is exceedingly difficult to see why the καί should be left when the two place names were removed. Though van Roon does not comment on it his conjecture accounts for the peculiar position of the geographical reference (see 4.1(i)) in the A text. It fails however to account for the disappearance of the original names and the appearance of Ephesus; it is not sufficient to say that it was omitted to create an ecumenical letter (cf. Rom. 1.7 and the omission of 'Rome' in G) for clearly the person who inserted 'in Ephesus' was unaware of an alleged tendency of the early church to universalize the letters of Paul. It also does not explain why Hierapolis is not mentioned in Col. 2.1 (2.1b would be a very roundabout way of referring to it) or why the Colossians should not have sent to Hierapolis (4.16) for a copy of the letter.

5.7. Santer[41] conjectures τοῖς ἁγίοις καὶ πιστοῖς[42] τοῖς οὖσιν ἐν Χριστῷ Ἰησοῦ and supposes 'καὶ πιστοῖς was omitted through haplography, put in the margin by a corrector, and then inserted in the wrong place thus producing' the B text. As he notes τοῖς οὖσιν ἐν Χριστῷ Ἰησοῦ is not found in any other Pauline address but he offers two parallels; neither is as close as he suggests: in 1 Thess. 2.14 the participle is more correctly linked to ἐν τῇ Ἰουδαίᾳ[43] and in Rom. 16.11 it could go with ἀσπάσασθε and it is in any case uncertain if Paul uses ἐν Χριστῷ Ἰησοῦ in the same way as he uses ἐν Κυρίῳ. In the position Santer puts it τοῖς οὖσιν would be unnecessary according to normal Pauline usage; e.g. 2 Cor. 12.2; Rom. 8.1; Phil. 1.14; 4.21; Rom. 16.7, 8. If Santer's conjecture were acceptable it would probably be better, as he suggests, to assume non-Pauline authorship. However the later we place the date of the writing the less time we allow for the extra variations in the text which have to appear before the process leading to the B, A and P texts begins. Why, moreover, should the second corrector

[41] M. Santer, 'The Text of Ephesians 1.1', *NTS* 15 (1968/9), pp. 247f.

[42] Although Santer does not note it the linking of two almost synonymous nouns or adjectives is in the style of Ephesians: cf. 1.4, 8, 17; 2.1, 19; 3.10, 12; 5.27; 6.4, 5.

[43] Cf. B. Rigaux, *Les Épîtres aux Thessaloniciens*, Études Bibliques (Paris/Gembloux, 1956).

insert the reference at the wrong point, showing an insensitivity to Greek?

5.8. Readings which presuppose a misreading of, or damage to, the original text. Many conjectures have been made, but probably only two are worthy of mention, the first because of its intrinsic value and the second because it is recent.

5.81. Ewald[44] conjectured τοῖς ἀγαπητοῖς οὖσι καὶ πιστοῖς and assumed that the corner of the manuscript was damaged and the letters απη were lost; ιοις was then surmised to replace them. However the use of ἀγαπητοί is unusual in the address of a Pauline letter; only Rom. 1.7 incorporates the word. Ewald's solution implies that the original letter had no direct address to a town or area and so may be held to accord with its general nature. It is however difficult to see how any one should create such a difficult text as the B form by the surmise Ewald supposes. It is then necessary to account for the appearances of the A form and the P form. All this requires a very complex and lengthy procedure.

5.82. Batey[45] conjectures as the original reading τοῖς ἀγίοις τοῖς ᾽Ασίας. A scribe mistook ᾽Ασίας for οὔσαις which he then changed to the masculine οὖσιν. This is far-fetched and as in 5.81 it has to be followed by a very complex process leading to the present text forms.

6. Few conclusions can be drawn other than that there is as yet no satisfactory solution. Certainly decisions taken on other grounds in respect of the variables eliminate some solutions, but not the same ones for every interpreter. It is difficult to conceive of the letter as existing in the Pauline corpus without some designation distinguishing it from other letters, but this designation need not have been in the text. The attachment of the name 'Ephesians' to the letter must therefore have been as early as the first collection of the letters which contained Ephesians. For this reason, if for no other, a process of development of text forms which contains as few steps as possible is essential, and this suggests one of the existing text

---

[44] P. Ewald, *An die Epheser, Kolosser und Philemon*, Kommentar zum NT, 2nd edition (Leipzig, 1910), pp. 15f.

[45] R. Batey, 'The Destination of Ephesians', *JBL* 82 (1963), p. 101.

forms, or if not, one which only adds one more step to the process; the more steps required the earlier the letter must be placed; complex theories therefore go best with Pauline authorship. While it might not settle the issue it would provide an important clue to it if we could determine why the name 'Ephesians' was originally attached to the letter. A full-scale study of this is required.[46]

---

[46] I have now attempted to supply this deficiency with 'Recipients and Title of the Letter to the Ephesians: Why and When the Designation "Ephesians"?' *ANRW* II, 25.4, pp. 3247–3279.

2

Ephesians 1.1 Again

In attempting to determine the original reading of Eph. 1.1 two other problems appear to require simultaneous explanation:
(1) the peculiar position of the phrase τοῖς οὖσιν (ἐν Ἐφέσῳ) which makes it refer only to τοῖς ἁγίοις;
(2) the insertion of ἐν Ἐφέσῳ and not some other geographical designation, assuming that the reference to Ephesus was not part of the original text.

We know from the evidence of Marcion and 2 Peter that at least by the middle of the second century a recognized collection of Paul's letters existed. But long before this there will have been an informal collection or collections of some, if not all the letters. Many scholars date the first formal collection as early as the end of the first century.[1] Whether this is so or not there were at least by this stage partial collections.[2] When Clement writes from Rome to Corinth he is aware of both Paul's letter to his own church and the first letter to Corinth; a copy of the latter must therefore have arrived in Rome by this time. Col. 4.16 shows awareness of a letter to Laodicea of which the Colossians are to obtain possession; they will then have had at least two

---

[1] E.g. W. G. Kümmell, *Introduction to the New Testament* (London, 1975), p. 480; D. Guthrie, *New Testament Introduction* (Leicester, 1976), pp. 654–7; W. Schmithals, *Paulus und die Gnostiker* (Hamburg-Bergstedt, 1965), pp. 175–200; C. L. Mitton, *The Formation of the Pauline Corpus of Letters* (London, 1955); A. von Harnack, *Die Briefsammlung des Apostels Paulus* (Leipzig, 1926).

[2] There are good grounds for arguing for a number of informal collections of Paul's letters which were later united to form the present corpus; see most recently, K. Aland, 'Die Entstehung des Corpus Paulinum', in his *Neutestamentliche Entwürfe*, Theologische Bücherei 63 (Munich, 1979), pp. 302–50.

letters. Once a number of letters come together problems of identification arise. In the ancient world most letters carried some identification on the outside, usually the name of the recipient or recipients.[3] It is, however, unlikely that Paul's autographs had any such outer address since they were taken by one of his associates to the church or churches to which they were directed; if they did have an external identification this, of course, has now been lost. The identification of letters by some word on the outside would, however, not be strange to the ancient world.

At Rome 1 Corinthians could either have had on the outside 'To the Corinthians' or 'To Corinth'. This would just give sufficient information to distinguish it from any others that might lie in the archive of the church in Rome. The full title, 'To the church of God which is at Corinth, to those sanctified in Christ Jesus, called to be saints together with all those who in every place call on the name of our Lord Jesus Christ, both their Lord and ours', would have been far too unwieldy and not necessary for identification. In view of later manuscript usage 'To the Corinthians' would seem the most probable, for all the early witnesses corroborate this as the heading to the letter. Once the letter became part of a codex the exterior identification would, of course, appear at the top of the first page.

If with most scholars we reject the view of Goodspeed[4] that Ephesians was written to be the introduction to the first collection of Paul's letters, we still need to enquire at what stage it was brought into association with other Pauline letters. Ignatius apparently knew and made use of both Ephesians and 1 Corinthians, though of course he does not identify either by name. The author of 1 Peter knows the thought of Romans and Ephesians. How then was Ephesians identified as over against the other two letters with which it was associated in different areas?

If the manuscript already contained the words ἐν Ἐφέσῳ then clearly a reference to Ephesians would be put on the

---

[3] O. Roller, *Das Formular der paulinischen Briefe* (BWANT IV, 6, Stuttgart, 1933), pp. 45 and n. 204, 392–4.

[4] See, e.g., E. J. Goodspeed, *The Meaning of Ephesians* (Chicago, Ill., 1933), pp. 10f.

outside, almost certainly πρὸς Ἐφεσίους. We cannot determine from its use by the author of 1 Peter (assuming he had used it), whether he knew it under this identification or not. It has, however, been argued that Ignatius knew it as addressed to the Ephesians because he uses it in his own letter to the Ephesians as if the Ephesians would be specially conscious of Paul's letter as a letter addressed to them.[5] We note however: (1) *Smyrn.* 1.1. may show acquaintance with Eph. 2.16; *Polyc.* 1.2 with Eph. 4.2 and *Polyc.* 5.1 with Eph. 5.25. It may therefore only be chance that there are two probable places in Ignatius' *Ephesians* (*the address* which recalls Eph. 1.3ff,[6] and Ignatius, *Eph.* 20.1 which recalls Eph. 2.15; 4.24) showing acquaintance with Pauline Ephesians. (2) Ignatius' *Eph.* equally probably displays acquaintanceship with 1 Cor. (cf. Ignatius, *Eph.* 16.1 with 1 Cor. 6.9f; and Ignatius, *Eph.* 18.1 with 1 Cor. 1.18, 20) and possible acquaintance with Romans (cf. Ignatius, *Eph.* 8.2 with Rom. 8.5, 8; and Ignatius, *Eph.* 19.3 with Rom. 6.4); indeed of all the letters of Ignatius his Ephesians is the one which shows the greatest acquaintanceship with various parts of the Pauline corpus.[7] (3) It is not certain that Ignatius does in fact use Ephesians in his *address*; this and the corresponding passage in Pauline Ephesians are both highly liturgical and may be dependent on a common tradition; Schenk[8] in fact argued that the existence of these two similar passages led someone in the early church to deduce erroneously that Pauline Ephesians was a letter addressed to the Ephesian church. (4) If Ignatius knew our letter as a letter addressed to the Ephesians, why did he make

[5] Cf. T. Zahn, *Geschichte des neutestamentlichen Kanons* (Erlangen, 1888), I, pp. 816–9. The attempt to deduce Ignatius' knowledge of Pauline Ephesians as addressed to the Ephesians from his *Eph.* 12.2 cannot be sustained; cf. T. K. Abbott, *Epistles to the Ephesians and to the Colossians* (ICC, Edinburgh, 1897), pp. ix–xi.

[6] E.g. H. Rathke, *Ignatius von Antiochien und die Paulusbriefe* (TU 99, Berlin, 1967), pp. 45f; cf. pp. 21–3.

[7] If we take the rating of the Oxford Society of Historical Theology, *The New Testament in the Apostolic Fathers* (Oxford, 1965) in respect of knowledge of particular New Testament writings and allocate numerical values to their ratings (A=4, B=3, C=2, D=1) and add up the results as a rough guide to the knowledge shown by the various letters of Ignatius of the ten letter Pauline corpus then *Ephesians* makes the highest score at 37 with *Romans* next at 14.

[8] W. Schenk, 'Zur Entstehung und zum Verständnis der Adresse des Epheserbriefes', *Theologische Versuche* (Berlin, 1975) VI, pp. 73–8.

the very vague reference in his *Eph.* 12.2 to Paul mentioning the Ephesians in all his letters when he could have been much more concrete and recalled them to the letter Paul had written to them? It therefore seems easiest to conclude that Ignatius did not know Pauline Ephesians as a letter addressed to the Ephesian Christians. Yet he knew it and other Pauline letters, so Pauline Ephesians must have had some identification. Of course if there were a number of minor collections which were later formed into a major collection of Pauline epistles it would only have been necessary for Pauline Ephesians to have been so identified in one of these collections for this identification to have been carried into the new total collection.

We may continue our further consideration of the identification given to our letter by beginning with the text of 1.1.[9]

The vast majority of manuscripts read τοῖς ἁγίοις τοῖς οὖσιν ἐν Ἐφέσῳ καὶ πιστοῖς and if this was the original text then it would have been perfectly natural to identify the letter as 'To the Ephesians'. There are, however, few today who contend for this as the original form of the text.[10] Not merely are there good witnesses which do not contain the reference to Ephesus but the position in the text at which it appears renders the text grammatically difficult to construe since by implication it attaches 'Ephesus' only to ἁγίοις and 'in Christ Jesus' only to πιστοῖς. Moreover the letter appears to be a general letter rather than one addressed to the specific situation of a particular church. For these and other reasons we reject this as the original text and therefore do not need to see the original identification as necessarily 'To the Ephesians'.

---

[9] For a fuller discussion of the extant text forms see Best, 'Ephesians 1.1' in *Text and Interpretation. Studies in the New Testament presented to Matthew Black*, ed. E. Best and R. McL. Wilson (Cambridge, 1979), pp. 29–41, *supra*, pp. 1–16 and the literature quoted there.

[10] A. Lindemann, 'Bemerkungen zu den Adressaten und zum Anlass des Epheserbriefes', *ZNW* 67 (1976), pp. 235–51. In a review of the Matthew Black *Festschrift* (see n. 9) J. K. Elliott, *TZ* 35 (1979), pp. 368–70, apparently argues for the originality of this reading. He criticizes me for not observing that the present participle of εἰμί is often followed in Paul by a prepositional phrase and instances 1 Cor. 1.2; 2 Cor. 1.1; Phil. 1.1. This is so but, leaving aside the difficulty that Ephesians may not be Pauline, Elliott has failed to grasp the real difficulty (seen in the multiplicity of unsatisfactory explanations) of the resulting dissociation of ἅγιοι and πιστοί.

Codex Vaticanus reads τοῖς ἁγίοις τοῖς οὖσιν καὶ πιστοῖς. The variety of explanations offered for the understanding of τοῖς οὖσιν shows that this text is even more difficult to understand than the previous one. If we commence with it we have to assume a stage at which 'in Ephesus' was added.[11]

The text of 𝔓⁴⁶ τοῖς ἁγίοις οὖσιν καὶ πιστοῖς is also difficult to translate and has little manuscript support.[12]

It has been conjectured that originally there was a gap left in the manuscript at the place where 'in Ephesus' now appears and that this was filled in with the appropriate name by the messenger as he took the letter round a number of churches or that a number of copies were sent with a lacuna in each for the local church to fill in its own name when it received the letter. However, there seems to be no evidence for the latter practice in the ancient world.[13] Even if the letter was taken round by Tychicus and he inserted the name of each church as he came to it, it is still the wrong point in the text at which to do this.

Thus none of the possible text forms which we have examined is easily explicable and only one of them possibly provides the geographical identification which we require.

It is now time that we looked at the nature of the letter. Its content does not suggest a precise geographical address. It is generally agreed that it is written to a wider audience than one church. This wider audience might have been identified as the church or churches in a particular district, e.g. Asia (cf. Gal. 1.2; 1 Pet. 1.1) or have lacked identification altogether (cf. Jas. 1.1). If there had been an original wide address 'The Churches of Asia' which was later reduced to 'Ephesus' this wide address would have appeared at the point where 'Ephesus' appears today in the great majority of manuscripts. But the grammatical difficulty would still exist even for such a wide form of address. It may then be better to assume that originally there was no geographical definition of the addressees. Since the forms of the text which lack geographical definition in Codex Vaticanus and 𝔓⁴⁶ are also difficult to construe it might be better to take as

---

[11] If a geographical identification had to be given no satisfactory explanation has as yet been offered why Ephesus was chosen.

[12] On this reading cf. P. Benoit, *DBS*, VII, pp. 195–211.

[13] Cf. Roller, op. cit., pp. 199–212, and n. 382, pp. 520–5.

the original form of the address τοῖς ἁγίοις καὶ πιστοῖς ἐν Χριστῷ Ἰησοῦ[14] and see if from this we can construct an evolution of the present text forms. It must be admitted that there is no manuscript evidence for this form of the text, but the suggestion we are about to make may account for the disappearance of the original form. Strong support for this as the original form is given if Colossians was the model for Ephesians;[15] if we were to generalize Colossians (i.e. issue a letter based on it but addressed to a wider audience) the first item in the address to disappear would be the reference to Colossae. The difference between the address in Colossians and Ephesians would then amount to the omission from the address in Colossians of the reference to 'Brethren' and the addition of 'Jesus' in Ephesians to the simple 'Christ' of Colossians. Such variations are typical of those we find elsewhere between Ephesians and Colossians.[16] Whether Ephesians is by Paul or not there is clearly some relation between it and Colossians of a general nature.

Sooner or later 'Ephesians' would be brought into contact with other letters of Paul and would need to be identified. The others would be identified with geographical names. Most of those who have discussed the question of identification have assumed therefore that the first identification of Ephesians would have been geographical,[17] but this may be an incorrect assumption. The first significant words relating to the addressees are τοῖς ἁγίοις. This phrase[18] might then have been written on the outside of the roll, or at the head of the page if the

[14] A number of writers have argued for this conjecture, e.g., J. Schmid, *Der Epheserbrief des Apostels Paulus* (Freiburg im Breisgau 1928), pp. 125ff; cf. M. Goguel, 'Esquisse d'une solution nouvelle du problème de l'épître aux Éphésiens', *RHR* III (1935), pp. 254ff, and 112 (1936), pp. 73ff at p. 254, n. 1; P. Dacquino, 'I destinatari della lettera agli Efesini', *Riv. Bib.*, 6 (1955), pp. 102–10; J. C. Kirby, *Ephesians, Baptism and Pentecost* (London, 1968), p. 170.

[15] If Paul wrote both Colossians and Ephesians he clearly allowed himself to be influenced in Ephesians by what he wrote in Colossians and our argument would still hold.

[16] Cf. the addition of καὶ κυρίου Ἰησοῦ Χριστοῦ in 1.2 and the alteration of ἁμαρτιῶν (Col. 1.13) to παραπτωμάτων (Eph. 1.7); see C. L. Mitton, *The Epistle to the Ephesians* (Oxford, 1951), pp. 279–315.

[17] E.g., T. Zahn, *Introduction to the New Testament*, vol. i (ET Edinburgh, 1909), p. 481.

[18] Or πρός with the accusative.

collection of letters was first made in the form of a codex. (However it is more probable that in those communities where a number of Pauline letters were beginning to be used these would originally be on separate rolls; only later would they be combined into a codex.) So on the outside of the letter we would find 'To the Saints'. It would be unnecessary to add καὶ τοῖς πιστοῖς for 'To the Saints' would be sufficient to distinguish the letter from other Pauline letters with their geographically oriented identifications ('To the Romans', etc.). In either case, however, the identification is through people – 'To the saints' and 'To the Romans (Corinthians, etc.)' – and not simply geographical and non-geographical.

At a later stage[19] in some unknown Christian community and for some unknown reason it was felt that the letter ought to have a geographical destination. For a reason again which is not clear to us and for which we do not now need to seek an answer 'Ephesus' was chosen as the appropriate identification. We suggest that for this purpose τοῖς ἁγίοις was expanded to πρὸς τοὺς ἁγίους τοὺς ὄντας ἐν Ἐφέσῳ. A number of other suggestions are possible:[20] τοὺς ἐν Ἐφέσῳ ἁγίους (cf. Col. 1.2); τοὺς ἁγίους Ἐφεσίων (cf. 1 Thess. 1.1; 2 Thess. 1.1); τοὺς ἁγίους τοὺς ἐν Ἐφέσῳ (cf. Jas. 1.1); τοὺς ἁγίους ἐν Ἐφέσῳ (τοῦ Ἐφέσου; cf. Gal. 1.2); but most of the letters of the Pauline corpus employ the present participle of εἰμί (Rom. 1.7; 1 Cor. 1.2; 2 Cor. 1.1; Phil. 1.1).[21] The earliest evidence for the association of Ephesians with other letters comes from 1 Peter where the author may know both it and Romans, and from Ignatius who probably knew both Ephesians and 1 Corinthians. The use of either of these as model would lead to the form we have suggested.

It is now possible to trace the further development of the text.

(a) The heading to the letter, probably once the letters had

---

[19] It is difficult to estimate how much later this would be.

[20] Assuming πρός in each instance.

[21] In the first instance the dative may have been retained and πρός with the accusative appeared only when the identification was reduced to a simple geographical destination; see below.

come together in codex form, was now abbreviated to πρὸς Ἐφεσίους.

(b) It was felt that the geographic destination should now be placed in the letter itself and so the phrase was carried bodily into the letter and changed to the dative. Thus the text of Alexandrinus came into existence with the unfortunate position of ἐν Ἐφέσῳ.

(c) Some scribes however remembered that the original letter had no geographical reference and so when they copied it they simply omitted the reference to Ephesus, thus creating the text of Vaticanus.

(d) The text of 𝔓⁴⁶ probably arose through the carelessness of a copyist faced with three words ending in οις.

This suggestion is independent of the question of Pauline authorship. Its strength lies in the way it accounts for the present very difficult forms of the text. Its weakness lies in the considerable amount of development, and therefore of time, which is necessary for the whole to be worked out. It does not solve the problem of the identification of the letter with the church at Ephesus but by dissociating this from the first identification of the letter it leaves greater flexibility for a solution to this problem.

3

Paul's Apostolic Authority—?

In recent writing on Paul there has been an increasing tendency to speak of and emphasize his apostolic authority. There is no doubt that he claimed to be an apostle; there is equally no doubt that he exercised authority. But when he exercised authority did he do so as an apostle? Almost without exception we answer 'Yes' but would Paul himself have so answered? Did he look on the source of his authority as deriving from his apostolic appointment? I ask this question because it has become almost axiomatic to treat certain actions of Paul as the exercise of his apostolic authority.[1]

A brief imaginary anecdote may open up the issue. Charles, now Prince of Wales, when five years old was at lunch with his parents. He is tardy in clearing up his plate. His mother says to him, 'If you don't finish up your greens you won't get any dessert'. Does she speak to him as his queen or as his mother? From which aspect of her being does she draw her authority?[2] When Paul exercises authority does he do so as apostle, teacher, prophet, pastor, missionary founder? Or, possibly, does he do so because he was a bossy kind of person by nature? In a family one sibling may order the others about though having no

---

* A lecture delivered at Commemoration, Westminster College, Cambridge, and in honour of R. Buick Knox on his retirement as Niveson Professor of Ecclesiastical History in that College.

[1] J. H. Schütz has even entitled his book *Paul and the Anatomy of Apostolic Authority* (SNTSMS 26; Cambridge, 1975).

[2] It is hardly necessary to say that this is an imaginary incident. I have no inside information as to what goes on in the palace.

recognized position of authority. I do not intend to enter into this last area. That is why I framed my question in the form, 'When Paul exercises authority does he envisage himself as doing so as apostle?' We do not have time to discuss the question of Paul's character, interesting as it may be, and whether the way in which he thought of himself as behaving corresponded completely with his real motivation.

There are a number of questions which must be treated, some more rapidly than others:

1. What is an apostle?
2. When did Paul become aware he was an apostle?
3. What led him to this awareness?
4. In what situations does he assert his apostolic position?
5. When Paul exercises authority under what picture of himself does he do so?
6. How has the stress on apostolic authority arisen?

I

The term 'apostle' is used in a number of different ways in the New Testament.[3] Though in the common mind the twelve apostles are the real apostles since they were chosen by the historical Jesus this is only one way, and that a relatively late way in the primitive church, of defining apostle. Clearly it is not a definition which would have appealed to Paul himself since it would automatically have excluded him. If we examine his own use of the word we see that he terms Epaphroditus who brought him money from Philippi an apostle (Phil. 2.25; cf. 2 Cor. 8.23), also Andronicus and Junia of whom we know nothing as to what they did (Rom. 16.7). At one point he appears to place Silvanus and Timothy as apostles alongside himself (1 Thess. 2.7) and he probably also regards Apollos and Barnabas as among the apostles.[4] When he lists the resurrection appearances of Jesus he apparently views the appearance to the Twelve as different from that to the apostles and as taking place at a different time.

---

[3] See C. K. Barrett, *The Signs of an Apostle* (London, 1970), pp. 71–3.

[4] The context of 1 Cor. 4.9 includes Apollos; 9.6 seems to imply that Barnabas has the same right as Paul of apostolic maintenance; cf. A. T. Hanson, *The Pioneer Ministry* (London, 1961), p. 95; W. Schmithals, *The Office of Apostle in the Early Church* (London, 1969), p. 63.

The Twelve are not then in his mind the same as the apostles.[5] As he continues the list he classes himself with this group of apostles (1 Cor 15.5ff), though without defining what determined its membership; the nature of the list proves that it cannot simply have been that its members had seen the risen Lord since others have done this but are not in the group. In particular the Twelve and the apostle group may have had some common members without being identical or one wholly including the other.

If then the use of the term leads to no clear definition as its meaning its origin is similarly shrouded in mystery. Traditionally it was assumed that when Jesus chose his twelve disciples he himself called them 'apostles'. This is highly unlikely. Mark and Matthew only use the word once each;[6] it is Luke in his Gospel and then in Acts who uses it regularly, in most cases apparently of the Twelve. Luke's understanding of the Twelve as the apostles may then be taken as a later formulation.[7] Thus the term does not go back to Jesus in any sense of defining a group, though we cannot exclude his use of it in a functional manner. As the name for a defined group of people it may have originated either in the primitive community in Jerusalem or among the first Christians in Antioch. Those who see its origin in the Jewish term *shaliach*[8] favour Jerusalem. Those who reject this origin probably favour Antioch. The evidence is difficult to assess.[9]

There is no need for us to explore these issues. It is sufficient to note that when terms appear in organizations they often come more or less simultaneously from diverse areas. The same

[5] Whether they actually were or not is irrelevant; we are only concerned with the way in which Paul conceived apostleship. J. A. Kirk, 'Apostleship since Rengstorf: Towards a Synthesis', *NTS* 21 (1974–5), pp. 249–65, wrongly concludes that the apostles include the Twelve. All we can say is that they may have shared some common members.

[6] Matt. 10.2; Mark 6.30. The word should probably not be read at Mark 3.14.

[7] Cf. R. Schnackenburg, 'Apostles Before and During Paul's Time', in *Apostolic History and the Gospel* (Essays presented to F. F. Bruce; ed. W. W. Gasque and R. P. Martin; Exeter, 1970), pp. 287–303.

[8] For a review of theories about *shaliach*, cf. J. A. Kirk, art. cit.

[9] For a recent assessment see C. K. Barrett, 'Shaliah and Apostle', in *Donum Gentilicium* (New Testament Studies in Honour of David Daube; ed. E. Bammel, C. K. Barrett, W. D. Davies; Oxford, 1978), pp. 93ff.

term may be used but those who use it because they derive it
from different areas may not intend it to signify the same thing.
The problem is intensified when the organization uses more
than one language and draws on more than one culture. In our
case the term probably always retains some sense of being sent,
whether by an individual, a group such as a church,[10] or by
Christ or God. It would not however be true to say that everyone
who carried out missionary work would have been called an
apostle (cf. Phil. 1.14–18). We can also be reasonably certain
that Paul was not the first to coin the term or to apply it within
the church. The way it appears in his letters implies that there
were those who had used it before he did. There was a pre-
existing group of apostles of which some would have denied
him membership. If he had introduced it no one would have
had any grounds for denying its application to him. If he had
introduced it we should probably also have been able to
discover a unitary conception of its meaning in his writings, and
as we have seen this is not the case.

II

There is no doubt that Paul traced his apostleship to his
encounter with the risen Lord on the way to Damascus but it is
very unlikely that he began to call himself an apostle immediately after that experience. When did he first become aware
that he was an apostle? We cannot suppose that Ananias burst
into the house of Jonas in the street called Straight in Damascus, raised his hands in greeting and cried, 'Hail, Apostle'.
Nor can we suppose that at the moment Paul's sight was
restored and he rose from his knees he thumped his chest and
proclaimed 'I'm an apostle!' It was at some later point that he
came to realize he was an apostle or, and we cannot exclude this
possibility, that for good theological and political reasons he
decided to claim to be an apostle.

It is not easy to determine when this happened for it is
inextricably bound up with the question of what constitutes an
apostle. In his earliest letter (1 Thess. 2.6) Paul describes

[10] See 2 Cor. 8.23; Phil. 2.25.

himself, Silvanus and Timothy[11] as apostles but while Peter and James later recognized his claim as an apostle they would certainly not have accepted Silvanus and Timothy as apostles in the same way. If then there is a doubt whether Paul claimed to be an apostle on a level with Peter at this stage, there is no doubt that he was making this claim by the time he came to write Galatians and the Corinthian correspondence. That the definition has changed is confirmed by Paul's failure to term Timothy an apostle in the address of 2 Corinthians. What was it then that triggered off the change in definition and the claim to parity with Peter?

III

It is highly unlikely that when Paul arrived in a new mission area that he began by announcing that he was an apostle. He would not have done this even in a synagogue for the term *shaliach* did not have for Jews any missionary significance.[12] He may of course have said that he had been 'sent' by God to bring the gospel but the use of a verbal form is not the same as the use of the noun. As we have seen the first occurrence of the term is in 1 Thess. 2.6 where Paul includes Silvanus and Timothy with himself as apostles. Before Paul eventually left Thessalonica he must have told the church that he and his fellow-workers had been sent to them by God, or Christ.[13] It is interesting that when he recalls to the Galatian Christians how they first received him he does not say 'You received me as an apostle of God' though he has been emphasizing his position as an apostle. Instead he says 'You received me as an angel of God' (4.14). An angel is of

[11] A few have denied that Paul intended to include Timothy as an apostle because there is no sense in which he could have seen the risen Lord; cf. A. M. Farrer in *The Apostolic Ministry* (ed. K. E. Kirk; London, 1946), p. 128 n. 1; A. Lemaire, *Les ministères aux origines de l'église* (Lectio Divina, 68; Paris, 1971), p. 71. For a more recent and thorough discussion refuting such views see Raymond F. Collins, *Studies on the First Letter to the Thessalonians* (Leuven, 1984), p. 183.

[12] Cf. H. Mosbeck, 'Apostolos in the New Testament', *StTh* 2 (1948), pp. 165–200 (169).

[13] It is just possible that he said they had been sent by the church in Antioch. This may have been Luke's opinion for it is only in Acts 14.4, 14 that he terms Paul an apostle; see Lemaire, op. cit., pp. 58–61.

course a messenger as in some sense an apostle is also. I do not
suggest that Paul deliberately avoided the word 'apostle' here.
He did not use it because it would not have reflected how the
Galatians received him; in the beginning of his mission they did
not think of him as an apostle.

But in the first two chapters of Galatians and in the letters to
Corinth he makes a great deal of being an apostle. What led
him to do so? He asserts his apostleship in Galatians because
some have argued that he was not an apostle and therefore
inferior to those who were apostles. It is unlikely that these
critics of his position would have been worried in the slightest
by his statement in 1 Thess. 2.6 where he set Silvanus and
Timothy on a par with himself; no one would have classed them
as on a par with Peter. It is equality with Peter, and some others
who cannot be identified with any certainty,[14] that is at the heart
of the argument over apostleship. Someone may have said to
him, 'Certainly, Paul, you are an apostle, but not one like Peter'.
Paul, however, claimed to be on a par with him and different
only in so far as his field lay with the Gentiles whereas that of
Peter lay with the Jews. While Paul uses the phrase 'apostle to
the Gentiles' (Rom. 11.12) it would be wrong to assume that he
arrived simultaneously at the two conclusions that his mission
was to the Gentiles and that he was an apostle on a par with
Peter. His mission to the Gentiles will have begun long before
he ever thought of himself as an apostle of the Peter-type. There
will have been others who would have been classed as apostles
alongside Peter. James may have been one but the ambiguity of
Gal. 1.19 does not allow us to draw any certain conclusion. In 1
Cor. 9.5f when discussing the right of apostles to maintenance
Paul speaks of 'the other apostles and the brothers of the Lord
and Cephas' which implies a recognized group of apostles even
if we do not know who were its members and its precise extent.
Since Paul discusses the right of Barnabas as well as himself to
upkeep it may be that at least in his eyes Barnabas would have
been a member of that group. No matter in what way the group
came to be acknowledged as a group it was one in which Paul
felt he ought to be included. Since we do not know the exact

---

[14] The names of the group are never listed; John, the son of Zebedee,
probably was one (cf. Gal. 2.9).

extent of this group and the names of all those in it we are at a loss to define the qualifications for inclusion in it. We know the claims Paul put forward at various times for his own inclusion. He had seen the risen Lord (1 Cor. 9.1; 15.8–11). His mission work testified to his position; the Corinthians are the seal of his apostleship (1 Cor. 9.2). He had displayed the signs, presumably miracles of healing etc., which were expected of an apostle (2 Cor. 12.12). There was however one qualification which he did not meet: he did not accept financial help from the churches in which he worked. We do not know if there were other qualifications. If there were and Paul met them they need never have been mentioned. The definition of the qualifications may also have changed from time to time. When his opponents found that Paul met a particular set of conditions they had proposed they may simply have changed the conditions in their attempt to eliminate him. Different groups of opponents may also have had different definitions. Finally no one of the conditions by itself would have been sufficient. The apostles were not the only ones who had seen the risen Lord or been successful missionaries or healed the sick. It is simplest to call the group over which there was dispute the Peter-group because he is the only person of whose membership we can be certain.[15]

IV

We must now examine the actual situations in which Paul claims to be an apostle. I detect a curious hangover from the days in which all the letters in the Pauline corpus were attributed to his personal authorship. It could then be said that he normally claimed to be an apostle of the Peter-group in each of them. Today scholars who accept only seven letters (Romans, 1 and 2 Corinthians, Galatians, Philippians, 1 Thessalonians, Philemon) continue to say the same. It is no longer true. Paul only claims to be an apostle in Romans, 1 and 2 Corinthians and

---

[15] Perhaps this group was known as 'the super-apostles'; these are mentioned in 2 Cor. 11.5; 12.11; cf. Barrett, op. cit., p. 38. This of course implies that 2 Cor. 11.13 refers to yet another group.

Galatians, four out of seven. This is not 'normally'. It is simply indeterminate.[16]

Turning to the letters it is easy to see why Paul makes the claim in the addresses of these four letters. In both Corinth and Galatia there have been those who denied he was an apostle and in the letters themselves he intends to advance reasons why he is. He therefore sets himself up as apostle from the outset. He uses the title in Romans because there he writes to a church which he has never visited and where he wishes to defend the gospel which he has himself linked to his apostleship. He can reasonably surmise after what has happened in other areas that suspicions about his apostleship may have been whispered in Rome. He mentions it therefore but does not make a major point of it as in the letters to Corinth and Galatia. He refers to it again only at 11.14 where in the course of the discussion of the position of Gentiles in the church he reminds his readers that he is the apostle to the Gentiles. Strictly speaking he only says here that he is *an* apostle to the Gentiles but all he writes suggests he believes that he has a special relationship to them and consequently most commentators and writers on Paul speak of him as '*the* apostle to the Gentiles'.[17]

Apart from terming himself 'apostle' in the address to Romans he also speaks there of his apostleship: 'Jesus Christ our Lord, through whom we have received grace and apostleship' (vv. 4f). Because Paul links χάρις and ἀποστολή together here many writers when they see another reference to Paul as given a χάρις of ministry assume that he is then also automatically referring to himself as an apostle.[18] In none of the other

---

[16] 'Normally' could well apply to ten instances out of thirteen. Two quotations taken at random from those who accept only seven letters show how easily the wrong conclusion can be drawn. Collins, op. cit., writes 'Paul normally identifies himself by name and title', i.e. in the addresses of his letters (p. 176). Victor Paul Furnish in his *II Corinithians* (The Anchor Bible; New York, 1984), puts the same point slightly differently when he writes, 'The *only* [italics mine] Pauline salutations in which the designation "apostle" is lacking are 1 Thess 1.1; Phil 1.1; Phlm 1'. We might with equal justification say that the term *only* appears in the addresses of four letters, those of Romans, 1 and 2 Corinthians and Galatians.

[17] I have discussed this in 'The Revelation to Evangelize the Gentiles', *JTS* 35 (1984), pp. 1–30 (19ff), and *infra*, pp. 103–38.

[18] This assumption underlies the otherwise very thorough study of A. Satake, 'Apostolat und Gnade bei Paulus', *NTS* 15 (1968–9), pp. 96–107.

passages however does he make that linking. In 1 Cor. 3.10 he is by God's grace a skilled master builder who lays the foundations of the church. There is no need to equate apostle and master builder. To do so only begs the question. Paul is an apostle and did lay foundations but that does not mean that when he laid foundations he thought of himself as an apostle. In 1 Cor. 15.10 he has just affirmed that he is an apostle when he says, 'By the grace of God I am what I am'. If he had stopped there we might well assume that he was referring to the grace of God in appointing him an apostle but he does not stop there. He continues by saying that it was the grace of God which enabled him to work harder than the other apostles, i.e. he relates God's grace to his activity and not to his apostolic position. In Gal. 1.6 the emphasis again lies on Paul as active in missionary work through the grace given to him and not on his position as apostle. In Gal. 1.15 where he says God had called him through his grace he stresses that he is what he is by God's grace without specifying what that is; the nearest reference indeed is to Paul as 'slave' of Christ. In Gal. 2.9 Peter, John and James perceive the grace that is in Paul; the immediate reference is to the valid mission he has to the Gentiles. In Rom. 15.15f Paul relates the grace given to him to his being a λειτουργός in the offering of the Gentiles. Again we do not find the word apostle. Paul thus attaches the idea of God's grace more generally to ministry than to apostolic ministry alone. So in Rom. 12.6 he writes of using the different gifts (χαρίσματα) we have according to the χάρις given to us. This leaves only 12.3 to be considered. Here Paul exhorts others by the grace given to him not to think more highly of themselves than they ought to. Many commentators write here of Paul speaking with apostolic authority.[19] But he does not introduce the word. As we have seen there is no necessary connection between grace and apostleship and if so there is no need to envision him speaking as apostle. It is sufficient that he holds a position of leadership. It is however perfectly correct that we should trace back both Paul's belief that he acts under God's grace and his claim to be an apostle to his experience on the Damascus road. But as we have seen there

---

[19] I shall not list names since I myself have been guilty of this very error; see my Cambridge Bible Commentary on Romans.

is no reason to think he left Damascus with the title 'apostle' ringing in his ears, though from that time onwards he will have seen himself a special recipient of God's grace.

We now turn from places where Paul does not use the term 'apostle' to those he does in order to determine in what situations he employs it. We have dealt with all the occurrences in Romans and 1 Thessalonians. In 1 Corinthians the word appears in the address. In 9.1ff we find it used three times. Here Paul asserts that he is an apostle of the Peter group because he saw the risen Lord. Clearly he uses it here because there have been suggestions that he is not an apostle of this group since he did not accept maintenance from the church in Corinth. No positive suggestions are made as to the activity of apostles other than that they preach. The word is used more generally without explicit reference to Paul himself at the conclusion of the discussion of the church as the body of Christ. A number of functions are listed, first apostles, second prophets, third teachers, then workers of miracles, etc., and it is said that not all are apostles, prophets, teachers etc. (1 Cor. 12.27f). Paul does not say that he is an apostle but his readers would certainly draw this conclusion. But what type of apostle has he in mind? An answer to this depends in part on how Paul conceives the body of Christ here. Does he compare the individual congregation to the body of Christ, in which case it would be the Silvanus-type apostle of whom he would be thinking, or does he compare the whole church, in which case he might be thinking of either the Peter-type or the Silvanus-type? Most commentators believe he has the individual congregation in mind.[20] We should also note that since every other 'title' in the list is oriented functionally apostle is probably also to be so taken; the emphasis then lies on function[21] rather than on position. Paul again uses the term in the plural and with a general reference in 4.9 where after

[20] It is just possible that Paul is thinking of the sum total of all congregations each of which taken by itself is a body of Christ. The plural 'apostles' could then denote the Peter group.

[21] There is a difference here between 'apostle' and the others in the list. In each of the others the function may be described as active, i.e. the prophet prophesies, but the apostle does not 'apostle'; he has been sent, i.e. the function is described in a passive manner; only at Rom. 11.13 where Paul calls himself the apostle to the Gentiles could the function be described as active.

sarcastically referring to the claims of some Corinthians that they have already attained to all that salvation has to offer he goes on 'I think God has exhibited us apostles as lowest of all, like men sentenced to death; because we have been made a spectacle to the world of angels and men'. Here Paul stresses the difference between what happens to those whom the Corinthians would presumably acknowledge as important, viz. apostles, with their own claims to be spiritually rich and spiritually kings. The sign of a true believer, of an apostle, is not strength but weakness. The final place where Paul uses the term 'apostle' is in 1 Cor. 15.8f where he applies it to himself as a witness of the resurrection. Here he certainly has in mind the Peter-type of apostle because of the resurrection allusion (cf. 9.1ff; at 15.7 he had mentioned apostles as a group). It is natural for him to include himself as a witness to the resurrection for some have linked this to apostleship and have doubted his apostleship. When we turn to 2 Corinthians it is again natural that Paul should use the term of himself in the address since there further questions have been raised about his apostleship. (That he uses it in 8.23 of those who take the collection to Jerusalem is irrelevant.) The word appears four times in the final four polemical chapters (10–13). On three occasions it is used of some who claim to be apostles, implying again that there is a recognizable group of apostles,[22] and Paul asserts that he is one no less than any of them, provided they are true apostles (11.5, 13; 12.11). The only evidence he offers for his own apostleship is his ability to perform signs (12.12). When he contrasts himself with these others it is in relation to missionary activity and Christ-like weakness. At one point the question of authority is raised; these false apostles have ill-treated the Corinthians even to the extent of striking them. Paul does not assert his authority in return but says he was too weak to do such a thing.

Paul opens the letter to the Galatians with a reference to himself as an apostle, not one appointed by men but by God. The ensuing discussion centres on the truth of the gospel he preaches rather than on his or others' authority. His gospel has

---

[22] Cf. Barrett; op. cit., p. 36.

been at stake but he leaves Jerusalem with this accepted and his own area of mission activity, his apostolate, among the Gentiles granted to him by those who claimed a position of importance among the Jerusalem Christians. Paul does not use the term in Philippians other than in relation to Epaphroditus as a conveyer of money and not at all in Philemon or in 2 Thessalonians, if it is by him.

We may sum up: when Paul uses the term of himself it is in contexts where there have been those who have said that he was not an apostle or contexts in which he stresses the weakness of those who are leading Christians or contexts in which there is some connection with either the truth or the proclamation of the gospel. At no point do we find him issuing instructions to others on the basis of his apostleship. But of course this may be implicit in his exercise of authority. He does not need to say that he is an apostle when he instructs others because everyone knows he is. It is appropriate then that we should turn now to examine his actual exercise of authority.

Before we turn to this it is important to note that it is not only apostles who exercise authority. In 1 Cor. 5.1ff and 6.1ff Paul expects other to do so. In 1 Cor. 16.15f he urges his converts to be subject to Stephanas (cf. 1 Thess. 5.12f). His envoys, Timothy and Titus, are expected to take action in their missions. Authority and apostleship do not then necessarily go together.

V

Paul did not come to a position of authority by inheritance or election as many do. He himself would have said that God gave him whatever authority he exercised and would have traced this back to his Damascus road experience. While Paul himself may have thought this others might have said that it was granted to him by Peter and the Jerusalem leaders, or at least was not valid until they recognized it. Some may even have said that he exercised it because of his tremendous activity (very active people often grab authority) or his dominating character. We do not need to weigh the relative merits of these possible views. It is however important to say a little about the areas in which authority may be exercised. Jesus exercised authority in exorcism and teaching. In discussing Paul we shall not be concerned with the first of these and only in part with the second. More importantly authority is exercised when rules are set down and where those who break these or other generally recognized rules are punished. We must now examine Paul's writings to see how he does exercise authority in these areas.[23]

We begin by noting that he expected obedience to himself. In such a simple and friendly letter as that to Philemon he can write that he is confident of Philemon's obedience (v. 21). To the Philippians he says, 'Therefore, my beloved, as you have always obeyed, so now, not only as in my presence but much more in my absence, work out your own salvation with fear and trembling' (2.12),[24] and the context shows that the obedience is to himself.[25] It is not then surprising that he should say to the contentious Corinthians that he is ready to punish their every disobedience, whenever they complete their obedience (2 Cor. 10.6).[26] If we regard the obedience as to Christ it is still offered to Paul as Christ's representative. If Paul expects obedience he is also not slow to issue commands to his converts. Again he writes in the friendly letter to Philemon that though in Christ he could have commanded him he will now only appeal to him (vv. 8f). That on this occasion he does not issue a command is beside the point; we learn that issuing commands was his normal practice. We learn the same when in respect of the collection he writes to the Corinthians, 'I do not say this as a command . . .' (2 Cor. 8.8). He would not need to stress that he was not commanding them if they were not accustomed to him doing so. We find the same authoritative note in 1 Thess. 4.2, 'you know what instructions we gave you through the Lord Jesus', or in 1 Cor. 11.17 when introducing the way in which the

[23] I have treated the manner in which Paul exercises authority in much greater detail in my Sprunt Lectures at Union Theological Seminary, Richmond, Virginia, *Paul and his Converts* (1985). Published under the same title, Edinburgh, 1988, pp. 73–95.

[24] Cf. 2 Cor. 2.9; 7.15. 7.12 should probably also be classed here.

[25] Cf. J. Hainz, *Ekklesia: Strukturen paulinischer Gemeinde-Theologie und Gemeinde-Ordnung* (Regensburg, 1972), pp. 221f.

[26] If it is said here that the obedience is to Christ, this is true, but Paul sees obedience to Christ as offered through himself, and therefore as obedience to himself. It is only because he so envisages it that he can think of himself as punishing those who disobey.

Eucharist should be celebrated he commences, 'In the following instructions'. Paul commands and expects that he will be
obeyed. If we accept 2 Thessalonians as Pauline this emphatic
tone is very explicit in 3.6ff where within a few verses Paul has
several times to recall the Thessalonians to the instructions he
gave them on his original visit about the need to work. At 1 Cor.
7.17 he says of the instructions he gives on marriage 'this is my
rule in all the churches' – note the '*my* rule'. He has rules for his
churches. The Corinthians asked him a number of questions
about behaviour and having answered some of these about
marriage, food sacrificed to idols, etc. he ends, 'about the other
things [presumably things about which they had asked] I will
give direction when I come' (1 Cor. 11.34). In respect of the
collection for Jerusalem he directs (ἐπιτάσσειν) them as he had
directed the churches of Galatia (16.1). Sometimes the authoritarian tone emerges when he only uses the simple word λέγω as
in Gal. 5.2.

I have drawn attention to these authoritarian passages in Paul
not to prove that he was an authoritarian person but in order to
inquire from where he thought he derived his authority. You
will have noted that in not one of them did he refer to himself
as an apostle; indeed in two of the letters, Philemon and
Philippians, he never described himself as an apostle. Surely if
he had been concerned about his apostolic authority we might
have expected him to have commenced at least once, 'As your
apostle I direct you'. In 2 Cor. 1.24 Paul denies that he lords it
over the Corinthians and we may take this to mean that he does
not regard himself as an authoritarian kind of person. To what
then, if not to his apostolic status or to his personality, does he
trace his authority?

We require now to examine a little more closely some of the
phrases he uses when advising and instructing his churches. We
begin with 1 Cor. 7.25 where he says that he has no command of
the Lord for the unmarried, but gives his own opinion (γνώμη)
as one 'who by the Lord's mercy is trustworthy'. It is clear from
this that one source of his authority might be a saying of the
earthly or exalted Lord. Occasionally he does use such sayings,
in relation to divorce (1 Cor. 7.10), to the right of those who
work for the Lord to support (1 Cor. 9.14) and to set out the

proper way in which the eucharist should be celebrated (1 Cor. 11.23, 'I received from the Lord what I also delivered to you ...'). By and large however he does not use sayings of Jesus as the basis of his authority.[27] The alternative is to give an opinion as one whom he believes the Lord trusts. His authority comes from the Lord but in some way other than through the teaching of the earthly Jesus. In very similar fashion in a later letter to the same Corinthians, who by now are no longer seeking his advice but doubting his right to control them, he warns them that when he comes he will not spare them so that they may 'have proof that Christ is speaking in' him (2 Cor. 13.2f). A few verses later he says he writes in this way before he comes so that when he arrives he may not have to be severe in the use of the authority given him by the Lord 'for building up and not for tearing down' (13.10; cf. 10.8). Earlier he had possibly been accused of lining his own pocket out of his missionary work and had retorted, 'we are not, like so many, peddlers of God's word; but as men of sincerity, as commissioned by God, in the sight of God we speak in Christ' (2 Cor. 2.17). He exhorts those with charismatic gifts to acknowledge that what he writes is a command (ἐντολή)[28] of the Lord (1 Cor. 14.37). He reminds the Thessalonians of the instructions (παραγγελίαι) he had given them through the Lord Jesus (1 Thess. 4.2).[29]

Just as in those statements in which Paul demanded obedience to himself, in none of these has there been any reference to himself as an apostle. Instead Paul regards himself as in close touch in some way with the exalted Christ and sees his authority deriving directly from Christ.[30] There are occasions when he appears to leave out the christological reference but probably he always expected it to be understood as present. Or possibly he was just an authoritarian kind of person whose authority found its basis in his own character. In either case his authority

---

[27] Even when he does use such sayings he adds his own interpretation as in 1 Cor. 7.11; cf. Hainz, op. cit., pp. 59f.

[28] The variant reading which omits ἐντολή does not affect the sense in which Christ is the origin of Paul's authority.

[29] See also 2 Cor. 12.19; 1 Thess. 2.13.

[30] Cf. Schütz, op. cit., p. 278, 'He bases his authority on his experience'.

was 'charismatic' in the sense of Weber[31] and did not derive from human appointment.

There are a number of places where Paul exercises or threatens to exercise it. The most interesting is 2 Cor. 13.10 where as we have seen he says he wishes to find things in order at his coming, for God has given him the authority both to build up and to tear down. He draws this phrase about building up and tearing down (he uses it also at 10.8) from Jer. 1.10 and 24.6 so that incidentally if he has any picture in mind as giving him authority it is that of the prophet[32] and not of the apostle. There is the same absence of a reference to 'apostle' in the way he treats the case of the incestuous man (1 Cor. 5.1ff). Paul calls on the church when it is assembled and his spirit is with it to make a decision (he even tells it what decision to take – to deliver the sinner to Satan). Note that he does not say 'when my apostolic spirit is with you'. On one occasion he had to confront Peter face to face. Peter had been getting along happily with Gentiles in Antioch until certain men came from James; he then separated from full fellowship with the Gentiles. Paul says that he rebuked Peter and those siding with him. He does not say that he uttered his rebuke because he was the apostle to the Gentiles but because he spoke for the truth of the gospel. Pushed to the limit Paul does not fall back on apostolic authority but on his understanding of the gospel.[33]

But if Paul does not envisage himself acting as 'apostle' when he instructs, advises and disciplines is there some other role which he sees himself as playing? We turn now to a passage

[31] See Schütz, op. cit., and B. Holmberg, *Paul and Power: The Structure of Authority in the Primitive Church as Reflected in the Pauline Epistles* (Lund, 1980), for the application of the insights of Weber to Paul. K. Kertelge, 'Das Apostelamt des Paulus, sein Ursprung und seine Bedeutung', *BZ* 14 (1970), pp. 161–81, regards Paul's apostolate as 'charismatic' in the New Testament sense.

[32] For the view that Paul may have regarded himself as a prophet see A.-M. Denis, 'L'Apôtre Paul, prophète "messianique" des Gentils. Étude thématique de 1 Thess., II, 1–6', *ETL* 33 (1957), pp. 245–318; T. Holtz, 'Zum Selbstverständnis des Apostels Paulus', *TLZ* 91 (1966), pp. 322–30; J. Murphy-O'Connor, *Paul on Preaching* (London and New York, 1964), pp. 104ff; J. M. Myers and J. D. Freed, 'Is Paul Also Among the Prophets?', *Interpretation* 20 (1966), pp. 40–53; David Hill, *New Testament Prophecy* (London, 1979), pp. 111ff.

[33] Cf. Schütz, op. cit., pp. 123, 145, 157f, 278, 284; Schmithals, pp. 39f, H. von Campenhausen, *Ecclesiastical Authority and Spiritual Power in the Church of the First Three Centuries* (London, 1969), p. 35.

about discipline previously omitted. It is the final section of his discussion of the different groups in Corinth and their failure to hold together recognizably as one church (1 Cor. 4.14ff). Paul says that some in the church are arrogant and threatens that he will come to them soon when they will find out the kind of person he really is. This is how the passage begins:

> I am not writing this to put you to shame, but to admonish you as my beloved children. Even if you have thousands of guides in Christ, you do not have many fathers. For I brought you to birth in Christ Jesus through the gospel.

and this is how it ends:

> What do you wish? Shall I come to you with a rod, or with love in a spirit of gentleness?

A rod is the way to keep children in order, or at least it was in the ancient world (e.g. Prov. 23.13f).

It is perfectly logical therefore for Paul to move from the image of himself as father and his converts as his children to that of the exercise of discipline.[34] His care for them in advising and directing them is indeed often set in terms of the parent–child relation. They are babes whom he has been forced to feed with milk and not solid food (1 Cor. 3.1–3). When he is worried about the Galatians and fears they may fall away into heresy he writes of them as his little children for whom he may have to suffer birth pangs a second time until Christ is formed in them (Gal. 4.19). Note here that it is the female aspect of the parent role which is to the fore. Paul indeed employs both aspects. Thus he writes to the Thessalonians that he and his colleagues were gentle among them like a 'nurse taking care of her children' (1 Thess. 2.7; 'nurse' means 'mother' and is so rendered in some English versions for in those days mothers nursed their own children). A few verses later in the same letter he reverts to the male image, 'You know how, like a father with his children, we exhorted each one of you' (2.11). The image is found also in 2 Cor. 6.13; 12.14 and in 1 Cor. 4.17, Phil. 2.22, Phlm 10 of individual Christians who have been converted by

---

[34] On this whole area see Pedro Gutierrez, *La paternité spirituelle selon saint Paul* (Paris, 1968).

Paul. When Paul then looks for the role which he fulfils towards his churches he does not use that of the apostle but that of the parent with his converts as his children. There is one other image he uses which is again associated with him as the one who has converted his readers. He is the master builder; his converts are what he has built (1 Cor. 3.9ff). It may indeed be because he views himself as builder that he uses the contrast of building up and destroying with which he threatens the Corinthians (2 Cor. 10.8; 13.10). It is however possible that he envisages himself here as playing the role of prophet. There is some other evidence that he may have so seen himself, e.g. in the language with which he describes his Damascus Road experience.[35] However he never explicitly claims to be a prophet.

It looks then as if the images which Paul acknowledges as motivating him when he comes to advise, instruct and discipline his churches are those that derive from his relation to them as the one through whom God brought them into being. The image of parent was of course widely used in the ancient world. In particular it was used in the Wisdom literature of the wise man, by Cynic philosophers of their relation to those whom they taught, of rulers towards their subjects and of colonists towards their founding cities. Confirmation that Paul's use of the image is no chance or haphazard affair can be seen in its absence from Romans.[36] Unlike his other letters Romans is not written to his own converts and it would therefore be inappropriate to employ it.

There is one other point which brings out some of the significance of this image in contrast to that of the apostolic. It has always been difficult to see why Paul refused financial help from his churches when apostles were entitled to it. Paul himself acknowledges their entitlement in 1 Cor. 9.3ff. His refusal to avail himself of this right landed him in repeated difficulties with his Corinthian Christians who because of it began to wonder whether he was a genuine apostle. Forced for the second time to defend his rejection he answered that it was not the duty of children to lay up money for their parents but of

[35] See note 32.

[36] Even if we accept Ephesians and Colossians as genuine Pauline letters this is confirmed for neither of them was written to those he had converted.

parents for their children (2 Cor. 12.14). In other words even to defend his apostolic position he goes to the parent image. It may well be that long before he came to claim a position as an apostle of the Peter-type he had already formed the practice of refusing financial aid from those to whom he ministered. Claiming the position he was later confronted with the right of apostles to maintenance; since he had already formed his own attitude and was unwilling to go back on it he justifies his position from the major image of parenthood which motivates his conduct.

It is time to recall the initial picture of the Queen, Prince Charles and his vegetables. Its appropriateness to the present discussion may now, perhaps, be more easily seen. The official title is not necessarily the motivating factor. Paul claimed to be an apostle of the Peter-type because it was necessary in order to maintain the truth of the gospel. But he only used the title when others disputed it or might dispute it. Basically he considered himself the parent of those to whom he wrote. The parent of those days had much more authority than the parent of today; he retained control over his children for a much longer period. In the extended family if a son brought home a wife they both came under the authority of the father. So Paul could expect continued obedience from his converts long after he had left them.

Perhaps parent is not quite the correct term. I would prefer to use that of 'founding parent'.[37] It is a well-known sociological phenomenom that those who found organizations tend to control them as long as possible. Though we may speak theologically of Christ as the founder of *the* church, if we were to use the sociological terms we would speak of Paul as the founder of the churches in Corinth, Galatia, Philippi, etc. It is then only natural that he should exercise authority in those churches. Now it may be said that founder and apostle are the same. Looking back from our vantage point in history we may equate them but would Paul have equated them? And if he would have

---

[37] The Greeks regularly used the term μητρόπολις of the city which founded a colony (our English transliteration no longer retains this meaning); occasionally the 'father' image is used. On cities and their colonies see A. J. Graham, *Colony and Mother City in Ancient Greece* (Manchester, 1964).

done so we have to ask further why he chose to use the idea of parent and not apostle in his actual control of his congregations? There seems no reason other than that was the way he thought. It might be suggested that he chose 'father' because 'apostle' would not have been easily understood by his Gentile converts. That that cannot be true can be seen in his use of the term for those who took the collection to Jerusalem (2 Cor. 8.23; cf. Phil. 2.25) and of Silvanus, Titus and himself as apostles of the non-Petrine type in his very earliest letter (1 Thess. 2.6). Moreover in the letters in which he argues strongly for his own Peter-type apostleship the readers apparently know what the term means. Yet it is in these very letters that he uses the parental image when exercising authority.

There is perhaps one further point which should be made before we leave Paul. If there is any way in which Paul regarded himself as unique then it might be from this sense of uniqueness that he derived his authority. If, say, he looked on himself as an 'eschatological' person whose task was to offer up the fulness of the Gentiles to Jerusalem and so consummate God's plans then he could be seen as giving himself a unique place. Even however if he only thought of himself as an exception among those who had seen the risen Lord ('one born out of due time'), as the last indeed to have done so, and as called to serve Christ in a most singular manner, he might have considered he had a special position before God and therefore possessed an authority different from that of the other apostles. In this way he would be an apostle, and would have to maintain that position if challenged, but would also have been more than an apostle and from that 'more' have derived his authority.[38]

VI

As we conclude it is not inappropriate to inquire how the emphasis on Paul's apostolic authority should have arisen. As is usual in such cases a number of factors will have contributed.

[38] We have made no use of Gal. 2.6 since this is a very difficult verse to understand. It has been used at times to suggest that being an apostle was an *adiaphoron* for Paul. For discussions of the verse see D. M. Hay, 'Paul's Indifference to Authority', *JBL* 88 (1969), pp. 36–44; H. D. Betz, *Galatians* (Hermeneia; Philadelphia, 1979), ad loc.

1. We begin by asking how far the exercise of authority is associated with apostleship in the parts of the NT not written by Paul.

Luke is the writer who gives the apostles their clearest position in the New Testament church. He depicts the apostles,[39] or some of them, initiating action, e.g. setting hands on the 'Seven' (Acts 6.6), imparting the Holy Spirit to Samaritan converts (8.14ff). It is the apostles and *brethren* who approve Peter's action in baptizing Cornelius. When the council meets in Jerusalem to consider Paul's mission to the Gentiles it is the apostles and elders who come together to discuss the matter and it is James, a non-apostle in Luke's eyes, who presides and issues the verdict (15.1ff). This itself is a decision of the apostles and elders (15.22; 16.4). Later when Paul came for the last time to Jerusalem it is again James who occupies the seat of authority (21.17ff). Luke does not therefore associate authority necessarily with apostleship but leave it open for such an association to appear.

In Matthew and Mark the apostles are given authority to exorcise and preach (Matt. 10.2; cf. Mark 6.7–13, 30).[40] Exorcism and preaching have not been areas of activity with which we have been concerned in discussing Paul but the idea of authority is there clearly related to apostleship. The exercise of authority in general also is envisaged for when James and John ask for the best seats in the Kingdom Jesus speaks of the way it is to be used (10.35ff); however the Twelve in this pericope probably represent in Mark's eyes disciples in general including those of Mark's own day and are not to be restricted to the apostles.[41] In Matt. 16.19 Peter is given the authority of the keys but in 18.18 this is given to all disciples. Whatever then that authority is it is not given to the apostles as apostles though it may have been given to one among them and it is not something which is necessarily associated with apostleship.

---

[39] The apostles appear in Acts primarily as witnesses and missionaries; cf. H. von Campenhausen, 'Der urchristliche Apostelbegriff', *StTh* 1 (1948), pp. 96–130.

[40] The authority that goes with the twelve thrones (Matt. 19.28; Luke 22.30) belongs not to this world but to the next.

[41] See the discussion in my *Following Jesus: Discipleship in the Gospel of Mark* (Sheffield, 1981), pp. 123ff.

There is a strange development of the apostolic concept in
Ephesians where they become the foundation of the church
and recipients of the mystery of Christ (2.20; 3.5); this should
not lead us to make a special claim for them for on each
occasion prophets are associated with them and these are
prophets of the New Testament and not of the Old. Whatever
authority belongs to apostles will also belong to prophets.[42]

In the Pastorals Paul is set out as an apostle[43] and instructs
and directs Timothy and Titus and through them various
churches. Apart from the addresses of the three letters and two
references which parallel apostleship with preaching and teaching his apostleship is not stressed in these any more than in the
genuine letters. Interestingly when Timothy and Titus are
themselves being instructed they are described as Paul's children (1 Tim. 1.2, 18; 2 Tim. 1.2; 2.1; Tit. 1.4). Thus these letters
remain faithful to one strand in Paul's pastoral approach.

There are no references to apostles in the Johannine literature apart from Revelation whereas in Luke they are equated
with the Twelve (21.14). When however we examine the letters
we find that the parent/child relationship appears repeatedly as
the writer (supposed to be the apostle John?) addresses his
readers (1 John 2.1, 18; 3.7, 18; 4.4; 5.21; 3 John 4).[44] There is
then no play on the writer as apostle.[45]

Thus there are few references to the apostles as possessing a
special apostolic authority in the non-Pauline parts of the New
Testament and a surprising amount of material that still leaves
authority in the area of fatherhood. We require to move on
outside the New Testament if we are to discover the source of
the stress on apostolic authority.

2. By the third century bishops were tracing their ancestry
back to the apostles. By this time bishops were people who

---

[42] Apostles and prophets may also be interchangeable terms in the Didache;
cf. Lemaire, op cit., pp. 139f.

[43] Some scholars claim that the Pastorals only recognize one apostle, viz. Paul;
cf. e.g. Misbech, art. cit., p. 199.

[44] This may not be the usage in 1 John 2.12, 14 where children are set
alongside young men and fathers. The use in 2 John 1, 4, 13 where we read of
the children of the 'elect lady' is difficult.

[45] In 2 and 3 John the writers claims only to be a *presbuteros* and not an
apostle.

exercised authority; it was then natural that they should see in the apostles figures of authority. If they had not, their own base would have been rendered insecure.[46]

3. One area in which the authority of the apostles became important in the second century lay in the upholding of orthodoxy over against gnostic heresy. The orthodox traced back their position to the authoritative teaching of the apostles.[47]

4. The process of viewing the apostles as figures of authority had however already begun by the end of the first century. Clement of Rome says that because the apostles realized that there would be strife after they died they appointed others to continue their work (1 Clem. 44.1f): only those who are regarded as possessing authority can make such appointments. Ignatius says twice that since he is a condemned prisoner he ought not to give orders like an apostle (*Trall.* 3.3; *Rom.* 4.3). He writes also of Christians being subject to the presbytery as to the apostles (*Trall.* 2.2; cf. *Smyrn.* 8.1) and of the instructions or commands given by the apostles (*Trall.* 7.1; *Mag.* 13.1). The apostles are thus beginning to be seen as figures of authority.

5. The modern ecumenical debate which has often centred on the question of the authority of the ministry has kept this aspect to the fore when discussing the ministry's New Testament origin. It is not however proper to force our views of the nature of ministry back on the first century. We can see how erroneous this can become if we look at another area of ministry. For us it is difficult to conceive of a ministry one of whose important functions is not the administration of the sacraments. Yet Paul minimizes his role in baptism, having baptized only a few of the Corinthians (1 Cor. 1.14ff). He gives instructions about the conduct of the eucharist but says nothing about who should preside and gives us no clue whether he himself did so in his own churches whenever he was present. Because we are interested in ministerial authority we should be wary of reading this back into the ministry of the original apostles.

6. There are also non-theological factors of which account must be taken. We are much happier dealing with 'offices' than

[46] Cf. Farrer, op. cit., pp. 197ff.
[47] Cf. von Campenhausen, *Ecclesiastical Authority*, pp. 158ff.

with 'functions'. If 'apostle' was originally descriptive of a function it was natural as time went by that it should be transformed into an office. Officials always exercise authority. So we connect authority with the apostolic office and then with those who exercise the function. From this it is only a short step to speak of Paul's apostolic authority. I find it an enlightening exercise when I am reading books about Paul and encounter the adjective 'apostolic' before some noun, say apostolic ministry, to omit it. Almost invariably the argument is not affected in any way. It is perhaps more habit then than anything else that leads us to speak of his apostolic authority. There is possibly also a more subtle factor. Paul, I am sure, was not an easy person to get on with. He dominated others; his language was over-vehement. It is so much easier to attribute such behaviour to the 'office' with its title than to a named person who is supposed to be of almost perfect character.

7. There is a sociological need to have some kind of authority. If one authority is rejected, as the Protestant reformers rejected that of the church in the sixteenth century, another must be found, and Scripture took the place of the church. In the first few generations an authority was equally necessary. 'As what was once shared becomes less and less common, the apostle becomes more and more differentiated from others. His status comes to look unique. His relationship to power is not one of interpretation, but one of application. A new sense of authority replaces the original one.'[48] I take it that the original authority was that of the gospel itself. But the gospel is a fluid concept and difficult to formalize. It is easier to see authority as residing in a few easily identifiable people. Hence the development of apostolic authority.

VII

We finish by returning to our starting point. There is no doubt Paul claimed to be an apostle, and that of the type of Peter. There is no doubt that he exercised authority. There must be doubt that these two ideas are necessarily related. Perhaps this

[48] Schütz, op cit., p. 280; cf. pp. 279, 283.

can be put in another way. When Paul is concerned with his relations with his converts he does not employ the term apostle; he does so only when he is concerned with his relations with other church leaders. He may then only have used the term when it was politically advisable.[49]

---

[49] My own awareness of the relative unimportance of the apostolic title for Paul came in the course of the preparation of my Sprunt Lectures (see n. 23). These treat Paul's pastoral relations with the churches he founded. When I looked back on them after I had finished I was surprised to discover that the term 'apostle' never featured.

4

The Use of Credal and Liturgical
Material in Ephesians

This is not another attempt to isolate credal and liturgical material in Ephesians but an examination of the material that various scholars have isolated in order to inquire after the way in which the author in using it has modified it and to discern if possible his reasons for doing so. I assume that Paul was not the author but there would be little need to modify any of my argument if in fact he were. It is difficult to draw precise lines between credal, liturgical and catechetical material since the same material may have been used for more than one purpose, but by limiting our examination to credal and liturgical we mean to exclude catechetical material intended primarily for ethical instruction. Credal material would certainly have been used when catechumens were taught.

When Paul quoted the little creed of 1 Cor. 15.3–5 he did so because it was one known to his readers and therefore could form a basis for an argument. But it was not merely one known to his readers which he may have created for them when he was with them; it was a creed belonging to the early church and carrying therefore an authority wider than Paul's personal authority. What he quoted was both known to his readers and was accepted by them as authoritative. When in the New Testament the Old is explicitly quoted it may be assumed that the readers knew it and that it carried authority in their eyes. Yet when the OT is quoted it is not always done so explicitly. If the quotation is reasonably long and drawn from a well known passage (e.g. Eph. 5.21; 6.2, 3) it may be assumed that at least some of the readers will realize from where it comes and recognize its authority. Shorter quotations and allusions need to be looked at differently. They may simply be incorporated into the course of an argument (1.22; 2.17; 5.25; 5.26; 6.14; 6.15) and may not even have been used consciously but have come naturally to the pen of the writer because he has been grounded in the OT and thinks in its terms. Many of these will have been recognized by, at any rate, some of his readers; even if they did not recognize them they may still have been impressed by them and regarded these words as authoritative because their words were 'biblical' words. We may compare the way in which older people respond to the language of the King James Version of the Bible. The words carry an aura when used, even though not in a quotation, and affect their hearers disposing them to accept whatever argument is being advanced through their use. Liturgical and credal words can have the same effect. We have also to recognize that the OT when quoted is often varied from the original. This may consist in no more than a change in person or number or in the tense of a verb. Sometimes the variations are much greater and when we are unable to account for them we suppose the writer is using a text unknown to us. This may be what has happened in Eph. 4.8. It is also often true that it is difficult to determine the OT passage an author has in view, and if it is difficult to do this when we have the text of the OT how much more difficult will it be to detect liturgical material whose text we do not have or only possess in variant form in another New Testament writing. For instance it becomes practically impossible to determine if a line in the original has been omitted by the NT author in using it.

One of the best discussions of a liturgical or credal passage has been given us by Dr R. P. Martin who, in his *Carmen Christi*[1] carefully unearthed the original text of Phil. 2.6–11 before its incorporation into the letter, examined the additions Paul made in quoting it and offered reasons for the alterations. In

[1] Ralph P. Martin, *Carmen Christi. Philippians 2.5–11 in Recent Interpretation and in the Setting of Early Christian Worship* (SNTSMS 4; Cambridge, 1967). From the earliest days of his work Dr Martin has shown his interest in our area as seen in his *Worship in the Early Church* (first published in 1954).

respect of the addition about the cross he writes 'For the
Philippians at least, the addition of θανάτου δὲ σταυροῦ would
emphasize the abject degradation of Christ's lowly obedience,
and drive home the lesson that His identification with men
reached the lowest rung of the ladder'.[2] And again, 'Paul thus
directs the drift of the hymn's soteriological teaching – in its
original form, somewhat vague and amorphous – into channels
which are known to us from the Pauline literature'.[3] In respect
of the addition (2.10) about the persons (things) in heaven and
on earth and under the earth, he writes 'The Christ-hymn
enables the Church to see beyond the present in which the
Head of the Church reigns invisibly and powerfully – but known
only to faith – to that full proof of His reign in the heavenly
sphere in which all the powers are veritably subject to Him and
His dominion is manifestly confessed'.[4] Finally, in respect of the
doxology to God the Father he writes,

> Yet, in both lines of thought which are interwoven in the hymn
> so that we should not be faced with the choice of either-or, the
> notion of a rivalry within the Godhead is scouted, and there is
> no thought that Christ is a usurper, nor any suggestion of a
> crude binitarianism. For the worship of the exalted Lord is 'to
> the glory of the Father'. The Biblical monotheism is safe-
> guarded; and the purpose of the Father-God is seen to be
> honoured in the high place accorded to His Son.[5]

In effect Paul's additions have not altered the meaning of the
hymn but sharpened its bite and brought it more fully into line
with his own theology. Those who knew the hymn and heard
the Pauline additions could not but be impressed by them and
understand their significance. This is what happens when we
ourselves use quotations; we often add little bits in order to
bring out the significance of the whole for our argument.[6]
Sometimes when we quote we do so simply to adorn what we are
writing or to impress others with our literary knowledge. We

---

[2] Martin, *Carmen Christi*, p. 221.
[3] Martin, *Carmen Christi*, p. 226.
[4] Martin, *Carmen Christi*, p. 270.
[5] Martin, *Carmen Christi*, p. 283.
[6] This general point remains true even if Phil. 2.6–11 was written by Paul and therefore contains no alterations.

can, I believe, acquit the author of Ephesians from making quotations with such ideas in mind. There are times also when we use quotations with the intention of refuting them; on these occasions we make our intention clear in the surrounding context and advance arguments explaining the errors in the quoted material. We have also to remember that sometimes when people quote they may in fact see a different meaning in what they quote from what the original author saw when he was writing. Can we detect anything similar to what happened in Phil. 2.6–11 in the way the author of Ephesians has used his credal and liturgical material? This material has normally been detected in 1.3–14; 1.20–23; 2.4–10; 2.14–18; 2.19–22; 4.4–6; 5.14.[7] We shall examine these in turn.

1.3–14

This was the first section of Ephesians to be suggested as based on a credal or liturgical *Vorlage*[8] and is also the most extensive.[9] Roughly speaking, those who have discussed it and detected in it almost always a liturgical *Vorlage* have tended either to see the passage as more or less identical with the *Vorlage*, possibly with a few variations, or to have sought within it a hymn which the author has considerably altered to suit his purposes. We consider first the former alternative. It is undoubtedly true that much of the language and style of the passage is elevated in tone and appropriate to a liturgy. But similar language and style are found in other parts of the letter.[10] Though 1.3–14 is an

[7] This is the list given by H. Merkel, 'Der Epheserbrief in der neueren exegetischen Diskussion', *ANRW* 2.25.4, pp. 3222ff.

[8] T. Innitzer, 'Der Hymnus in Eph 1.3–14;, *ZTK* 28 (1904), pp. 612–21.

[9] An almost complete list of those who have discussed the possibility of a *Vorlage* here is given in Merkel, 'Der Epheserbrief in der neueren exegetischen Diskussion', pp. 3224–7. To these we may add J. C. Kirby, *Ephesians: Baptism and Pentecost* (London, 1968), pp. 103–10, 126–38; R. C. Bankhead, *Liturgical Formulas in the New Testament* (Clinton, S. Carolina, 1971), pp. 91–101; K. Usami, *Somatic Comprehension of Unity: The Church in Ephesus* (AnBib 101), pp. 80–91; J. Schattenham, *Studien zum neutestamentliche Prosahymnus* (Munich, 1965), pp. 1–10; G. Castellino, 'La dossologia della lettera agli Efesini (1, 3–14)', *Salesianum* 8 (1946), pp. 147–67.

[10] E.g. N. A. Dahl, 'Addresse und Proömium des Epheserbriefes', *TZ* 7 (1951), pp. 241–64; C. Maurer, 'Der Hymnus von Epheser 1 als Schlüssel zum ganzen Briefe', *EvT* 11 (1951/2), pp. 151–72.

abnormally long and complicated sentence the letter contains other lengthy and complex sentences. The thought of the passage is not out of accord with what we find in the remainder of the letter; indeed some commentators believe that 1.3–14 was composed in order to introduce the main ideas of the letter. There are however other issues which are important here. An author might be expected to quote from a liturgy if this was known to his readers for it would then have more effect on them. If Ephesians had been written to one community which the author knew we could well imagine him using material known to that community so that his points would come across more easily. But Ephesians is a general letter written to a number of communities. Would all of these have been using the same liturgy? Was the liturgy as settled in form and wording as this towards the end of the first century even in as limited an area as Asia Minor, assuming Ephesians was directed to that area? Most of those who regard 1.3–14 as derived from a liturgy suppose that it was part of a baptismal liturgy. In the *Didache* prayers are given in relation to the eucharist but not for the celebration of a baptism, though baptism is discussed. Even in the case of the eucharist prophets are left free to use their own prayers. Baptism may have been a much more unorganized service than it became later. Paul does not appear to have thought it important that he should baptize his converts (1 Cor. 1.13–16). We do not know who did baptize. There was probably then at this time no regular order of service and no baptismal liturgy. It may however be said that the author was using the language of the liturgy of his own community. Yet this does not overcome the difficulty of the similarity of the language and style of 1.3–14 with that of the remainder of the letter. We might get round this by saying that the author of the letter had himself composed his community's liturgy. He would then be the author of the passage and there would be no *Vorlage*.

The liturgical language of vv. 3–14 may be accounted for in quite another way. Much of the language of Ephesians reflects that of Colossians, but if we did not possess Colossians we would never have been able to argue that the author of Ephesians was indebted to another letter and still less able to reconstruct Colossians from Ephesians. The author of Ephesians combines material from different sections of Colossians, sometimes in the process imparting fresh meaning to a word or phrase, but he does not take a section of Colossians and interlace it with his own comments. This provides a useful clue to the way his mind works, though perhaps more applicable to some of the later passages to be discussed. What it means is that when he writes 1.3–14 he may reflect the language of a liturgy without it ever being possible for us to reconstruct that liturgy.

The second of our possibilities, that the author of the letter utilized an existing piece of tradition which he considerably reworked, has led to a number of attempts to recover the original. Almost all of these attempts have sought an underlying hymn. This has led to the elimination from the existing text of words, clauses and even whole verses in order to create a poetic form. Those who have approached the problem in this way have also had to take into account the thought of the passage in comparison with that of the rest of the letter and so have sought in the passages they have retained as deriving from the *Vorlage* theological views at variance with those in the letter and therefore sentiments for which the author of the letter could not have been responsible. Thus Fischer[11] omits from his reconstruction vv. 8b–11 because these verses allot to Christ a central and cosmic position whereas the beginning and end of the passage deal with the redemption of believers. Yet when Fischer comes to reconstruct the hymn underlying 2.14–18 he supposes the author of Ephesians added clauses emphasizing the redemption of believers and obscuring the cosmic position of Christ. It would be possible to take up and discuss here the many other attempts to discern an underlying hymn but this article would then become a book. All it is possible to do is to raise the general question as to the purpose of the use here of an underlying hymn. If the hymn is known to the readers then clarificatory amendments as Martin has shown in the case of Phil. 2.6–11 will serve to bring home to them points which the author wishes them to see as important. Large additions which alter the thought will hardly do this and in the course of them

---

[11] K. M. Fischer, *Tendenz und Absicht des Epheserbriefes* (FRLANT 111; Göttingen, 1973), pp. 111–18.

the readers may well forget that the hymn is being quoted and so lose the thread of the argument.

1.20–23

It is relatively easy to extract from these verses four lines which could have formed the core of a credal or liturgical statement:

20a [who] raised Christ from the dead
20b and set him at his right hand in the heavenlies
22a and put all things under his feet
22b and made him head over all things.

Sanders[12] argues that these lines have hymnic traits. Deichgräber[13] also settles on them but points out that they may be only a portion of a longer hymn which dealt with the pre-existence of Christ, his incarnation, sufferings and death in common with what seems to be a general pattern in early hymns about Christ. Other interpreters add to the four lines given above varying portions of what remains. Schille[14] is alone in rejecting part of this suggested hymn preferring instead a structure consisting of 20a, 20b, 21a, 22a. All are agreed that v. 21b with its 'not only' 'but also' is in a wholly other style and must be regarded as an addition of the author who wishes to make sure that the list of 21a may not be incomplete. All also agree that the reference to the church in 22b comes from the author. Fischer[15] adds 21a to the four lines. Those who do not add it would regard it as the author's interpretation of 'the heavenlies'; the latter phrase, ἐν τοῖς ἐπουρανίοις, is one of his favourite expressions (1.3, 29; 2.6; 3.10; 6.12) and this ought to lead to its elimination from the core in 20b; if so v. 21 would be automatically eliminated as its expansion. Ernst[16] would appear to wish to add the whole of v. 23 with the cosmos understood as

---

[12] J. T. Sanders, 'Hymnic Elements in Ephesians 1–3', *ZNW* 56 (1965), pp. 214–32.

[13] R. Deichgräber, *Gotteshymnus und Christushymnus in der frühen Christenheit* (Göttingen, 1967), pp. 161–5.

[14] G. Schille, *Frühchristliche Hymnen* (Berlin, 1963), p. 103 n. 4.

[15] Fischer, *Tendenz und Absicht des Epheserbriefes*, pp. 118–20.

[16] J. Ernst, *Pleroma und Pleroma Christi* (Regensburg, 1970), pp. 106f.

the body of Christ. Although other commentators do not agree with Ernst in accepting v. 23 or part of it as belonging to the *Vorlage* they are in agreement that the hymn originally referred to the cosmos as the body of Christ and that the author of Ephesians adapted it to his own ecclesiological purposes. We shall return to this supposed adaptation of the hymn but before doing so we note that there is no citation formula introducing the hymn and that the hymn would have followed more easily without the first words of v. 20; instead of the personal pronoun of 20a there could then have been the name 'Christ'. Many commentators have noted that 1.20–23 has affinities with 1 Cor. 15.20ff; most of the statements of the alleged hymn are in fact recognized christological statements which the author of Ephesians could have drawn on on his own. He did not then need to go to a hymn to obtain them. But the principal difficulty in accepting a hymn here must lie in the changed meaning which it has received on being incorporated into Ephesians. If we assume that his readers knew the original hymn or creed they must have been confused by his change in its meaning. If they did not know it, it was pointless to quote it without drawing attention to the fact that it was a citation (at 5.14 the author tells us he is quoting a hymn). It is also important to ask if the writer disagreed with the cosmic meaning of the original hymn; elsewhere he shows that he has an interest in the cosmic significance of his faith (cf. 1.10; 2.7; 3.10, and 4.6 if the forms of πᾶς in 4.6 are understood as neuter and not masculine). If then the author of Ephesians took up an original piece of tradition which referred to the cosmos and inserted the reference to the church, he was modifying it in an entirely different way from the modifications made in the Philippian hymn. We conclude that there is no deliberate and extensive quotation of a section of traditional material in 1.20–23.

2.4–10

Most of this is couched in the first person plural but vv. 5b, 8 are in the second plural, and v. 9 in the third singular; it is generally agreed that this verse should be eliminated from any hymn, creed or liturgy found in the remainder of the passage.

Sanders[17] attempts to give the passage hymnic structure but the lines he suggests are of unequal length and have no rhythmic structure.[18] It is probably then better to regard it with Fischer[19] as part of a prose liturgy, and Stuhlmacher[20] suggests (Schille had already proposed regarding it as an initiatory hymn)[21] that it represents what those who were being baptized said (the sections in the first plural) while the sections in the second person are addressed to them by those who are already Christians. Here we need to remember that Ephesians is not directed to a particular community but is a general letter. We have already raised the question whether there was an accepted baptismal liturgy at this time so that the reference to baptism would have been recognized in a number of diverse communities. Moreover the author of the letter writes as if he has not visited the communities to which he is writing (1.15) and so may well not have known their form of liturgy. But could he not have been using the baptismal liturgy of his own community? Some of the language is similar to what he himself uses (e.g. 'the heavenlies', the use of a verb and its cognate noun in v. 4).[22] However if we are to attribute the liturgy to the composition of the letter's author it is easier to think of him as composing it to fit its context, and therefore as not part of a liturgy.[23] The reference to the mercy of God in v. 4 follows on the discussion of human sin in vv. 1–3 and the first words of v. 5 repeat part of v. 1. The placing of the resurrection of Christians in the past (v. 6) has been already said in Col. 2.12; 3.1 and our author draws heavily on the language and ideas of Colossians (note how the words of Col. 2.13f have been used in our passage).[24] Another factor confirming the view that the author of Ephesians wrote

---

[17] J. T. Sanders, 'Hymnic Elements in Ephesians', *ZNW* 56 (1965), pp. 214–32.

[18] So Fischer, *Tendenz und Absicht des Epheserbriefes*, p. 121.

[19] Fischer, *Tendenz und Absicht des Epheserbriefes*, pp. 121–31.

[20] P. Stuhlmacher, *Gottes Gerechtigkeit bei Paulus* (FRLANT 87; Göttingen, 1965), pp. 216f.

[21] Schille, *Frühchristliche Hymnen*, pp. 53–60.

[22] Cf. E. Percy, *Die Probleme der Kolosser- und Epheserbriefe* (Lund, 1946), p. 32.

[23] Cf. A. Lindemann, *Die Aufhebung der Zeit* (Gütersloh, 1975), pp. 116f.

[24] Cf. U. Luz, 'Rechtfertigung bei den Paulusschülern' in *Rechtfertigung*, ed. J. Friedrich, W. Pohlmann, P. Stuhlmacher (FS E. Käsemann; Tübingen, 1976), pp. 365–83.

our passage is the way in which it picks up the ideas of 1.20–23 relating to resurrection and heavenly session and applies them to believers. We conclude that our author wrote this passage though he was of course heavily dependent on expressions and thought current in the early church.

2.14–18

More discussion has taken place over a possible *Vorlage* to this passage than over any other in Ephesians. It is cast in the first person plural whereas both 2.11–13 and 2.19–22 are in the second person. The subject of 2.11–13 is resumed in 2.19–22 with words that are common. Haupt[25] therefore suggested that 2.14–18 is parenthetical to the main thrust of 2.11–22. Accepting this many from Schlier[26] and Schille[27] onwards have sought to unearth in it a hymn. The argument for the existence of a *Vorlage* has been supported by the number of words and concepts not found elsewhere in Ephesians and by features common to hymnic material, e.g. participles, relative clauses, *parallelismus membrorum*. The passage also appears to have an implicit ambiguity in that the author seems unable to decide whether his main emphasis lies on reconciliation between God and humanity or between two human groups. It also sets out Christ as the subject of the action of what happens whereas elsewhere God is regarded as initiating redemption. Taking these features as clues assisting decision as to what belonged to or did not belong to the original *Vorlage* a considerable number of attempts have been made to recreate it, none of which agree in detail.

Limitations of space prevent a full listing and examination of all the attempts and we shall only look at two representative samples. These two unlike many others succeed in producing a good line structure. Before examining them there are several general observations to make. There is no agreement on the precise passage in which we should look for the *Vorlage*.

[25] E. Haupt, *Die Gefangenschaftsbriefe* (KEK 7th edn; Göttingen, 1902).

[26] H. Schlier, *Der Brief an die Epheser* (Düsseldorf, 7th edn, 1971; 1st edn, 1957).

[27] Schille, *Frühchristliche Hymnen*, pp. 24–31.

Although the initial examination of the passage suggested that all of vv. 14–18 should form the basis more recent work has limited consideration to either vv. 14–17 or even to vv. 14–16. This means that the change of person and the parenthetical nature of vv. 14–18 which were the initiating cause for the search for a *Vorlage* are no longer relevant; they seem indeed to have been forgotten by those who choose one of the smaller sections on which to base their solution; they do not even seem to see the need to explain why the author continued v. 18 or vv. 17f in the style of the *Vorlage* and did not revert to the earlier style of vv. 11–13 until v. 19. Again while attention has been drawn to the *hapax legomena* some of these are often omitted from the proposed reconstructions; the number of *hapax legomena* is in fact not statistically significant: 10 in a passage of 80 words where the average would suggest 7. The ambiguity in relation to reconciliation which runs through vv. 14–18 is not unique to it; in particular it is present in v. 13 where the Gentiles are said to have been made near without it being specified whether they have been made near to God or to the Jews. This ambivalence may be deliberate on the part of the author who sees the two as related and who thus allows the two aspects of reconciliation to penetrate what he writes next.

The first example is that of Gnilka:[28]

Αὐτός ἐστιν εἰρήνη ἡμῶν
ὁ ποιήσας τὰ ἀμφότερα ἕν
καὶ τὸ μεσότοιχον λύσας
τὴν ἔχθραν ἐν τῇ σαρκὶ καταργήσας
ἵνα κτίσῃ ἐν αὐτῷ καινὸν ἄνθρωπον
ποιῶν εἰρήνην
ἀποκτείνας τὴν ἔχθραν ἐν αὐτῷ
καὶ ἐλθὼν εὐηγγελίσατο εἰρήνην
[τοῖς μακρὰν καὶ τοῖς ἐγγυς]

The essential thing to note here is that Gnilka has preserved the consistency of his *Vorlage* by excluding from it those elements in vv. 14–18 which imply that human beings are reconciled to one another. The only reconciliation is that between God and the human sphere, and this reconciliation is only

---

[28] J. Gnilka, *Der Epheserbrief* (Freiburg: Herder, 1971), p. 149.

implicit, for Gnilka makes the writer of Ephesians responsible for the introduction of the term. Christ has broken down the wall separating heaven and earth, and this apparently by his incarnation as indicated by the reference to 'flesh'. Leaving aside all questions as to the origin of the term 'middle wall' and assuming as is highly probable that the author has used this hymn because the hymn was known to his readers, has he not introduced hopeless confusion into it by his references to the law, to the body which is the church, and to the cross so that the latter now governs the meaning of 'flesh'? The new man which in the hymn was the cosmos as *makroanthropos* has now become the corporate Christ. If the author of Ephesians was attempting to correct what he took to be bad theology in the *Vorlage* were there not easier ways to go about this? He could have stated the bad theology and controverted it. Without such a deliberate argument would his readers have been able to realize what he was about? If, to take the less probable position, the hymn was not known to the readers it is difficult to see why he should express himself through its use when he had to alter it so much.

The second example is that of Wilhelmi:[29]

I   Αὐτὸς ἐστιν ἡ εἰρήνη
      ὁ ποιήσας τὰ ἀμφότερα ἓν
      καὶ

II   τὸ μεσότοιχον τοῦ φραγμοῦ λύσας
      τὸν νόμον τῶν ἐντολῶν καταργήσας
      ἵνα

A   τοὺς δύο κτίοῃ εἰς ἕνα καινὸν ἄνθρωπον
      ποιῶν εἰρήνην
      καὶ

B   ἀποκαταλλάξῃ τοὺς ἀμφοτέρους ἐν ἑνὶ σώματι
      ἀποκτείνας τὴν ἔχθραν.

Of all the suggested underlying hymns this is probably the best so far as rhythmical balance goes. Wilhelmi has taken considerable care to ensure that the lines are of similar length

[29] G. Wilhelmi, 'Der Versöhner-Hymnen in Eph 2,14ff', *ZNW* 78 (1987), pp. 145–52.

and that there is a proper *parallelismus membrorum*. The only feature breaking a proper hymnic structure is the ἵνα separating the two strophe. In the hymn God is the acting subject throughout. In I-II the reference is cosmic with the wall that between heaven and earth; in A-B it is human. The differences between the two strophe are considerable and Wilhelmi speculates that they may have had different origins. Two however of the original clues to the existence of a *Vorlage*, the change of person from second to first at v. 14, and the reverse at v. 19, and the mixture of heaven/earth and human/human reconciliation no longer operate so strongly to support the existence of the *Vorlage*. The first has simply disappeared; the second is still present, though in a less confusing way. But the major change when the hymn is used in Ephesians is the appearance of Christ and not God as the subject of the action. Some of the other changes, e.g. the reference to the cross, might be regarded as clarificatory but they are so extensive that it may be reasonably asked whether the readers of Ephesians, supposing they knew the hymn, would ever have recognized that the author was using it? If, however, the readers were not acquainted with the hymn some of these difficulties disappear since the author might be regarded as simply using it as a framework on which to hang his own thoughts. But then the whole point of the search for underlying traditions seems to disappear. Finally it should be noted that both the attempts of Gnilka and Wilhelmi and indeed of many others imply that the author of Ephesians used an interlacing technique in altering the *Vorlage* which we have seen was contrary to the manner in which he used material from Colossians.[30]

---

[30] Other attempts at formulating a *Vorlage* to this passage are discussed in J. T. Sanders, 'Hymnic Elements in Ephesians', and *The New Testament Christological Hymns* (Cambridge, 1971), pp. 14f, 88–92. Deichgräber, *Gotteshymnus und Christushymnus in der frühen Christenheit*, pp. 165–7; E. Testa, 'Gesù pacificatore universale. Inno liturgico della Chiesa Madre (Col. 1,15–20 + Ef. 2,14–16)', *SBFLA* 19 (1969), pp. 5–64; J. Gnilka, 'Christus unser Friede – ein Friedens-Erlöserlied in Eph 2,14–17', *Die Zeit Jesu* (FS H. Schlier; Freiburg, 1970), pp. 190–207; K. Wengst, *Formeln und Lieder des Urchristentums* (Gütersloh, 1972), pp. 181–6; Fischer, *Tendenz und Absicht des Epheserbriefes*, pp. 131–7; P. Stuhlmacher, ' "Er ist unser Friede" (Eph 2,14). Zur Exegese und Bedeutung von Eph 2,14–18', *Neues Testament und Kirche* (FS R. Schnackenburg; Freiburg, 1974), pp. 337–58; C. Bürger, *Schöpfung und Versöhnung: Studien zum liturgischen Gut in*

2.19–22

W. Nauck[31] has argued that these verses are drawn from a baptismal hymn and points to parallels with 1 Pet. 2.4ff which he also regards as such a hymn. This view of 1 Pet. 2.4ff has been disputed by the majority of recent commentators.[32] Nauck makes no emendations to the text of 2.19–22 and the text as it stands lacks many hymnic characteristics.[33] Moreover it is fully in the author's style. We may dismiss it from our discussion.

4.4–6

This section is not listed as possible liturgical material in Merkel's survey. Many recent commentators however find traditional material within it. Mussner[34] in the introduction to his commentary lists 4.5f. Almost all recent writers see v. 6 as deriving ultimately from Stoic formulae but reflecting passages like 1 Cor. 8.6; Rom. 11.36. They also see v. 5 as carefully constructed (note the appearance of the three genders of εἷς) and coming either from a baptismal liturgy or baptismal instruction. They are not clear whether the writer of Ephesians brought these two verses together or if they previously existed as a unit. Verse 4a, 'one body and one Spirit' is regarded as containing traditional material (the two phrases appear in close

---

Kolosser- und Epheserbrief (Neukirchen-Vluyn, 1975), pp. 117–39, 144–57; Lindemann, *Die Aufhebung der Zeit*, pp. 156–8; W. Rader, *The Church and Racial Hostility. A History of Interpretation of Eph. 2:11–22* (Tübingen, 1978), pp. 196–201; H. Merklein, 'Zur Tradition und Komposition von Eph 2,14–18', *BZ* 17 (1973), pp. 79–102; and the commentaries ad loc. R. P. Martin, *Reconciliation: A Study of Paul's Theology* (London, 1981), pp. 167–76, assumes a much longer underlying piece of tradition running from v. 12 to v. 19, the core being vv. 14–16, which 'was a hellenistic hymn of cosmic transformation' (p. 171); his reconstruction does not seem to escape the objections we have raised to the attempts of Gnilka and Wilhelmi.

[31] 'Eph. 2,19–22 – ein Taufleid?', *EvT* 13 (1953), pp. 362–71.

[32] E.g., L. Goppelt, *Der erste Petrusbrief* (Göttingen, 1978), pp. 139f.

[33] For detailed criticisms see Bankhead, *Liturgical Formulas in the New Testament*, pp. 107f; H. Merklein, *Das kirchliche Amt nach dem Epheserbrief* (Munich, 1973), pp. 119f. The revised structure suggested by G. Klinzing, *Die Umdeutung des Kultus in der Qumrangemeinde und im Neuen Testament* (Göttingen, 1971), p. 190 n. 61, does not overcome most of these criticisms.

[34] F. Mussner, *Der Brief an die Epheser* (GTB 509; Gütersloh, 1982), p. 19.

proximity in 2.16, 18). The stumbling block to taking v. 4 in its entirety as traditional is its final clause. This is written in the author's normal style (in particular he is fond of καθώς clauses, 1.4; 3.3; 4.4, 17, 21, 32; 5.2, 3, 25, 29) and is completely different from the other brief phrases all of which begin with 'one'. If the whole were pre-existing tradition it seems to some very peculiar that it should begin with a reference to the church and not to God or Christ, but this strangeness may arise only from the way in which we have become accustomed to the traditional but later creeds. The order, 'Church, Christ, God', may be the order of importance in the mind of the author of Ephesians as fitting his theology[35] and so have been created by him. When we look at vv. 4–6 there is a quite remarkable change in style at the beginning of v. 4, broken only by v. 4b. At v. 7 we return to the author's normal argumentative style. So far as I can trace only F. F. Bruce looks on vv. 4–6 as a pre-existing unit: 'This section [vv. 4–6] has the nature of an early Christian *credo*'.[36] It is worth exploring this further. We do not need to look for any modification of a *Vorlage* in vv. 5, 6. If v. 4b is in the author's style then part of it may need to be eliminated to reach the original. This is easily done and we end with a verse containing three units each commencing with 'one' in harmony with the following verse; this enables us to conjecture a pre-existing unit:

One body, one Spirit, one hope,
one Lord, one faith, one baptism,
one God and Father of all,
    who is over all and through all and in all.

This unit has a total of seven (a sacred number) units each introduced by 'one' and concludes; in the final unit (v. 6) with three all containing 'all' (in fact there are three 'threes'). Its emphasis on 'one' suits the author's purpose which at this point is to stress the unity of the church before going on to concentrate on the variety within it (4.7–16). But he needs to link this to his ongoing discussion. This began at 4.1 with an emphasis on the call (note the verb and its cognate noun) which

---

[35] So K. Wengst, *Formeln und Lieder des Urchristentums*, pp. 141f.
[36] F. F. Bruce, *The Epistles to the Colossians, to Philemon, and to the Ephesians* (NICNT; Grand Rapids, 1984), p. 335.

Christians have received. In 1.18 the author has already linked hope and calling; it is therefore natural for him to do so again; so he writes v. 4b tying in the tradition to his major purpose, and because v. 4b is now much longer he modifies the first half of it by introducing καί between its two units. Thus what we have here is the kind of modification which we might expect from someone who is using a piece of existing material and needs to relate it to his general argument.

5.14

At only two points in his letter does the author of Ephesians say that he is quoting, 4.8 and 5.14, using on both occasions the same introductory formula, 'therefore it (he) says'. In 4.8 he cites the OT. Many attempts[37] have therefore been made to trace the quotation in 5.14 to the same source but all have proved unsuccessful and today it is generally agreed that a Christian hymn, or a portion of one, is being used, though it must be realized that since we do not know how our author defined Scripture he may have thought he was quoting it here; in any case it is certain that he was quoting. No one, so far as I know, has suggested any amendments to the existing text, though it may be that there was another strophe in the hymn; the strophe with which Clement of Alexandria continues it in *Protrepticus* 9.84.2 and 1 Tim. 3.16 have both been suggested. It has also been suggested that it may have had a different meaning in its original usage from its meaning in Ephesians.[38] There is no need then to look for an underlying *Vorlage* and speculate how and why our author may have changed it. We need to be careful here and not draw a wrong deduction from the fact that our author states he is quoting at this point but does not say so in relation to the other passages which have been suspected as quotations. We cannot automatically conclude that he is not quoting at those points, for he quotes the OT at points other than 4.8 but does not use an introductory formula. However the quotation he uses in 4.8 is not the normal

---

[37] See the commentaries.

[38] B. Noack, 'Das Zitat im Ephes. 5,14', *StTh* 5 (1951), pp. 52–64, believes it had an originally apocalyptic intention.

biblical text and he may have used the introductory formula so that his readers would know that he was quoting something which was authoritative. The same may be true at 5.14. The hymn, perhaps one spoken by a Christian prophet inspired by the Holy Spirit (cf. 5.19), may not have been known to many or even all his readers (remember this is a general letter) and so he gives it authority by his introductory formula.

3.5; 5.25–27

In addition to the passages enumerated by Merkel, M. Barth[39] suggests two other possibilities: 3.5; 5.25–27. In the case of 3.5 he points to the parallelism of its two halves and to non-Pauline terms ('sons of men', 'holy apostles and prophets'). This latter argument is of course only valid if Paul is the author of Ephesians. As to the former it is true that there was a tradition about a commission to go to the Gentiles given to the Twelve or a similar group (Mt. 28.16–20; Lk. 24.47–49; Jn 20.21b; Acts 1.8). It is expressed in different terms in each of these references and it is impossible to derive a common *Vorlage* from them.[40] If one could be deduced it would only cover 3.5b, which itself is in a different form from any of those mentioned. It is therefore easier to assume that the author of Ephesians knew the tradition, reformulated it in his own words and added v. 5a, and created the parallelism (he has many such passages containing parallels). In the case of 5.25–27 Barth sees a hymn which the author of Ephesians quotes without modification. However when Barth sets it out he does so in English translation and the lines he suggests in English do not correspond to possible lines in the Greek (to get his English lines he alters the order of the Greek words!). He is however probably correct in seeing 5.25b, 'he loved the church and gave himself for her', as a brief credal form. We find equivalents in 5.2, 'he loved us …', with a brief expansion suiting the context and in Gal 2.20 where it is in the first person singular which again suits the context. When we examine the supposed hymn in 5.25–27 we see that it

---

[39] M. Barth, *Ephesians* (AB; New York, 1974) I, pp. 331f.; II, pp. 621ff.
[40] See E. Best, 'The Revelation to Evangelize the Gentiles', *JTS* 35 (1984), pp. 1–30; and *infra*, pp. 103–38.

itself is an expansion of this brief creed adapted to fit the marriage context.

Before leaving the subject we should note that Kirby[41] understands the whole letter to be based on a liturgical text which the author transformed into a letter by the addition of 1.1–2; 1.14–22; 3.1–13 and a number of smaller additions in the paraenetic section 4.1ff. This text was used in a renewal of the covenant service at Pentecost and was related to baptism. His argument depends in large part on the liturgical fragments which others have detected and which we have discussed. If these are not so easily detected as he assumes his thesis becomes difficult. It also has its own difficulties: why was the liturgy turned into a letter? who would have recognized the underlying liturgy so that it would have had authority for them?

Finally, a brief look at Col. 1.15–20 may be interesting, since like Phil. 2.6–11 it is generally assumed to have been a preexisting hymn. As with the latter, various suggestions have been made in relation to modifications the author of Colossians may have made to his *Vorlage*; most of these are expansions, e.g. v. 20b, but one, the addition of the reference to the body in v. 18 is said to alter the meaning so that while 'body' in the original referred to the cosmos it now refers to the church. Is it likely that this simple addition would have been sufficient to change the meaning in a way easily appreciated by the readers, whom it is to be supposed knew the hymn with the original reference? Surely the author would have needed to make much clearer his new understanding of the hymn and have shown in some way that the original was incorrect? There are two other possibilities: the explicit reference to the church may always have been there in which case there is no problem; alternatively the hymn lacking the explicit word 'church' may always have been intended to refer at this point to the church and the author, having found out that some of the community to which he was writing were misunderstanding it as a reference to the cosmos, has inserted the reference to the church to remove that misunderstanding.

[41] Kirby, *Ephesians: Baptism and Pentecost, passim* and especially p. 132.

5

Dead in Trespasses and Sins
(Eph. 2.1)

Eph. 2.1–3 are anacolouthic; at v. 2 the author breaks off one explanation of the pre-Christian life of his readers to present it in a different way. In v. 1 it had been described in terms of personal sins; in vv. 2, 3, while the reference to personal sin remains, emphasis is placed instead on the condition of the readers as one arising from supernatural evil powers. At v. 4 the author realizes he has diverged and begins again with what should have been the principal clause to which v. 1 would have been subordinate; then in v. 5 after repeating v. 1 in a modified form he goes on to develop the new condition of his readers as Christians. The phrase of v. 5, καὶ ὄντας ἡμᾶς νεκροὺς τοῖς παραπτώμασιν is almost identical with that of Col. 2.13, the only important variation being that between first and second person plurals; the phrase of v. 1 in which we are interested has greater and different variations.

What is the relation of Ephesians and Colossians at this point? Some scholars argue that a hymn or a section of liturgical material underlies Col. 2.8–15. Did our author draw directly on this, did he use this and the existing text of Col. 2.8–15, did he use Col. 2.8–15 alone, or did he write in total independence of both Colossians and pre-existing material? Lohse[1] sees the

---

[1] E. Lohse, *Colossians and Philemon* (Hermeneia; Philadelphia, 1971), pp. 106f.

traditional material as beginning in Col. 2.13c with the change of person and including almost all of vv. 14–15 (he has doubts about τοῖς δόγμασιν). Wengst[2] also sees vv. 13–15 as based on a piece of tradition, probably part of a baptismal liturgy, but unlike Lohse he includes most of v. 13, omitting only the reference to the circumcision of the flesh. Schille[3] sees a more extended section of liturgical material underlying 2.8–15 and to it he attributes vv. 9, 10b, 11b, 13b–15. Burger sees vv. 8–15 largely as the creation of the author of Colossians who is reflecting on the hymn he has used in chapter 1; into this a redactor has made some insertions, including τοῖς παραπτώμασιν in v. 13; he also used existing material in vv. 14, 15.[4] Hanson,[5] following Boismard,[6] sees baptismal material underlying 1 Pet. 1.3–5 and Tit. 3.4–7; he also finds some of this material in Eph. 2.2, 3 but none of it in v. 1; the author of Colossians did not know this common material.[7] Because of the divergent results about underlying liturgical material Gnilka[8] is sceptical whether we can assume the existence of such material and it is difficult to do other than agree with him. If there was any traditional material v. 13a was not part of it.[9] The change from the reference to the wiping away of sin (v. 13) to the victory over the powers (vv. 14, 15) is not unsuitable in the context of the whole letter but would be in an isolated liturgical section.[10]

There appears to be a break in thought between Col. 2.12

[2] K. Wengst, *Christologische Formeln und Lieder des Urchristentums* (SNT 7; Gütersloh, 1971), pp. 186ff.

[3] G. Schille, *Frühchristliche Hymnen* (Berlin, 1962), pp. 31ff. For criticism see especially C. Burger, *Schöpfung und Versöhnung: Studien zum liturgischen Gut im Kolosser- und Epheserbrief* (WMANT 46; Neukirchen–Vluyn, 1975), pp. 81ff.

[4] Op. cit., p. 108.

[5] A. T. Hanson, *Studies in the Pastoral Epistles* (London, 1968), pp. 78ff.

[6] M.-E. Boismard, 'Une liturgie baptismale dans la Prima Petri', *RB* 63 (1956), pp. 182–208 and 64 (1957), pp. 161–83. See also his *Quatre Hymnes baptismales dans la première Épître de Pierre* (Lectio Divina 30; Paris 1961), pp. 15–56.

[7] So Hanson, op. cit., p. 89. In his *Studies in Paul's Technique and Theology* (London, 1974), pp. 1–12, Hanson argues that vv. 14f reflect Num. 25.1–5.

[8] J. Gnilka, *Der Kolosserbrief* (Herder X, 1; Freiburg-Basel-Wien, 1980), p. 120.

[9] Cf. R. Diechgräber, *Gotteshymnus und Christushymnus in der frühen Christenheit* (SUNT 5; Göttingen, 1967), pp. 167f.

[10] Gnilka, op. cit., p. 121.

and 2.13. The connection is not made logically but through the catchword νεϰϱός.[11]

There is also a change of subject; in vv. 9–12 the subject has been 'you', but certainly in v. 12c the real subject has become God;[12] God is the actual subject in vv. 13–15. Because of the use of the second plural in vv. 9–12, v. 13 begins with ὑμᾶς but changes to ὑμῖν at the end[13] for this suits vv. 14–15 better. The change from 'you' to 'we' does not then arise because Paul as a Jew was not dead in uncircumcision.[14] Logical connections are much less frequent in Colossians than in the genuine Paulines,[15] so the change of content between v. 12 and v. 13 and the use of ϰαί at the beginning of v. 13 is not surprising; v. 13 is only lightly tacked on to v. 12; there is a similar connection at 1.21.[16] In vv. 11f death and resurrection, in so far as these referred to the believer, referred to him in his death and resurrection in baptism, an act rather than a state of being; in v. 13a the 'death' of the believer refers to his pre-baptismal non-believing period and thus to a state of being; in 2.20 we return to the view of death in vv. 11f.

We thus conclude that the only possible connection between Eph. 2.1 and Col. 2.13 is either one of pure chance or one of interdependence; Ephesians and Colossians are not both dependent on the same piece of liturgical material. Van Roon[17] would apparently argue for chance when he speaks of 'stereotype (*sic*) phraseology'; if however we decide for some kind of

---

[11] W. Bujard, *Stilanalytische Untersuchungen zum Kolosserbrief als Beitrag zur Methodik von Sprachvergleichen* (SUNT 11; Göttingen, 1973); E. Lohmeyer, *Der Brief an die Kolosser* (Meyer IX[8]; Göttingen, 1929), p. 113; J. Lähnemann, *Der Kolosserbrief: Komposition, Situation und Argumentation* (SNT 3; Gütersloh, 1971), p. 124.

[12] Not Christ. See the discussions in T. K. Abbott, *The Epistles to the Ephesians and to the Colossians* (ICC; Edinburgh, 1897), pp. 253ff and J. B. Lightfoot, *Colossians and Philemon* (London, 1900), p. 183. Even Hanson, *Studies*, pp. 1–12, who argues strongly that in vv. 14f the subject is Christ, allows (p. 8) that God is the subject of συνεζωοποίησεν.

[13] Bujard, op. cit., pp. 83f.

[14] So Lähnemann, op. cit., p. 125, n. 62.

[15] Bujard, op. cit., pp. 71–6.

[16] Lohse, op. cit., p. 107, n. 87, says it reflects 'preaching style'; Gnilka, op. cit., p. 120, says it is in line with the style of the author of Colossians.

[17] A. van Roon, *The Authenticity of Ephesians* (Suppl. *NT* 39; Leiden, 1974), p. 419.

relationship between the two letters then the dependence by Ephesians on Colossians is by far the easier solution.

Eph. 2.1 and Col. 2.13 are linked not only through the presence of our phrase but also because after the diversion of Eph. 2.2f the phrase of Col. 2.13 is taken up again in Eph. 2.5 and leads on to the key thought expressed by συνεζωοποίησεν (Eph. 2.5) which is also found in Col. 2.13.[18] In Eph. 2.1, as we shall see, the καί at the beginning is difficult but can be accounted for most easily by its use in Col. 2.13. ἐν αἷς ποτὲ περιεπατήσατε at the beginning of Eph. 2.2 recalls the beginning of Col. 3.7 and the reference to the wrath (of God) in Eph. 2.3 recalls Col. 3.6, though, of course, Col. 3.6f has a quite different context from Eph. 2.1.[19] If we read ἐπὶ τοὺς υἱοὺς τῆς ἀπειθείας in Col. 3.6[20] then we have another contact with Eph. 2.2. The use of πληρόω in Col. 2.10a may also account for its use in Eph. 1.20–23. It is difficult therefore to reject the conclusion that our phrase has been suggested to the author of Ephesians by Col. 2.13.[21] Otherwise we must suppose that the connection between the resurrection of Christ in Eph. 1.20 and the thought of new life out of death for the believer in Eph. 2.1, 5f comes from a fixed link in thought either in a common author's mind[22] or in the existing tradition.[23] It must be allowed however that the context of our phrase in 2.1 and in Col. 2.13 is different, but this is true of many of the literary connections between the two letters. In Col. 2.11f baptism leads on to our text; if baptism is present in the context of Eph. 2.1 it is only so in an obscure and indirect way.

What then is the meaning of our phrase in Col. 2.13? In Eph.

---

[18] The verb is found only in Col. 2.13 and Eph. 2.5 and in later writings dependent on them. The simpler form ζωοποιεῖν is however used regularly by Paul.

[19] E. Percy, *Die Probleme der Kolosser- und Epheserbriefe* (Lund, 1946), p. 374.

[20] P. Benoit, 'Rapports littéraires entre les épîtres aux Colossiens et aux Éphésiens' in his *Exégèse et Theologie* III (Paris, 1968), pp. 318–34, at pp. 323f, argues strongly for the words.

[21] Cf. Benoit, art. cit., and C. L. Mitton, *The Epistle to the Ephesians* (Oxford, 1951), pp. 60, 65f. We find it difficult to see a dependence here of Colossians on Ephesians as argued by J. Coutts, 'The Relationship of Ephesians and Colossians', *NTS* 4(1957/8), pp. 201–7.

[22] Percy, op. cit., pp. 363, 374f.

[23] Van Roon, op. cit., p. 419.

2.1 and Col. 2.13 τοῖς παραπτώμασιν is associated with different concepts; that of Eph. 2.1, 'sins', is really a synonym;[24] that of Col. 2.13 with its reference to uncircumcision can hardly be so regarded. Here the reference probably follows from the immediately prior reference to circumcision in v. 11 where it is used metaphorically of baptism. 'Uncircumcision' must therefore refer to the readers' pre-Christian life and since it is used metaphorically in v. 11 it is probably to be taken also in the same way in v. 13, though the metaphor may have changed. This has been the generally accepted line of interpretation since Theodore of Mopsuestia;[25] it was already beginning to be used metaphorically in varying senses in the Old Testament,[26] in Judaism[27] and in earlier Christian writings.[28] If the readers were Gentiles then the reference is particularly relevant but is not necessarily to be understood physically; it signifies their alienation from God.[29] In the school of Hillel[30] it was said 'He that separates himself from his uncircumcision is as one that separates himself from the grave'.[31] A clear connection is made here between 'death' and 'uncircumcision' and this may underlie the phrase of Col. 2.13. Unlike τὰ παραπτώματα which relates to individual sins 'the uncircumcision of their flesh' refers to a condition, the condition of their not being Christian. For this reason the dative cannot be causal[32] or instrumental[33] but is rather one descriptive of circumstances,[34] and this will apply

---

[24] See below.

[25] Ad loc. (Swete, I. p. 289).

[26] E.g., Jer. 4.4; Ezek. 44.9; Deut. 10.16.

[27] E.g., 1QS 5.5; 1QH 11.5; 18.20; 1 QpHab 11.13; *Jub.* 1.23.

[28] Rom. 2.29; cf. Phil. 3.3. For discussions of circumcision see the articles by H. C. Hahn, in *NIDNTT*, I, pp. 307–12 and R. Meyer, *TDNT*, VI, pp. 72–84.

[29] C. F. D. Moule, *The Epistles to the Colossians and to Philemon* (CGT; Cambridge, 1957), p. 97.

[30] See D. Daube, *The New Testament and Rabbinic Judaism* (London, 1956), pp. 108ff; J. C. Kirby, *Ephesians, Baptism and Pentecost* (London, 1968), p. 155.

[31] *M. Eduyoth* 5.2 (Translation from H. Danby, *The Mishnah*, Oxford, 1933); cf. *M. Pesahim* 8.8.

[32] So e.g., Lightfoot, op. cit., p. 184; Lohse, op. cit., p. 107, n. 90.

[33] So F. F. Bruce in E. K. Simpson and F. F. Bruce, *Commentary on the Epistles to the Ephesians and Colossians* (NICNT; Grand Rapids, 1957), p. 236, n. 57.

[34] So Moule, op. cit., p. 97. Parts of the manuscript tradition add ἐν (𝔓⁴⁶ADG, etc.). See also Moule, *An Idiom-Book of New Testament Greek* (Cambridge, 1953), p. 45 and N. Turner in J. H. Moulton, *A Grammar of New Testament Greek*, Vol. III (Edinburgh, 1963), pp. 240f.

also to τοῖς παραπτώμασιν.[35] The latter are probably the sins spelt out in 3.5, 8.[36]

Assuming that the author of Ephesians is indebted to Colossians for the origin of the phrase we need to note the two important changes he has made: the omission of the reference to circumcision and the addition of τοῖς παραπτώμασιν. Circumcision plays no part in the discussion in Ephesians; baptismal ideas, wherever they enter (e.g. 1.13, 18; 4.5, 30; 5.25–27), are presented under other images and baptism is never treated with the same direct attention which it receives in Col. 2.11f. In particular the metaphorical reference to circumcision in Col. 2.11 does not reappear in Ephesians[37] though the associated idea of 2.12, 'rising with Christ' (see Eph. 2.6), does. If there is a deeper connection between 'death' and 'uncircumcision' than appears on the surface[38] the author of Ephesians has missed it, which would be surprising since he displays a good knowledge of Jewish ways and thought, or else he has deliberately omitted it because in his mind there is a direct connection between 'uncircumcision' and 'Gentiles' as in 2.11, and he does not wish to limit 2.1 to Gentiles.

The reference to uncircumcision (Col. 2.13) has been replaced in Ephesians with one to 'sins'. The double expression 'trespasses and sins' is not out of keeping with the way in which the author uses synonymous nouns and adjectives coupled by 'and' (cf. 1.1, 4, 8, 17; 2.19; 3.10, 12; 5.27; 6.4f); but are these two words indeed synonymous?

The plural ἁμαρτίαι is unusual in the Pauline corpus, apart from the Pastorals where it appears three times (1 Tim. 5.22, 24; 2 Tim. 3.6; the singular is not found in the Pastorals). In the remainder of the corpus we have the singular 54 times and the plural 7 times. Of the latter, two appear in pre-Pauline credal formations (1 Cor. 15.3; Gal. 1.4); one is in an OT citation (Rom. 4.7), one appears under the influence of the OT (1 Th. 2.16; see Gen. 15.16 and cf. Dan. 8.23; 2 Macc. 6.14f). 1 Cor.

---

[35] We see no reason with Burger, op. cit., pp. 99f, to regard τοῖς παραπτώμασιν καὶ as a redactional gloss.

[36] So Lähnemann, op. cit., p.124.

[37] Circumcision and uncircumcision are used at 2.11 simply as a means of distinguishing Jews and Gentiles.

[38] See above, *M. Eduyoth* 5.2.

15.17 is probably due either to the influence of 1 Cor. 15.3 or to the prior use of the plural by the Corinthians from whom Paul has picked it up; in Rom. 7.5 it is clearly concrete acts of sin which are in mind;[39] in Col. 1.14, the only occurrence of the word in that letter, we may have a liturgical formation, but in any case the reference to forgiveness requires that we understand it again of concrete acts of sin, for it is never abstract 'sin' which is forgiven but only actual 'sins'. Again in Eph. 2.1, the only occurrence of the word in Ephesians, the reference must be to individual sins and not to their totality regarded as a single concept. (The use of the plural suggests but does not entail non-Pauline authorship.) The plural παραπτώματα is not unusual and causes no problems. The word is used both of Adam's transgression (Rom. 5.16–20) and of Israel's (Rom. 11.11f), and carries the idea of rebellion against God. It appears however also in liturgical contexts (Rom. 4.25; possibly also 2 Cor. 5.19) where it loses its particular flavour of 'rebellion' and becomes a general word for sin (cf. Col. 2.13 (*bis*); Eph. 1.7; 2.1, 5). Attempts have been made in varying ways to distinguish 'sins' and 'transgressions' in Eph. 2.1, mostly along the lines of a division into sins of omission and commission,[40] but within the context it is better to regard them as together intended to indicate the fullness and variety of sins. Their acceptance as synonyms in the NT church may be seen in their use in similar liturgical formulae (Rom. 4.25; 1 Cor. 15.3), in the Lukan form of the Lord's Prayer (11.4) when compared with Mt. 6.14f and Mk. 11.25, in Rom. 5.12–20 where the singulars of both words are used and in Eph. 1.7; Col. 1.14; 2.13 where their plurals are used; in Eph. 2.5 'transgressions' can function alone without loss of meaning.

Barth[41] argues that since the two words 'trespasses' and 'sins'

---

[39] The genitive may be either one of quality or of object; cf. C. E. B. Cranfield, *Romans*, Vol. I (ICC; Edinburgh, 1975), p. 337.

[40] F. A. von Henle, *Der Epheserbrief des hl. Apostles Paulus* (Augsburg, 1908), pp. 115f; cf. (for other ways of distinguishing the words) J. E. Belser, *Der Epheserbrief des Apostels Paulus* (Freiburg im Briesgau, 1908), p. 48; H. von Soden, *Die Briefe an die Kolosser, Epheser, Philemon. Die Pastoralbriefe* (Freiburg I.B., 1891), p. 113; E. Gaugler, *Der Epheserbrief* (Zürich, 1966), pp. 84f. Abbott's (op. cit., p. 39) analysis and rejection of all such distinctions still stands.

[41] M. Barth, *Ephesians* (2 vols.; AB, 34, 34A; New York, 1974), pp. 83f, 212f.

do not necessarily imply any transgression of the Law they were carefully chosen to suit the case of Gentiles. It is true that etymologically neither word involves a transgression of a law but the determination of their meaning in Eph. 2.1 must depend not on their etymology but on their context and contemporary Christian usage. ἁμαρτίαι is regularly used of the sins of the Jews (e.g. Mt. 1.21; Mk. 1.4f; Lk. 1.77; Jn. 8.21ff; 19.11; Acts. 5.31); Jews cannot be excluded from the formula of 1 Cor. 15.3. παράπτωμα is used of Jews in Rom. 4.25. In Rom. 5.15–19 the 'transgression' of Adam is contrasted with the righteous act and obedience of Christ, thereby implying disobedience on Adam's part to God's command. Finally when in Eph. 2.5 our author repeats the formula using the first person plural he certainly does not exclude Jews. The two words do not then provide any justification for a limitation of 2.1 to Gentiles.[42]

The whole question of the use of 'we' and 'you' in Ephesians is complex. If we assume, probably correctly, that the letter is addressed to Gentile Christians, does this mean that when the author uses the second person plural their Gentile nature is uppermost in his mind or is it simply used because they are being addressed and the second person plural is the only possible construction? We cannot attempt here to give an overall answer to this question for the letter as a whole. Indeed a satisfactory answer can only be evolved as each use of the first and second person plural is separately examined, for usage may vary from text to text. Does then the author imply in 2.1 that it is only Gentile Christians who were once dead in trespasses and sins or does he imply that it was all Christians? Do we have a picture of a man as man prior to salvation or of Gentiles as Gentiles?

The problem is raised by the initial καί of the chapter if we

---

[42] J. T. Beck, *Erklärung des Briefes an die Epheser* (Gütersloh, 1891), pp. 111f, equating παράπτωμα with παράβασις, argues the opposite view that it implies a transgression of a law and therefore is an appropriate term for Jews; ἁμαρτία does not and therefore applies to Gentiles. So in v. 2, where the reference (for Beck) is to Gentiles, ἐν αἷς picks up ἁμαρτίαι alone and in v. 5 where the reference is to Jews we find παράπτωμα alone. This is ingenious but distinguishes too clearly between the words, lays too much emphasis on αἷς as feminine and ignores the fact that v. 5 covers both Jewish and Gentile Christians.

assume, as we assuredly must, a period and not a comma at the end of 1.23.[43] We do not need to list the various views that have been put forward. Some take the καί closely with ὑμᾶς, 'God has raised Jesus who was dead (1.19ff) and so he will make alive you who are dead';[44] but the type of the death of Christ and that of the readers was quite different. The majority however regard καί as a continuative particle indicating both a new stage in the argument (see Acts. 1.15; 2.1; 6.7; 15.1; Rom. 13.11; 1 Cor. 2.1; 3.1 for similar uses of καί) and the connection of that new stage with what precedes, a connection indicated by the catch-word 'dead'. In neither of these views is there a necessary connection with Gentiles, though for other reasons many commentators make the connection. Barth[45] renders it 'you, especially' where the 'especially' relates to Gentile Christian readers and he refers vv. 1, 2 to Gentile Christians but v. 3 to Jewish Christians. We have already seen that Barth's argument for limiting 'trespasses and sins' to Gentiles is weak; equally weak, though we do not have time to discuss it, is his argument limiting v. 3 to Jews, and if καί has the meaning he gives it we would normally expect it to be the second word in the verse. If also, as we have seen, Eph. 2.1 depends on Col. 2.13 where the phrase also begins with 'and', then it is much more probable that the 'and' in Eph. 2.1 is not to be explained in any of these ways but simply as a reminiscence of Col. 2.13;[46] in so far as it has a function in 2.1 it is continuative, but its presence ought not to be overemphasized nor too much meaning drawn from it. Where the phrase is

---

[43] The possibility of a comma is fully discussed and refuted by H. A. W. Meyer, *Critical and Exegetical Handbook to the Epistle to the Ephesians and the Epistle to Philemon* (ET of Meyer[4]; Edinburgh, 1880), pp. 90f. From time to time, however, this suggestion is revived, most recently by W. H. Denbow, 'A Note on Ephesians II.1', *Congregational Quarterly* 35 (1957), pp. 62–4. He translates '. . . what is the exceeding greatness of his power . . . which he wrought in Christ whom he raised from the dead, and you, who were dead in trespasses and sins'. Quite apart from the way in which this makes 1.20b–23 parenthetical, Denbow's solution makes the death of Christ parallel to that of believers, i.e. a death in trespasses and sins.

[44] E.g., Beck, op. cit., pp. 110f; Belser, op. cit., p. 48; Gaugler, op. cit., pp. 82f; von Henle, op. cit., p. 115; C. Hodge, *A Commentary on the Epistle to the Ephesians* (London, 1856), pp. 58f.

[45] Op. cit., pp. 211f.

[46] Wengst, op. cit., pp. 187f.

repeated in 2.5 the καί again causes trouble;[47] it is probably present there also as a reminiscence of Col. 2.13 (and of course now also of 2.1). We cannot therefore use the καί as an argument that Gentile Christians are addressed in v. 1. We note further that in 2.5 where the phrase is repeated it is changed to the first person plural; it seems probable that our author used the phrase from Col. 2.13 (where it is second person plural) in 2.1 and then when he came to repeat it in 2.5 realized that the second person plural might be misleading and so moved to the first plural. Whether his mind worked in this way or not he certainly cannot have regarded the phrase as applicable to Gentiles only or else he would never have used the first plural in 2.5. We should note that Col. 2.13 also begins in the second person and moves to the first, thus producing problems for the scribes as the varying tradition shows. Mitton comments 'No consistent meaning can be attached to this changeable use of the pronouns'.[48] We conclude that v. 1 describes the pre-Christian condition of humans as such and not of Gentiles only.

But what is that pre-Christian condition? It is described here as that of being dead. What significance is to be given νεκρός in this connection? Because of the previous reference to death in 1.20 and the succeeding references to life and resurrection with Christ in 2.5, 6 it might be thought that 'death with Christ' is in mind here but the latter concept is quite different from death in relation to sin.[49] The association of death with sin is however quite natural within a Jewish-Christian context and not impossible even in the Hellenistic sphere.[50] While death was continually regarded in the OT and later Judaism as biologically

---

[47] See the commentators, especially P. Ewald, *Die Briefe des Paulus an die Epheser, Kolosser und Philemon* (Zahn[2]; Leipzig, 1910) and E. Haupt, *Die Gefangenschaftsbriefe* (Meyer, VIII and IX[9]; Göttingen, 1902).

[48] Op. cit., p. 226.

[49] W. Grundmann, *TDNT*, VII, p. 785, wrongly plays down the distinction between death with Christ and death in sins.

[50] On 'death' see R. Bultmann, *TDNT*, III, pp. 7–25, IV, pp. 892–5; G. F. Moore, *Judaism* I (Cambridge, Mass. 1927), pp. 474ff; A. Feuillet, 'Mort du Christ et mort du chrétien d'après les épîtres pauliniennes', *RB* 66 (1959), pp. 481–513; G. Schunack, *Das hermeneutische Problem des Todes* (Tübingen, 1967); P. Hoffmann, *Die Toten in Christus* (Münster, 1969); L. Coener and W. Schmithals, *NIDNTT*, I, pp. 429–47.

natural there gradually developed a connection between sin and death based in part on an interpretation of Gen. 3. This latter view of death was becoming widely accepted in Judaism just prior to the advent of Christianity, e.g. *4 Ezra* 3.7; Wisd. 2.24; Sir. 25.24; *2 Baruch* 17.3; 19.8; 23.5; Sifré Deut. para. 323 (on Deut. 32.32); Deut. R. 16.6; Eccles. R. 7.13. At the same time and often in the same circles and probably in dependence on Ezek. 18.20, 'the soul that sins shall die', a man's death is connected to his own sin, e.g. *4 Ezra* 3.25f; 8.59f; *2 Baruch* 54.15, 19; *1 En.* 69.11; *2 En.* 30.16; Exod. R. 3(70a); *Shab.* 55a. Biological death is thus related to sin in Judaism and of course death is then viewed as more than a biological event. But the death to which Col. 2.13 and Eph. 2.1, 5 refer is hardly biological death, for those who are addressed have been dead and are now alive; by implication these who have not become Christians remain dead. The idea is probably best explained as a realized eschatological conception of death.

The three passages, Eph. 2.1, 5; Col. 2.13, are not the only places where this idea appears in the New Testament; we find it also in a fragment of a hymn in Eph. 5.14 and in the Johannine literature (Jn. 5.24; 1 Jn. 3.14). In Mt. 8.22 = Lk. 9.60 its use is simply metaphorical. However in 1 Tim. 5.6 and Rev. 3.1f it is used of members of the Christian community who are failing gravely in their Christian profession; this use differs from that in the Captivity Epistles and the Johannine Literature where it is used of non-Christians.

Probably a number of factors worked together to produce the idea of a 'realized' death. Within the Johannine literature it is consistent with the idea of new birth. If at a certain point believers begin to 'live' then either they did not previously exist or else they had a non-real existence which might be described as death. In Romans chs. 5–7 the death which is connected to sin is still future but there are passages which approach the idea of it as 'realized', e.g. 6.13 (but note the ὡσεί) and 7.10, 13; in each of these instances there is really a three-stage process: life, death through sin, life through Christ. In Rom. 11.15 most modern commentators take ζωὴ ἐκ νεκρῶν as a reference to the future resurrection at the parousia because of the 'fixed' phrase ἐκ νεκρῶν. However Paul is not writing at this point about his own mission (cf. v. 13)[51] and if there was a reference to the resurrection we should expect ἀνάστασις and not ζωή.[52] Is he then using the word metaphorically here or is there as in Eph. 2.1, 5; Col. 2.13 something more? The former is more probable but even if this is so it in itself would be a powerful factor formative of the phrase and concept in the Captivity Epistles. There are passages in the OT (e.g. Ps. 30.3; 33.19; Jon. 2.6), referring originally probably to biological death, which could come to be spiritualized when combined with a view of death which saw it as more the end of life. So in some later Jewish writings we come on passages verbally similar to the earlier but carrying a 'spiritual' overtone (e.g. *Ps. Sol.* 16.1–8; 1QH 3.19f).

Perhaps the nearest approach to the 'realized' death idea outside the NT is in 1QH 11.10–14, 'For the sake of Thy glory Thou hast purified man of sin ... that bodies gnawed by worms may be raised from the dust ... that he may stand before Thee ... to be renewed together with all the living ...'.[53] In 'gnawed by worms' the reference is not to actual physical death but to a state of seeming death related to sin; the text does not refer to the resurrection but to the entrance of the new member of the community into a state of salvation, a kind of realized eschatology corresponding to an earlier realized death. 'Thus the author of this hymn understands his entrance into the community as an eschatological event. He has been brought from the realm of death and alienation from God to life, knowledge of God, and the presence of the angels. He belongs to the eschatological community of the holy'.[54] In Judaism, as we have

---

[51] F. J. Leenhardt, *The Epistle to the Romans* (ET, London, 1961), pp. 284f.

[52] See the discussion in *Die Israelfrage nach Röm 9–11* (ed. Lorenzo de Lorenzi; Monographische Reihe von 'Benedictina', Biblisch-ökumenische Abteilung, 3; Rome, 1977) and in particular the contributions of W. M. Bédard, pp. 152–4, P. Benoit, pp. 154, 176, 231f, S. Lyonnet, p. 174, A. Vögtle, pp. 191f.

[53] Translation as in G. Vermes, *The Dead Sea Scrolls in English* (London, 1962), p. 186.

[54] G. W. E. Nickelsburg, *Resurrection, Immortality and Eternal Life in Intertestamental Judaism* (Harvard Theological Studies XXVI; Cambridge, Mass., 1972), p. 156. Cf. S. Holm-Nielsen, *Hodayot: Psalms from Qumran* (Aarhus, 1960), pp. 184–9; H. Lichtenberger, *Studien zum Menschenbild in Texten der Qumrangemeinde* (SUNT 15; Göttingen, 1980), pp. 219–24; H.-W. Kuhn, *Enderwartung und Gegenwärtiges Heil* (SUNT 4; Göttingen, 1966), pp. 78–90. On the connec-

seen, we also encounter the view of the Gentiles as 'dead' (cf. *M. Eduyoth* 5.2);[55] other passages of more doubtful date give the same view.[56] While not making specific reference to the Gentiles there are a number of occasions when the Rabbis of a later period describe the godless as dead: we find the saying, 'The wicked, who even in their lifetime are called dead',[57] in both Midr. Qoh IX 5 para 1 and Gen. R. XXIX 7.

It might be argued that the one reference to the connection between uncircumcision and death may be the actual point of entry into Christianity of the idea of the pre-Christian condition as death since in Col. 2.13 these two are connected, but as we have already seen the idea is also found in the Johannine literature in total independence of uncircumcision. Eph. 5.14 is a liturgical fragment, again unconnected to uncircumcision, probably part of a hymn associated with baptism;[58] the dead and those asleep are non-Christians who are just about to be baptized. We note also that as in 2.1, 5; Col. 2.13 no connection is made between the awakening or coming to life of the Christian and the resurrection of Christ.[59] In Eph. 5.14 the image is associated with light; the contrast of light and darkness and the idea of the redeemed as the children of light and the unredeemed as the children of darkness was already widely accepted. 'Sleep' was an even more widely accepted metaphor both for death (in the NT cf. 1 Thess. 4.13–18; 5.10; 1 Cor. 7.39; 11.30; etc.)[60] and for an unspiritual life; in the New

---

tions between this Qumran hymn and Eph. 2 see F. Mussner, 'Beiträge aus Qumran zum Verständnis des Epheserbriefes' in his *Praesentia Salutis* (Dusseldorf, 1967), pp. 197–211.

[55] Quoted above.

[56] See Daube, op. cit., pp. 110ff; Kirby, op. cit., p. 155.

[57] ET as in Soncino edition. See also Billerbeck, *Kommentar zum NT*, I, p. 489 (on Mt. 8.22) and III, p. 652 (on 1 Tim. 5.6).

[58] Cf. J. Gnilka, *Der Epheserbrief* (Herder, X 2; Freiburg-Basel-Wien), pp. 259f; Barth, op. cit., II, pp. 574f; H. Schlier, *Der Brief an die Epheser*[7] (Düsseldorf, 1971), p. 240. B. Noack, 'Das Zitat in Ephes. 5.14', *StTh* 5 (1951), pp. 52–64, while accepting it as a hymn gives it an apocalyptic rather than a baptismal orientation.

[59] Cf. P. Siber, *Mit Christus Leben* (ATANT 61; Zürich, 1971), pp. 199–202.

[60] Cf. A. Oepke, *TDNT* III, pp. 431ff; R. E. Bailey, 'Is "Sleep" the proper biblical term for the Intermediate State?', *ZNW* 55 (1964), pp. 161–7; L. Coenen, *NIDNTT* I, pp. 441–3.

Testament it is used in Rom. 13.11f and 1 Thess. 5.5f of Christians who are insufficiently awake to the parousia, but this is an adaptation of its use for non-initiates (e.g. Poimandres 1.27).[61] To return to the contrast of light and darkness; this already implies a 'realized eschatology'; we note incidentally that the light/darkness contrast was strong in Qumran where in 1QH 11.12 we have found the closest parallel to the NT concept.

There were then a number of factors operating in the Jewish and Christian spheres which could produce the idea and it could have appeared spontaneously and independently in more than one area. 'Death' is naturally contrasted with 'life'; once new life is accepted as a present reality and not just a future hope and it is also accepted that life or a new life begins at a particular point (admission into the community) the period prior to 'life' could be envisaged as 'death' rather than as non-existence. Because in the Johannine literature life begins with new birth it was natural for the idea to appear there. In Col. 2.13 and Eph 2.5 we note the use of συνεζωοποίησεν to describe the passage from non- Christian existence; converts are 'made alive' by God; if the church is the sphere of life whatever is outside the church will be the sphere of death.

The Hellenistic world also was accustomed to the use of death as a metaphor in relation to our area of conceptuality. The poor pupil in moral behaviour was termed 'dead' (Epict. I.9, 19, M. Aur. 4.41; 9.24; 12.33), as was the ineffective philosopher (Epict. III.23, 28). Philo viewed as dead the man who lived falsely (e.g. *Somn.* II.66; *De Fuga* 55, 58, 59; *Quis. Div. Rer.* Her. 290, 292). In some strands of Gnosticism the non-initiate, corresponding to the Christian before redemption, was termed 'dead': Hipp. *Ref.* VI. 35.6; *Corp. Herm.* I.19; VII.2; (Clement) *Exc. Theod.* 58.1; 80.1; *Apoc. Ad.* 66.2f; 67.12–14; *Gosp. Phil.* 70.10–17; *Book Thom.* 141.31; 143.26. The idea here however was often related to the body as 'tomb' and therefore as 'dead' (cf. Iren. *Adv. Haer.* I. 30, 9; Hipp. *Ref.* V.19, 16) and so would be foreign to the precise meaning of Eph. 2.1, 5; Col. 2.13, where death is related to sin

---

[61] On the metaphor see H. Jonas, *The Gnostic Religion* (Boston, 1963), pp. 68ff. The background to Eph. 5.14 may therefore be in part gnostic; cf. P. Pokorný, *Der Epheserbrief und die Gnosis* (Berlin, 1965), pp. 119f.

and new life is characterized not as redemption from the body but as good works (2.10).[62]

The idea of Eph. 2.1 is however continued in Christian thought and we find it in writings from the early second century onwards. Ignatius twice used the idea without using the actual words of either Eph. 2.1, 5 or Col. 2.13; he writes of non-Christian Gentiles who interpret Judaism as στῆλαι καί τάφοι νεϰρῶν (Philad. 6.1) and of docetics as νεϰροφόροι. 2 Clement 1.5 speaks of Christians who have received their spiritual sight as previously living a life which was nothing other than death (θάνατος). Hermas writes of semi-faithful Christians as half-alive and half-dead (τὸ δὲ ἥμισυ νεϰρόν ἐστι; Sim. VII 8.1) or as those whose words are alive but whose deeds are dead (Sim. IX 21.2); here he approximates to the idea we have found in 1 Tim. 5.6 and Rev. 3.1f. However in Sim. IX 16.3–4 he describes baptized Christians as those who have been previously 'dead'. When, slightly later, Eph. 2.1 is used in citations there is little to tell us how it was understood (cf. Tertullian, *Adv. Marc.* V. 17.7; Novatian, *Trin.* 7.5).

Taking all this background into account we can now return to the full phrase of Eph. 2.1. The transgressions and sins which are mentioned, since they are plural, are not those of Adam, but those of the unredeemed (note the ὑμῶν). They are not sins of an especially heinous nature but the whole generality of the sins of non-Christians. Eph. 2.1 is primarily concerned with those who were once dead in trespasses and sins and are now alive but it does not envisage a three-stage process: life, a slow (or fast) dying through sin and then finally life through Christ. It is not the loss of a spiritual life which was present at an earlier stage or the hardening of the spiritual life through indulgence in sins and trespasses, for these ideas would refer to a change in the Christian life and not to pre-Christian existence. It is not a process of slow dying[63] or of 'moral degeneration'[64] in which death begins in every man as he starts to sin and continues in it. Equally the assertion of a death in trespasses and sins is not the result of the observations of the author of Ephesians on the lives

---

[62] Cf. J. L. Houlden, *Paul's Letters from Prison* (Pelican; London, 1970), p. 281.

[63] Cf. R. W. Dale, *The Epistle to the Ephesians* (London, 1890), p. 160.

[64] C. L. Mitton, *Ephesians* (New Century Bible, London, 1976), p. 81.

of those around him; it may be true that sin atrophies the
impulse toward good so that the higher life dies as men sin, but
the author is not drawing conclusions from what he has seen
happening in his own or other lives; he does not preface his
remarks as Paul often does 'Do you not know that ...' and
appeal to the experience of his readers. He is making a
theological[65] and not an experiential judgment (if there is
anything of the latter it only comes in v. 3 and then only
implicitly). Psychological questions as to the age at which sin
begins and therefore the age at which death takes place are far
from the mind of the author. To say that a man is dead from the
moment he is born[66] probably goes too far since it appears to
involve a 'psychological' judgment. Our author is only interested in asserting that before a man becomes a Christian he was
dead; he makes no statement about when the death occurred.
In the non-Christian and pre-Christian life sin is present; so also
is death. For these reasons we can no more here than in Col.
2.13 take the dative 'trespasses and sins' in a purely causal
manner. Sins and trespasses cause death but the life (if the
paradox may be pardoned) which continues thereafter is characterized by sins and trespasses: the lifestyle of the dead is one
of sins and transgressions. Whoever is dead in this way cannot
bring himself or herself to life, and so the sequel tells how God
brings to life. Finally we should note that our understanding of
νεκρός as indicating a realized eschatological death accords
with the further discussion in vv. 2, 3 of the state of man apart
from redemption. However we interpret the first clause of v. 2
the remainder of the verse describes man as under alien
supernatural powers and the final clause of v. 3 says that he is
τέκνον φύσει ὀργῆς. The 'wrath' is the eschatological wrath of
God to which those outside the community are subject[67] as
'human beings'; this interpretation of φύσις is to be preferred
to that which regards it as a description of the 'character' of
those who are mentioned. The contrast of 'death' with 'life'

---

[65] Hanson, *The Wrath of the Lamb* (London, 1957), p. 105, describes it as 'a
spiritual condition'.

[66] J. Calvin, *Ephesians*, ad. loc.

[67] Here I must with all due respect disagree with Hanson's interpretation (op.
cit., pp. 104f) of 'wrath'.

which is the new condition of the believer and which follows in v. 5 (συνεζωοποίησεν) is also most appropriate. One matter in relation to v. 1 lies unresolved. The strict interpretation of the idea would imply that there was no goodness at all in the 'dead', the non-Christian. Our author is not making careful and precise theological statements at this point about a problem which probably never occurred to him.

6

Ephesians 2.11–22: A Christian View of Judaism

There have been many Christian views of Judaism down the centuries, some of them framed in very unfriendly terms. That of Eph. 2.11–22 comes from almost the beginning but is not expressed in a hostile manner, although the author (I take him not to have been Paul, although whether he was Paul or not has no bearing on the nature of the view expressed here) clearly believes that his Christian faith is superior to Judaism. Before we examine his view it is appropriate first to enquire if it was one that would have been readily recognizable in the ancient world. The readers of the Ephesian Epistle came largely from a Gentile background (cf. 2.11; 3.1), probably in Asia Minor; to what image of Judaism had they been accustomed in their pre-Christian days?

This question can only be answered in very general terms for all of us are affected both by the general beliefs of society about any group of people and by the actual contacts we have with individual members of it in forming our opinion of the group. Gentiles of the time who had been helped in some way by Jews would have thought very differently from those who believed they had been cheated in business by them. There are, however, some general points that we can make, for many Greek and Roman authors have commented on the Jewish people, and Jewish writers such as Josephus and Philo, by the rebuttals they make of what they take to be slanders on their people, indicate

views held by others.[1] We need, however, to remember that the
views pagan authors express, often in passing, are those of
educated people, and the less well-educated may have judged
differently. Those, moreover, who had never encountered Jews
would depend very much for their opinions on rumour, and
rumour rarely preserves good views. Allowing for all this, we can
say that it was widely known that Jews were circumcised.[2] Even if
a few were not circumcised (a few proselytes were excused
circumcision for one reason or another)[3] the great majority
were, and were probably despised because of their circumcision. It was also generally accepted that they kept one holy day
in the week and did not eat pork. Authors either deduced from
these beliefs, or learnt from deliberate enquiry, that the Jews
were controlled by an unusual system of law or custom.[4]
Apparent also, and partly arising from these practices, was a
view that the Jews kept to themselves and did not mingle in
society as others did; they formed an exclusive community
within the general populace, a community which was centred
on their place of worship. It would also have been widely
recognized that they did not take part in the normal religious
rites and ceremonies (i.e. what went on in every city and village)
but worshipped only one God of whom they made no images;
indeed there were those who called them atheists because they
did not worship the generally recognized gods or the gods
specific to their area.[5] Their exclusiveness, combined with their

---

[1] On views held about the Jews in the ancient world see, e.g., M. Whittaker,
Jews and Christians: Greco-Roman Views (Cambridge, 1984), pp. 14–130; M. Stern.
'The Jews in Greek and Latin Literature', in *The Jewish People in the First Century*,
II (ed. S. Safrai and M. Stern; Amsterdam, 1976), pp. 1101–59; *idem, Greek and
Latin Authors on Jews and Judaism* (3 vols.; Jerusalem: The Israel Academy of
Sciences and Humanities, 1974–1984); V. Tcherikover, *Hellenistic Civilisation
and the Jews* (New York: Atheneum, 1979), pp. 344–77.

[2] It is true that other peoples practised circumcision; Paul may have known
this since he had lived in Arabia (see L. Gaston, 'Israel's Enemies in Pauline
Theology', *NTS* 28 [1982], pp. 400–23) but in the ancient world circumcision
was regularly connected only with Jews.

[3] Cf. N. J. McEleney, 'Conversion, Circumcision and the Law', *NTS* 20
(1973–74), pp. 319–41.

[4] Diodorus Siculus, *World History*, 34/35.1.3; 1.94.1–2; 40.3.3; Josephus, *Ant.*
16.162–5.

[5] Cf. H. Conzelmann, *Heiden–Juden–Christen* (Tübingen, 1981), pp. 43–6,
130–1, 231–2.

rejection of the worship of their pagan neighbours, could also lead to such wild rumours as that they secretly worshipped pigs (so Petronius, *Satyricon*, frag. 37) or asses (as reported by Josephus, *Apion* 2.114; 2.80).

If it is difficult to determine the opinion of non-Jews on Jews and their beliefs, it is equally difficult to determine the way in which first-century Jews would have described themselves and their faith in distinguishing themselves from others. There were then a number of groups within Judaism, each of which might have characterized Judaism in different ways and might not have been prepared to acknowledge the Jewishness of all the other groups; but in practice, most of the groups seem to have been prepared to accept most of the other groups.[6] The leaders of the Qumran community were probably hesitant to acknowledge as true Jews those who controlled the temple, and the Jewishness of the Samaritans may not have been widely recognized. While it may be true that the later rabbis disenfranchised other groups, that would take us beyond our period. It is, however, clear that the exclusion of some who did not come up to recognized standards began to appear within the first century, as the existence of the *birkat ha-minim* testifies, and this holds true whether the relevant prayer is regarded as directed against Christians or sectarian Jews.[7] The Qumran community practised both partial (1QS 6.25–27; 7.15–16) and total (6.27–7.2; 7.17, 22–25) exclusion from its membership, but whether in the latter case the Jewishness of the excluded member was denied is not certain. The exclusion of some from Judaism did take place, or was at least advocated in one earlier period. Ezra compelled Jews who had married non-Jews to put away their wives; presumably if they had not done so he would no longer have acknowledged them as Jews (Ezra 9; 10; cf. Tob.

---

[6] On the whole area see *Jewish and Christian Self-Definition. II. Aspects of Judaism in the Graeco-Roman Period* (ed. E. P. Sanders with A. I. Baumgarten and A. Mendelson; London, 1981), and a series of papers by N. J. McEleney, 'Orthodoxy in Judaism of the First Christian Century', *JSJ* 4 (1973), pp. 19ff.; D. E. Aune, 'Orthodoxy in First Century Judaism', *JSJ* 7 (1976), pp. 1–10; L. L. Grabbe, 'Orthodoxy in First Century Judaism?', *JSJ* 7 (1976), pp. 149–53; N. J. McEleney, 'Orthodoxy in Judaism of the First Christian Century: Replies to David E. Aune and Lester L. Grabbe', *JSJ* 9 (1978), pp. 83–8.

[7] See the articles by R. Kimelman and E. E. Urbach in Sanders *et al.* (eds), *Jewish and Christian Self-Definition*, II, pp. 226–44, 268–98.

4.12; 6.15). The basis for his judgment seems to have been behaviour rather than belief. This raises one of the basic issues in relation to the definition of Judaism: is it more a way of life than a way of thought, or to put it differently, is Judaism to be conceived as an orthopraxy or an orthodoxy? But even to put the alternatives in this way is not sufficient. Being a Jew is not just a question of believing a certain number of doctrines (e.g. that there is only one God) and/or practising a certain number of rules (e.g. not eating pork) but of belonging to the Jewish group either through birth, or exceptionally, through conversion, in which case the children of the converts are Jewish. Thus one of the Maccabaean martyrs speaks of dying for his *patris* as well as for the law (2 Macc. 8.21).

One of the more important factors which made it difficult for one group of Jews to deny the Jewishness of another group was birth; so long as its members had been born within the nation, their Jewishness could hardly be denied. Christian churches have regularly made decisions defining their membership through a legal process of some type, but there was no body in the Judaism of the first century which was able to determine in particular cases whether a person was or was not a Jew. Yet for practical purposes, for example marriage, Jews needed to know who were Jews and who were not. In the Mishnah, we find clear instructions about the differing attitudes that should be adopted to Jews and non-Jews. A benediction is not to be said over the lamp or spices of Gentiles (*Ber.* 8.6). A Jewish woman may not assist in the birth of a child of a Gentile woman, although a Gentile woman may assist in that of a Jewess ('*Abod. Zar.* 2.1). The same practical concern is found in one of the Qumran writings (CD 12.6–11), probably because this writing was designed for members living outside the actual community who would be in contact with both other Jews and Gentiles. The need to identify who was a Jew and who was not would also arise in the case of the conversion of someone who had been previously held to be non-Jewish. The ritual connected with conversion may or may not at this period have included immersion, but if it did there was no way afterwards of determining whether a person had been immersed or not except through the testimony of eyewitnesses. The same difficulty would apply in relation to the offering of sacrifice at the temple (or after AD 70 of the readiness to sacrifice). But someone who had been circumcised could always be thereafter identified. Also required of converts was acceptance of Torah; this would not mean that every prescription of the law was observed but only the more important,[8] for example charity, and the avoidance of pork and idolatry. The avoidance of pork and idolatry were two easily observable indicators and were regarded as important as can be seen from the stories of the martyrs or possible martyrs (Dan. 3.1–18; 6.1–15; 2 Macc. 6.18–31; 7.1–42). Another obvious sign of the Jew was his joining with other Jews in worship, although this in itself would not serve to determine whether a person was a Jew or not since there were others than Jews who attended synagogue. Also, although it is not often expressed, probably because it was so obvious, all Jews would have been believers in the God of the Old Testament.

I now turn to Eph. 2.11–22. It is, in fact, a discussion of the disadvantages under which Gentiles suffered as seen from the position of a Jewish Christian, assuming that Ephesians was written by such a person. The Jewishness of the author is not certain, yet even if Paul is not the author, it is still very probable; but granted this Jewishness we do not know whether he (or she) was a first-generation Christian, that is, converted directly from Judaism, or a second-generation Christian, one whose Jewish parent(s) had been converted and who, while aware of their Jewish inheritance, had never in fact personally lived as a Jew. As a discussion of the disadvantages under which Gentiles suffered it may be read in mirror fashion to disclose the advantages of Jews. It is also not a sociological presentation; for example, it does not deal with the moral failures of the Gentile world, an approach which is made at two other points in the letter (4.17–24; 5.13–14). It is rather a theological characterization of the Gentile world and so, in mirror-image, it provides a theological characterization of Judaism.

It begins not unnaturally with circumcision and we have seen

---

[8] Cf. L. Schiffmann in Sanders *et al.* (eds.), *Jewish and Christian Self-Definition*, II, p. 124.

how largely this featured in Gentile views of Judaism and in Jewish views of itself. In 2.1–10 both Jewish and Gentile Christians have been depicted as once dead in trespasses and sins; Gentile Christians however lacked the physical sign by which, despite this, Jews knew they belonged to God's people, and the author of Ephesians is writing to Gentile Christians for he explicitly identifies his readers as Gentile by birth, τὰ ἔθνη ἐν σαρκί. Left to themselves, Gentiles would not have distinguished themselves in any essential way from Jews; Jews were just another race or nation among the many on earth; educated Gentiles would have been more concerned to distinguish themselves from barbarians than from Jews. Only the presence of Jews among them would have made them aware of Jewish feelings on Gentile identity as being on a different plane from Jewish identity and in some way inferior to it. Why the author of Ephesians should have thought it necessary to remind Gentile Christians of the distinction Jews drew between themselves and others is not clear; perhaps as one from Jewish stock he felt Gentile Christians too easily forgot their origins, although he can hardly be said to feel his own Judaism with the same emotional involvement as does Paul in Rom. 3.1–2 and 9.1–5. From Marcion onwards, Christians have regularly ignored their Jewish origin, or forgotten it, or taken it for granted without understanding its implications.

So far as circumcision goes, the author does not wish to emphasize it as an important part of the distinction between Jews and Gentiles; it is only a physical (ἐν σαρκί) thing, made by human hands, χειροποιήτου. In the LXX this word is used of idols (Lev. 26.1, 30; Isa. 2.18; Dan. 5.4, 23; cf. Acts 17.24) and in the New Testament of the Jewish people (Mk 14.58; Acts 7.48; 17.24; Heb. 9.11, 27), and always with the intention of stressing the inadequacy of that to which it refers. Paul himself had already said that neither circumcision nor uncircumcision was of any value (Gal. 5.6; 6.15) and one of his school who particularly influenced the writer of Ephesians had spoken of a circumcision 'not made with hands' (Col. 2.11). But the writer of Ephesians does not go as far as Paul in making a positive attack on the practice (Phil. 3.2) or spiritualizing it (Rom. 2.29), nor does he suggest baptism as a substitute for it as many have done. It is the physical rite separating Jews and Gentiles. Since, for our author, this distinction no longer exists within the Christian community, he does not have to find a place for it and can simply give up speaking about it.

There is a sense in which 2.11 is really parenthetical. Its author had begun by calling on his Gentile readers to 'remember'; it is not, however, circumcision that he wished them to remember but certain other factors to which he moves in v. 12. In recalling their past their non-circumcision had been relatively unimportant; what had been important was their separation from the messiah, their alienation from the commonwealth of Israel, their non-participation in the covenants of promise, and the fact that they had been without hope and without God in the world. Their pre-Christian condition is thus not described in sociological or moral terms but in theological. That the writer had a dim view of their earlier moral behaviour is seen in 4.17–24; 5.3, 14. They had come from a sinful past described in the way many a Jewish moralist would have viewed Gentile life. But this aspect of their past existence is not the author's concern at this point. We now need to look item by item at the description he gives of their previous condition.

Of the five items, the second and third are coupled by 'and', as are the fourth and fifth. There is no reason to take this 'and' as indicating that the third and fifth items explain the second and fourth or are their consequences.[9] Nor should the first be understood as qualifying what follows, 'you (in the time when you were) without Christ were alienated ...',[10] but taken predicatively, that is, as a distinct item in the chain. It is not surprising that the reference to the messiah should be set first, for throughout the letter it is the relation of the readers to Christ which is positively stressed. They have been redeemed by him, they are 'in him', they are members of his body, they have been made alive with him, raised with him and sit with him in the heavenlies. We may note here the difference from the list of

[9] So H. Merklein, *Christus und die Kirche: Die theologische Grundstruktur des Epheserbriefes nach Eph 2,11–18* (SBS, 66; Stuttgart, 1973), pp. 17–18.
[10] So J. A. Robinson, *St Paul's Epistle to the Ephesians* (London, 1909); C. Masson, *L'épître de saint Paul aux Éphésiens* (Commentaire du Nouveau Testament; Paris, 1953).

Jewish advantages which Paul gives in Rom. 9.4–5 where the reference to Christ is the climax. In Ephesians all begins from Christ.

I commence with the first phrase: what does it mean to be 'without Christ'? Christ can be conceived as being present with Israel in his pre-incarnate state (cf. 1 Cor. 10.4; 1 Pet. 1.11; Jn 12.14)[11] or as the Jesus who lived and died as a historical person in Israel[12] or as the messiah for whom Israel hoped.[13] As for the first possibility, there are no indications elsewhere that the author of Ephesians believed in a pre-incarnate presence of the messiah with Israel. To limit the reference to the historical Jesus makes only a trivial point and one which would have been true for only a limited period. Thus the third view is to be preferred. There is, however, a sense in which it cannot be separated from the second; for Gentiles there had never been a time when they had hoped for a messiah; when they first came to hear of a messiah he was already identified as Jesus. Although our author begins his list with a reference to a messiah it is important to note that in the brief summaries I gave of Gentile and Jewish views of Judaism there was no reference to such. It would be natural that Gentiles would know little about Jewish expectations of a messiah (before their conversion Gentiles would probably never even have heard the word 'Christ' and if they had they would have thought it referred to someone anointed with oil after a hot bath!) What emerges here then is now much more important to Christian views of Judaism than to Jewish views was the messianic expectation.

It is more difficult to give an exact significance to the second item in the list, 'outside the πολιτεία of Israel'. 'Outside' is the translation of the perfect participle from ἀπαλλοτρίοω (the use of the word here probably derives from Col. 1.21) more usually

---

[11] So H. von Soden, *Die Briefe an die Kolosser, Epheser, Philemon* (Hand-Commentar zum Neuen Testament; Leipzig, 1893); M. Barth, *Ephesians 1–3* (AB; New York, 1974); for the idea see A. T. Hanson, *Jesus Christ in the Old Testament* (London, 1965).

[12] So E. Haupt, *Die Gefangenschaftsbriefe* (KEK; Göttingen, 1902); H. Rendtorff, *Der Brief an die Epheser* (NTD; Göttingen, 1955); Merklein, *Christus*, p. 18.

[13] So H. Schlier, *Der Brief an die Epheser* (Düsseldorf, 1971); J. Gnilka, *Der Epheserbrief* (Freiburg, 1971); F. Mussner, *Christus, das All und die Kirche* (Trier, 1955), p. 77.

rendered by something like 'alienated' or 'excluded'; such translations would wrongly suggest a definite action in which Gentiles had been excluded or that there had once been an original harmony from which they had alienated themselves. They have always been outside. But of what are they outside? πολιτεία has a wide range of meanings.[14] Since it does not appear in the LXX as the translation of any Hebrew word but only in the Jewish texts for which we have no underlying Hebrew it probably entered Judaism in the Hellenistic period when Jews had to explain their life and nation to others. It can signify 'constitution' (Josephus, *Ant.* 4.45; 13.245) or 'way of life' (2 Macc. 8.17; 4 Macc. 8.7). The former is too legalistic for the present context; in any case at this time the Jews did not have a constitution. The latter by itself hardly goes with the idea of being outside, excluded or alienated. A meaning therefore which suggests membership of a community with the rights, privileges and way of life associated with that membership seems most suitable, and in 2 Macc. 13.14 Jews are bidden to struggle for their laws, temple, city, country and πολιτεία; cf. 4 Macc. 17.9. This understanding would make it accord with the 'fellow-citizens' of v. 19 if the 'saints' mentioned there are the Jews, though such an identification of the 'saints' in v. 19 is doubtful; there is in fact no need for it to accord; words coming from the same root but formed differently can vary in meaning within a paragraph provided always that both are customary meanings. Our term is not, however, the equivalent of 'nation'. In modern parlance it has both a political and a religious (including moral) aspect. In our context it means that Gentiles were once outside the community of Israel. Israel is not of course here a substitute for the church.[15] Whenever it denotes anything other than the Jewish people, or a part of that people, this is made clear (for example, Gal. 6.16; even here it is not clear if the

---

[14] Cf. LSJ; W. Bauer, *Wörterbuch zu den Schriften des Neuen Testaments* (Berlin, 1952); C. Spicq, *Notes de lexicographie néo-testamentaire* (Friburg, Switzerland, 1978–82), II, p. 710; Strathmann, *TWNT*, VI, pp. 516–55; R. Schnackenburg, 'Die Politeia Israels in Eph 2,12', in *De la Torah au messie: Etudes d'exégèse et d'herméneutique bibliques offertes à Henri Cazelles pour ses 25 annés d'enseignement à l'Institut Catholique de Paris* (Paris, 1981), pp. 467–74.

[15] S. Hanson, *The Unity of the Church in the New Testament. Colossians and Ephesians* (Uppsala, 1946), p. 142.

church is intended).[16] The phrase used in Eph. 2.12 is not out
of keeping with the indefinite way in which, as we have seen,
Jews tended to describe themselves, and for the writer as for the
Jews it is clearly a description intended to give honour.

The third phrase in the series 'strangers to the covenants of
promise' is again unusual, perhaps because it is intended to
carry a lot of meaning. Like the preceding phrase, it expresses
the condition of the Gentiles in Jewish terms (for Gentiles as
strangers or foreigners see Jer. 5.19; Mt. 27.7). The plural
διαθῆκαι with the meaning 'covenants' is unusual; in the New
Testament it is found only at Gal. 4.24, where only one of the
two covenants which are mentioned refers to Israel, and Rom.
9.4.[17] Generally speaking the view of the Old Testament is that
God had one covenantal relationship with Israel which he
renewed on a number of occasions and the plural is not used to
describe this.[18] Often the plural means 'promises' but this is
impossible here, as it is also at Rom. 9.5, where we have
covenants and promises as separate items in the list. Probably,
then, we have to recognize an unusual use of the plural. This
may be occasioned because Christians thought of two covenants, the old first one made with Abraham and a new second
covenant made with Christ (Jer. 31.31–34; cf. 32.40; Isa. 55.3;
Ezek. 37.26) of which they were reminded every time they
celebrated the Eucharist. It is possible, although highly unlikely,
that the covenant made with Noah has occasioned the plural.
More probable, but still unlikely, would be the idea that the
author of Ephesians looked on the covenant, originally made
with Abraham, when renewed with Isaac and Jacob as being a
new covenant. Wherever the covenantal idea appears in the Old
Testament, a promise, or promises, is associated with it,
although the term 'promise' is not an Old Testament term,
appearing only in later Jewish writing (2 Macc. 2.17–18; 3 Macc.
3.15; *Ps. Sol.* 13.8; Josephus, *Ant.* 2.219; 3.77; etc.) But what
within our context is the content of the promise? Although

---

[16] Evidence for the description of the church as Israel is scarce; cf. P.
Richardson, *Israel in the Apostolic Church* (SNTSMS 10; Cambridge: 1969), pp.
70ff.

[17] The singular is an alternative reading here but should be rejected.

[18] Cf. C. Roetzel, 'Diathekai in Romans 9,4', *Bib* 51 (1970) pp. 377–90.

Christians may associate the covenant with the Eucharist, and see in Christ the fulfilment of the promise of the new covenant, this can hardly be the idea here, for Christ has already featured in the list as its first item. The word recurs at 3.6 and is again undefined and may refer either to the total promise of the Old Testament with its many aspects as promise of salvation, or the particular promise made to Abraham on which the position of the Jews as the people of God depended and which Paul argues can be understood as including Gentile Christians (Gal. 3.29). The style of the author of Ephesians suggests that he may be expressing in fresh words what he had already said in the previous phrase ('strangers' to some extent parallels 'outside') but pushing it in a new direction. From the Christian point of view there is something inherently forward-looking in the community of Israel; not only is there the expectation of a messiah but also that of the creation of a new community, the community of the new covenant (2 Cor. 3.6; Heb. 8.6; 12.24), and indeed a great part of Ephesians is taken up with describing the nature of this new community; the passage with whose beginning we are dealing ends with such a description (2.19–22).

The final two phrases 'having no hope and without God in the world' do not appear to be directly related to Israel[19] and therefore sound more like value judgements than theological descriptions. However, to Jews looking out on the Gentile world, they would appear as indicating its non-spiritual condition and their judgment would not change in this respect if they became Christians.[20] Most Gentiles, while they would not have worried very much about their failings in respect of the first three phrases, would, however, have rejected the final two charges as untrue. The reference to hope follows naturally after that to promise, for promises give hope. Hope should not be limited to the hope of an afterlife but taken in the broadest way

[19] Cf. Schnackenburg, 'Zur Exegese von Eph 2,11–22 im Hinblick auf das Verhältnis von Kirche und Israel', in *The New Testament Age. Festschrift B. Reicke* (ed. D. Brownell and W. C. Weinrich; Macon, GA, 1984), pp. 467–91.

[20] It is interesting to note that when the early fathers refer to our verse it is largely the second and third phrases which they quote as a brief glance at *Biblia Patristica*, I–III will show. Moderns would probably choose the fourth and fifth as descriptive of the world outside the church.

possible in line with the promise. If, as is possible, 'in the world' also qualifies it, then every material thing is rejected as the object of hope. If hope follows on promise it is also linked to belief in God. Atheism,[21] without God, could be an accusation that Gentiles were godless or impious, but this would be a value judgment (see 4.17–24 for Gentiles as impious), and therefore more probably means they did not worship the true God, the Jewish God, or had been abandoned by him. The description of Gentiles as without hope and God would be one that the readers of Ephesians would themselves have made about those around them who were neither Jews nor Christians. I am not concerned to evaluate its truth as a judgment on Gentiles; most of them would have denied that they were without God; genuine atheism was on the whole rare at that time. Hope was also not something confined to believers in Yahweh.

Thus we see that all five phrases, when taken as they stand, give a description of the Gentile world, yet their mirror-images are a description of Judaism as at least one Christian saw Judaism. It looks forward to the messiah, it is the community of God's people with whom God has entered into covenants with their promise, it believes in the true God and has hope. Before we begin to compare this with pagan and Jewish views of Judaism we need to turn to the one other place in the New Testament where we have a description of Judaism. In Rom. 9.4–5, the privileges or advantages of Judaism are set out directly and there is no need for mirror reading. On this occasion they are detailed also by someone, Paul, whose relationship to Judaism is known and of whose firsthand experience of it in its rabbinic and Hellenistic forms we can be certain. This list runs

> They are Israelites, and to them belong the sonship, the glory, the covenants, the giving of the law, the worship, and the promises; to them belong the patriarchs, and of their race, according to the flesh, is the Christ. God who is over all be blessed for ever.

[21] On atheism in the ancient world see J. Thrower, *A Short History of Western Atheism* (London, 1971), pp. 37–48; Conzelmann, *Heiden*, pp. 43–6, 130–1, 231–2.

The list appears to be carefully constructed[22] yet is probably not pre-Pauline but his own creation since it contains so many of his favourite concepts; he may, of course, have formulated it prior to the writing of Romans. There are elements here which correspond to the list of Eph. 2.11–12: the reference to Israel, the covenants, the promises, Christ (he is now the climax of the list), God, if we include the final clause of v. 5 and do not regard it as a statement of Christ's divinity, or if we regard the 'glory' as that of the Shekinah indicating his presence, or if we regard him as the object of the worship. Unique to Romans then are the giving of the law,[23] sonship, worship, and the fathers, though our understanding of πολιτεία would probably suggest that both the worship and the fathers would fall under that heading. Unique to Ephesians is the reference to hope.

The two lists of Ephesians and Romans serve different purposes.[24] In the latter, they form part of an argument that God has not forsaken Israel and that it continues to have a place in his purpose. The words are set with a verb in the present tense and so are to be regarded as still being true after Christ. In Ephesians, the list is set in a once/now contrast; Christian Gentiles once were without Christ, etc., but now they have him. No conclusion is drawn as to the Jews, although certainly Christ, etc., was once theirs. It is not at this point said that Jews no longer enjoy the listed privileges; all that can be said is that Gentile Christians now enjoy the privileges that once belonged to Israel. In Romans, of course, nothing is said at that point to suggest that Gentile Christians participate in what are the privileges of Israel. Finally, we should note that there are no extant equivalent lists of Jewish privileges compiled by Jews. The nearest approaches are found in 2 Macc. 2.17–18; *4 Ezra*

[22] Cf. M. Rese, 'Die Vorzüge Israels in Röm. 19,4f. und Eph. 2,12: Exegetische Anmerkungen zum Thema Kirche und Israel', *TZ* 31 (1975), pp. 211–22; F. Dreyfus, 'Le passé et le présent d'Israël (Rom. 9,1–5; 11,1–24)', in *Die Israelfrage nach Röm 9–11* (ed. L. de Lorenzi; Rome, 1977), pp. 131–51; J. Piper, *The Justification of God* (Grand Rapids, 1983), pp. 6–7.

[23] E. J. Epp ('Jewish–Gentile Continuity in Paul: Torah and/or Faith? [Romans 9:1–5]', in *Christians among Jews and Gentiles: Festschrift K. Stendahl* [ed. G. W. E. Nickelsburg with G. W. MacRae; Philadelphia, 1986], pp. 80–90) argues that Paul has deliberately used a word which refers to the giving of the law so as to avoid a direct reference to the law.

[24] Cf. Rese, 'Vorzüge Israels'.

3.13–24; *2 Bar.* 57.1–3. In them, however, the activity of God is stressed rather than actual privileges.[25]

The picture of Judaism which Eph. 2.11–22 presents is very different from that which Gentiles held, and it is also, though not to such a great extent, different from that of Judaism itself. The only factor common to all three is circumcision. The differences between Judaism's own picture or pictures and that of Ephesians must lie in the reason why the latter's author wishes to give a picture at all. Before looking at that, we note that the factors he has picked out are those of which he can make positive use as a Christian. The church believes in a messiah, sees itself as in some way related to Israel, as enjoying the promises, understood in a Christian way, made to Israel, as related to God in a new covenant, as believing in the same God as Israel believed in and not some other, and as having a hope of salvation just as Israel had. Since the letter is a round letter written to a number of Christian communities, none of which can be identified, we know little about its recipients. The stress, however, on continuity with Judaism (for this in fact is what the list indicates) suggests that there were those in these communities who were forgetful of the rock from which they were hewn. It would go too far to say that they were renouncing their Jewish heritage as Marcion did, but the probable absence of many Jews among them had left them in a position similar to that of many Christians today who seem unaware of their Jewish inheritance. Our author might have chosen to remind them of this by copious quotation from the Old Testament in the manner of the author of Hebrews but instead has chosen another and more subtle approach. It is interesting that when we first find the early fathers quoting this section of Ephesians they sometimes use it to refute Marcion and various Gnostics and to demonstrate the link between Christianity and Judaism.[26]

I have suggested that our author selected those concepts from Judaism which suited him as a Christian, those, moreover,

---

[25] For references to possible lists see L. Cerfaux, *Recueil Lucien Cerfaux*, II (BETL, 7; Gembloux, 1954), pp. 339–64 (p. 340 n. 1).

[26] Cf. W. Rader, *The Church and Racial Hostility* (Tübingen, 1978), pp. 12–16; Irenaeus, *Adv. Haer.* 5.14.3; Tertullian, *Adv. Marc.* 5.11.13.

which he could take up and use in expressing his Christianity; it is therefore interesting to note what he has left out that a Jew might have inserted. Surprising is the omission of any reference to the law and in this our list contrasts with that of Rom. 9.4–5. There is in fact very little about the law in Ephesians; it is mentioned only in 2.15 where it is said to be abrogated. Commentators differ here as to whether 'the law of command-ments and ordinances' means the many commandments of the ceremonial law or is intended to refer to the whole law. The matter was apparently not important enough for the author to spell out. This absence of reference to the law is in striking contrast to what we find in Paul. Indeed there is an almost total absence of hostility towards Judaism. The author is not con-cerned with the continuing existence of Judaism and the fate of unbelieving Jews as was Paul in Romans 9–11. There is nothing to suggest that Jews are rejected as God's people, but nothing either to suggest that they remain his people.

Yet the author should not be taken to be indifferent to Judaism. He goes on directly after this list to deal with the relation of Gentile and Jewish Christians. The Gentiles who were once far off (2.13, 17) are now near; but this nearness is not a nearness to the Jews but of both Jewish and Gentile Christians to God. Gentiles on becoming Christians have not thus become Jews. With Jewish believers they have been formed into a new group, the community of believers (2.15, 16).[27]

[27] The position which M. Barth has argued for in a number of writings as well as in his commentary on Ephesians (e.g. *Israel und die Kirche im Brief des Paulus an die Epheser* [Munich, 1959]; 'Conversion and Conversation: Israel and the Church in Paul's Epistle to the Ephesians', *Int* 17 [1963], pp. 3–24; *The People of God* [JSNTSup 5; Sheffield, 1983]) that Gentile Christians have entered Israel, the Israel of v. 12, is thus to be rejected. For criticism see Schnackenburg, 'Exegese'; A. T. Lincoln, 'The Church and Israel in Ephesians 2', *CBQ* 49 (1987), pp. 605–24. See also E. Grässer, *Der alte Bund im Neuen Testament* (WUNT 35; Tübingen, 1985), pp. 25–34.

7

The Revelation to Evangelize the Gentiles

Who first received this revelation? When did he or they receive it? There are a number of traditions about this in the New Testament. Two appear together in Eph. 3.1–13, where, at least on the surface, Paul is claimed to have received the revelation about the Gentiles (3.3) and the holy apostles and prophets are also said to be its recipients (3.5). We begin our examination with the Gospels and Acts. At the conclusion of each Gospel, except Mark, and at the beginning of Acts, there is a command to go with the gospel into all the world. It is not always easy to distinguish between commission and revelation. A commission may involve a revelation, if those commissioned are sent to a group from whom what they are commissioned to preach had previously been withheld on doctrinal grounds. There is then an implied revelation to those who are sent that their message relates to a group who they had previously thought should be excluded from it.

The disciples would not necessarily have needed a command to go to Israel, nor would any such command necessarily imply a revelation. Within his own lifetime Jesus had sent out disciples two by two; they had returned and reported what happened, but this would not necessarily entail the need for a new instruction after his death; in any case the commission of Mark 1.17 ('fishers of men') is much more general. When this was originally given, 'men' will have been understood as 'Israelite men'. To be a disciple was to have a commission, but not a commission to all the world. The preservation or creation of particularist sayings like Matt. 10.5f, 23 shows that the Christians did not at first see the need for a universal mission.

The best-known of the gospel passages implying a revelation that the gospel is for Gentiles is Matt. 28.16–20, the so-called great commission. It has been extensively discussed in recent years.[1]

What is its *Gattung*? Is the unit verses 16–20 or 18b–20? Is it a summary of Matthew's theology? Did Matthew compose it? We do not need to resolve most of these issues. At least five views are theoretically possible: (1) Matthew received vv. 16–20 in the tradition and used them more or less unchanged. (2) He received a core which he expanded into its present form. (3) He received a number of isolated logia which he brought together and expanded. (4) He knew of a tradition that the risen Jesus sent his disciples on mission and formulated this in his own words, outlining their activity in terms of baptizing and teaching. (5) He composed the whole independently of all tradition. The verses are Matthaean in language, yet it is difficult to see him creating the triadic baptismal formula and thrusting it on his church; almost certainly it was already in use there.[2] Probably therefore one of (2), (3), or (4) is correct but in the case of (2) or (3) we must allow for considerable reformulation in Matthew's own language.[3] Because of the parallels in Luke, Acts, and John we assume that Matthew knew a tradition about the risen Lord relating to a commission to disciples to spread the Gospel; this excludes (5). In

---

[1] B. J. Hubbard, *The Matthean Redaction of a Primitive Apostolic Commissioning: An Exegesis of Matthew* 28:16–20 (SBLDS 19; Missoula, Mont., 1974); J. Lange, *Das Erscheinen des Auferstandenen im Evangelium nach Matthäus* (Würzburg, 1973), pp. 349–54; B. J. Malina, 'The Literary Structure and Form of Matt. 28.16–20', *NTS* 17 (1970/1), pp. 87–103; J. P. Meier, 'Two Disputed Questions in Matt. 28.16–20', *JBL* 96 (1977), pp. 407–24; S. Brown, 'The Twofold Representation of the Mission in Matthew's Gospel', *StTh* 31 (1977), pp. 21–32; H. Frankenmölle, *Jahwehbund und Kirche Christi* (Münster, 1974), pp. 42ff.

[2] Cf. Meier, art. cit.

[3] E.g., see most recently O. S. Brooks, 'Matthew 28.16–20 and the Design of the First Gospel', *JSNT* 10 (1981), pp. 2–18.

his reformulation[4] he probably used or was influenced by his own previous words, 1.23; 11.27, and possibly by Mark 13.10 and certain OT passages. μαθητεύσατε παύτα τὰ ἔθνη, his expression of the traditional command, he reformulated in his own language.[5] Who are πάντα τα ἔθνη?[6] The Gentiles alone or the Gentiles plus Israel? Lange settles for the former;[7] if he is correct, then we have a distinct difference from Acts 1.8 and, implicitly, from Luke 24.47.[8] Even if he is correct this does not tell us how the underlying tradition, which probably used τὰ ἔθνη, regarded its content. Most scholars, however, correctly choose the alternative view that the Gentiles plus Israel are intended.[9] A serious problem relating to particularistic and universalistic interpretations of mission-commands crops up here; in 10.5f. Jesus sends the disciples to Israel only, and much else in the Gospel is in harmony with this; there are also some earlier passages which may imply a world mission (e.g. 5.14; 12.18–21; 26.13). The resolution of this difficulty would take us further into Matthaean theology than we need to go.

Luke 24.47–49 and Acts 1.8 may be taken together. We begin with the latter as the shorter. Here we have the promise of the risen Lord to the eleven apostles that they will receive power through the Holy Spirit and will be his witnesses in Jerusalem, in all Judaea and Samaria, and 'to the end of the earth'. Although the promise is given only to the Eleven we may assume the Twelve are meant for when the choice of a successor to Judas is made he is selected on the basis of his ability to witness. Though Luke may have picked up and employed here an earlier piece of

---

[4] For attempts to recreate the original see Hubbard, op. cit., pp. 122, 131; Meier, art. cit., pp. 415f; J. D. Kingsbury, 'The Composition and Christology of Matt. 28.16–20', *JBL* 93 (1974), pp. 573–84.

[5] It may be that the original tradition was based on a word like 'Go' (cf. πορευθέντες here) or 'Send' (cf. John 20.21) rather than on μαθητεύσατε.

[6] If Dan. 7.14 is held to have affected 28.18, then the phrase may come from it; but it is such an expected phrase in the Matthaean context that even if Daniel affected v. 18 the phrase may not come from there. On the relationship to Dan. 7.14 see A. Vögtle, 'Das christologishe und ekklesiologischen Anliegen von Mt 28,18–20', *SE* 2.1 = *TU* 87 (Berlin, 1964), pp. 266–94.

[7] Op. cit., pp. 302f; see especially nn. 142, 144, where the views of others are listed and rejected.

[8] See below.

[9] Hubbard, op. cit., p. 85.

tradition[10] there are signs of his hand in 1.8.[11] The first half of the verse repeats the promise of 1.5 in a more Lucan form;[12] the second provides the structure for the remainder of the book.[13] In the geographical formula of verse 8b we do not need to work out whether we have a fourfold division, a threefold (so most commentators), or a twofold (Jews/Gentiles; Palestine/beyond Palestine).[14] We can also leave unresolved the question whether 'the end of the earth' means Rome or, more probably, the furthest extent of the inhabited world.[15] The reference is in any case to the Gentiles,[16] for if Rome is intended it represents the centre of the Gentile world. The phrase itself is derived from Isa. 49.6, and is used again in Acts 13.47 in relation to the Gentile mission. Acts 1.8 is often taken imperatively, but both finite verbs are future and the imperatival sense is implicit and secondary. The verse is a promise, but as a promise it also contains a revelation: what is witnessed to, the gospel, the risen Lord, is for the whole world, Jews and Gentiles. To whom is the commission given? to the Twelve alone, to the Twelve plus Paul, or to the church as a whole, Luke taking the Twelve as representative of the church? Since in Acts Paul is later given an individual commission the second possibility is unlikely. In the

[10] See below.

[11] E.g. the connection of δύναμις and πνεῦμα (Luke 1.17, 35; 4.14; 24.49(?); Acts 10.38), the concept of witness. John is much more interested in the activity of 'witnessing' than in 'witness'. See L. E. Keck, 'Listening To and Listening For', *Interpretation* 27 (1973), pp. 184–202 (at pp. 190f). Luke uses the noun μάρτυς far more often than any other New Testament writer. S. G. Wilson, *The Gentiles and the Gentile Mission in Luke–Acts* (SNTSMS 23; Cambridge, 1973), p. 93, writes, 'It (1.8) is best understood as a Lukan creation'.

[12] G. Schneider, *Die Apostelgeschichte* (Herder V. 1, Freiburg–Basle–Vienna, 1980), vol. 1, ad loc.

[13] Possibly it only provides the structure for chs. 1–8 if the suggestion of C. G. Thornton, 'To the end of the earth: Acts 1.8', *ExpT* 89 (1977–8), pp. 374f, is accepted that Ethiopia is the end of the earth. However we agree with Schneider's criticism (ad loc.) of this view and reject it. Even if Thornton's view is correct the geographical areas selected relate to what follows.

[14] C. Burchard, *Der dreizehnte Zeuge* (FRLANT 105; Göttingen, 1970), p. 133 n. 309.

[15] There are exhaustive discussions in H. J. Hausner, *Strukturen der Abschlusserzählung der Apostelgeschichte (Apg. 28.16–31)* (AnalBib 86; Rome, 1979), pp. 206ff and W. C. van Unnik, *Sparsa Collecta*, Part I (Suppl. NT; Leiden, 1973), pp. 386–401.

[16] This is so even on the view of Thornton, art. cit., for then the Ethiopian eunuch is regarded as a Gentile.

actual mission activity of the church, if we leave aside Paul and his co-workers, the only evangelists Luke presents are Peter and John, Stephen and Philip; the apostles remain in Jerusalem at 8.1. There is no point in which we are shown the general activity of the church in mission. Stephen and Philip are not given a commission to evangelize but to serve tables (6.1–6). Perhaps the solution lies in a double understanding of the role of the apostles in Acts. On the one hand they function as a historical and fixed group connecting the church to Jesus. On the other hand they are representative believers. Luke sees them then first as the group which received the promise/commission/revelation – this would be unrepeatable since there could be no more 'witnesses' to the life, death, and resurrection of Jesus – and secondly as representing all the church in its mission activity, which is to be directed to Jerusalem, Judaea, Samaria and the end of the earth, for the Twelve are not depicted by Luke as missionaries outside Palestine; Paul and others are.

At the end of his Gospel Luke has a somewhat similar commission to that of Acts 1.8, which again reflects his thought and style.[17] Luke omitted Mark 13.10 from between his 21.13 and 21.14. Has he transferred it to 24.47, at the same time adapting it, or is 24.47 his substitution for it, which he has either freely composed or adapted from another strain of the tradition? Neither alternative may be correct. More probably Luke used a saying or other fragment of tradition and amalgamated it with Mark 13.13, expressing it in his own terminology as he did so.[18]

There are a number of differences from Acts 1.8. Luke 24.47–49 lacks a geographical list but refers to the content of the Gospel and founds witness-bearing εἰς τὰ ἔθνη on scripture. The mission of the church is thus made to rest both on Jesus' word (as in 1.8) and the Old Testament (verses 45, 46).[19] In Acts 1.8 we saw that the reference to the end of the earth was

---

[17] E.g. ἐπὶ τῷ ... ἁμαρτιῶν, μάρτυρες. Cf. I. H. Marshall, *The Gospel of Luke* (NIGTC; Exeter, 1978), ad loc.; Wilson, op. cit., pp. 47ff; V. Taylor, *The Passion Narrative of St. Luke* (SNTSMS 19; Cambridge, 1972), pp. 112f; Burchard, pp. 130–3; etc.

[18] For discussion see Burchard, op. cit., p. 132; F. Hahn, *Mission in the New Testament* (SBT 47, London, 1965), pp. 130f, etc.

[19] Cf. Hahn, op. cit., p. 130.

probably drawn from Isa. 49.6 (cf. Acts 13.47); though no Old
Testament texts are given, Acts 10.43 and 26.22, 23 indicate that
a mission including both Jews and Gentiles had been prophesied in the Old Testament. Already also the concept of a
universal mission based on the Old Testament had appeared in
earlier parts of the Gospel (3.6, cf. 2.10, 30–32) in statements
about Jesus.

Unlike Acts 1.8, Luke 24. 47–49 contains no explicit sending
of the Eleven; ('beginning from Jerusalem', however, implies
departure elsewhere). It is not said that they are (will be?)
preachers but that they are witnesses to Christ's suffering and
resurrection and to the universal mission; again we have an
indicative rather than an imperative, and again the indicative
carries an implied imperatival sense. As witnesses they are
guardians of the tradition;[20] their commission is thus centred on
mission.

As in Acts 1.8 there is a reference to the Spirit in Luke 24.49,
though it is veiled as 'the promise of the Father' (cf. Acts 1.4);
Acts regularly depicts the presence of God with disciples as
made real through the Spirit. Matt. 28.20 makes the same point
through the promise of the presence of the exalted Christ. In
Luke the commission does not become immediately effective,
but only after the coming of the Spirit at Pentecost.

The commission in the Fourth Gospel is the least detailed
and precise. It is found in John 20.21b, 'As the Father sent me
so I send[21] you.'[22] The language is Johannine and very similar to
that of 17.18.[23] We should note, however, also a number of
similarities in the passage as a whole to Luke 24.36–47:[24] (i) the

---

[20] Cf. Burchard, op. cit., p. 132.

[21] There was no distinction for the Fourth Evangelist between ἀποστέλλειν
and πέμπειν; cf. C. K. Barrett, *The Gospel According to St. John* (London, 1978); R.
E. Brown, *The Gospel According to John* (AB; New York, 1970), vol. ii, ad loc. See,
however, F.-M. Braun, *Jean le Théologien*, vol. iii. 2 (Paris, 1972), pp. 58–61.

[22] Whether by ὑμᾶς John intends us to understand the church or the Twelve is
for the moment irrelevant.

[23] So Bultmann, *Das Evangelium des Johannes* (KEK II; Göttingen, 1950), p. 536;
Braun, op. cit., pp. 1029f; R. Schnackenburg, *Das Johannesevangelium* (Herder
IV; Freiburg–Basle–Vienna, 1975), vol. iii, p. 381.

[24] John is much closer to Luke than to Matthew; cf. B. Lindars, *The Gospel of
John* (NCB; London, 1972), p. 597; Brown, op. cit., pp. 1028f; H. Kästing, *Die
Anfänge der urchristlichen Mission* (Munich, 1969), pp. 44ff.

display by Jesus of his wounds (John 20.20; Luke 24.39); (ii) a reference to the Holy Spirit (John 20.22; Luke 24.49), though the way in which this reference is made is very different;[25] (iii) a reference to sin (John 20.24; Luke 24.47).[26] It is improbable that the Fourth Evangelist has used Luke[27] but very likely that both Luke and John depend on a tradition[28] which after it had diverged from that of Matthew again divided. Because both have heavily worked over this tradition, and because they may not have used it at the same point in its transmission, it is impossible to determine its actual content with any accuracy. In passing, we may note the absence of any statement in John 20 about those to whom the disciples are sent; however, the universalistic outlook of John implies that both Jews and Gentiles are in mind, Finally, it is not clear 'who' they are who are sent. Is it the Twelve, the Ten, the apostles, a larger group of disciples, or the church as a whole?

If we now set these four expressions of the commission alongside one another, we see that in each case the way in which the particular commission is expressed reflects the wording, style, and characteristic viewpoint of the Evangelist. There is, however, enough in common to reject the idea that each independently thought up the idea of including a commission in his Gospel and Acts. While denying any literary interdependence we have to acknowledge some basic similarities: the commission is given by the risen Jesus; it includes Gentiles; Luke, in both his Gospel and Acts, and Matthew state this explicitly; John's universalism implies it. Because of the great

---

[25] In Luke the Spirit is only mentioned implicitly in 'the promise of the Father'.

[26] Lindars, op. cit., depending on J. A. Emerton, 'Binding and Loosing – Forgiving and Retaining', *JTS* 13 (1962), pp. 325–31, argues that John's reference means the preaching in mission of the forgiveness of sin. Clearly John 20.23 uses a saying from the tradition (cf. Matt 16.19; 18.18) but it goes too far to argue with E. Haenchen, *Das Johannesevangelium* (Tübingen, 1980), ad loc., that the 'completer' of the Gospel drew it from the synoptic tradition.

[27] Burchard, op. cit., p. 130 n. 293, supplies a multitude of references to other scholars, though curiously he omits C. H. Dodd, *Historical Tradition in the Fourth Gospel* (Cambridge, 1963), pp. 144ff. One of the few who doubt John's literary independence is J. A. Bailey, *The Traditions Common to the Gospels of Luke and John* (Suppl. NT 7; Leiden, 1963), pp. 92–4.

[28] Lindars, op. cit., p. 597; Brown, op. cit., pp. 1029ff; Burchard, op. cit., pp. 130f.

differences between the Evangelists it is impossible to determine the earliest wording of the commission.[29]

The group to which the commission or revelation is given differs in each case; in Matt. 28.16 it is the Eleven; in Luke 24.33, 36 it is the Eleven and those with them; in Acts 1.8 it is the apostles;[30] in John 20.19 it is the disciples, certainly not the Eleven because Thomas was not there (20.24), but not necessarily the Ten since John's use of 'disciples' does not imply their identity with 'the Twelve'; John probably means the commission to apply to the church as a whole.[31]

So far we have not referred to Mark.[32] He presents a very different picture. There is no missionary commission to the disciples by the risen Jesus unless it was present in a conclusion now lost (16.15 is not, of course, this commission; it represents the view of a period later than any of the canonical Gospels). C. F. Evans[33] argued that the place of a commission similar to those of Matthew, Luke, and Acts is taken by 14.28 and 16.7, where Galilee signifies the Gentiles. If 14.28 is a commission then it is one given by the earthly Jesus and not the risen Christ; in so far as it is repeated after the resurrection in 16.7 it is not spoken by Jesus but by the young man at the tomb. Other references in the Gospel to the Gentiles suggest that Mark differs from Matthew and Luke in that he saw the earthly Jesus as teaching the disciples the need for this Gentile mission. 7.24–8.26 depicts a journey of Jesus in Gentile territory; it is omitted by Luke. Matthew modifies the geographical references

---

[29] Hubbard, op. cit., pp. 101–22, is altogether too confident about his own ability to do so.

[30] Assuming οἱ μέν of 1.6 continues the reference to them in verse 2.

[31] Cf. Schnackenburg, op. cit., p. 385; Bultmann, ad loc.

[32] We do not need to consider Pseudo-Mark at this stage. It is difficult to determine whether it is based on Matthew and Luke or represents another strand of the tradition. In 16.15 the commission is addressed to the Eleven, there is no mention of the Gentiles, but the Eleven are sent to preach to all men. The language of v. 15 is, however, in many respects different from that of the parallels (κηρύσσειν, κόσμον, ἅπαντα, εὐαγγέλιον, πάσῃ τῇ κτίσει). If Pseudo-Mark is a separate witness to the strand of the tradition we have found in Matthew, Luke, Acts and John, it does not help us in determining its origin.

[33] C. F. Evans, 'I will go before you into Galilee', *JTS* NS 5 (1954), pp. 3–18.

so that the Gentile nature of the area is decreased.[34] Within this section Matthew also modifies the story at 15.24 to include a firm rejection by Jesus of a mission to the Gentiles; Mark could be used to justify such a mission (Mark 7.24–30). In the sandwich Mark created of the cursing of the fig-tree and the cleansing of the temple he expressly refers to the temple as a place of prayer 'for all the Gentiles' and the cursing implies a rejection of Israel. Both Matthew (21.13) and Luke (19.46) omit the reference to the Gentiles. The cursing of the fig-tree disappears in Luke and in Matthew loses its significant place around the cleansing. In the parable of the vineyard (12.1–12) the vineyard (Israel) is taken from some, apparently the Jewish leaders, and given to others; there seems to be a lack of consistency here in that we would expect new leaders to be given to the Jews; probably Mark intends us to see a replacement of old Israel by new Israel, the Church, but not necessarily of Jews by Gentiles, though everything indicates that Gentiles are in the Church.[35] 13.10 and 14.9 (both of which have probably been shaped by Mark)[36] speak of a preaching of the Gospel to all the Gentiles; in 13.10 this is governed by δεῖ,[37] indicating a divine necessity laid on the church. Probably the rending of the veil (15.38) symbolizes that the gospel applies to Gentiles.[38] Finally the first person to confess Jesus after his death is a Gentile, the centurion (15.39). Mark often works on a double level; on the one hand the disciples are the historical disciples, on the other they represent the community of Mark's

[34] Tyre in Mark 7.24 becomes Tyre and Sidon (Matt. 15.21); the healing of the deaf-mute in the Gentile area of the Decapolis (Mark 7.31–37) becomes a generalized healing by the sea of Galilee (Matt. 15.29) and probably is therefore no longer envisaged as taking place in Gentile territory; where Jesus goes after the feeding of the four thousand cannot be accurately identified in either Matthew or Mark; the healing of the blind man at Bethsaida (Mark 8.22–26) disappears in Matthew. Tyre and Sidon may indeed be mentioned (15.21) because Matthew wrote for the church in that area, cf. G. D. Kilpatrick, *The Origins of the Gospel according to St. Matthew* (Oxford, 1946), pp. 130ff.

[35] For detailed discussion see Best, *Following Jesus* (JSNTSup 4; Sheffield, 1981), pp. 218–20.

[36] Note the absolute use of εὐαγγέλιον; this is a Marcan characteristic; cf. Best, op. cit., p. 218.

[37] This disappears in Matt. 24.14 and is replaced by a future.

[38] See Best, *The Temptation and the Passion* (SNTSMS 2; Cambridge, 1965), p. 99.

own day. In this latter role they have a commission to the Gentiles, and awareness of the need for this commission must therefore be set back into the life of the historical Jesus[39] and Jesus be pictured as working among Gentiles. Mark is saved from any ambiguity because he gives no resurrection appearances and no commission from the risen Lord. Neither Matthew nor Luke wholly evade this difficulty, in part because at times they take over without modification what Mark has written (e.g. Mark 13.10 in Matt. 24.14)

If Mark suggests Jesus taught disciples to go to the Gentiles, is there any evidence that he did so teach? Did Jesus make any clear statements about this? Are the post-resurrection Gospel commissions merely a spelling-out of an original instruction of the earthly Jesus? The question of Jesus and a mission to the Gentiles has been examined on many occasions and with the majority of scholars we assume that with rare exceptions the earthly Jesus limited his own activity to Jews, that he sent out his disciples, but again to Jews, and that his activity and message were not out of accord with a development at a later period into a universal mission. Before this could become explicit something more was required.[40]

If Jesus did not explicitly teach his disciples to go on a mission to the Gentiles was there anything in his teaching which after his resurrection might lead them to draw this conclusion? There are at least two possibilities:

(1) Jeremias[41] argues that, although Jesus did not go to the Gentiles or send his disciples to them, yet he foresaw a time at the end when the Gentiles would stream to Zion to render homage to Israel. This Jesus deduced from the Old Testament. Evidence that he held such a view is found in sayings like Matt. 8.11f, and in those parables which speak of Messianic times. Thus Jeremias sees Jesus as teaching two successive events: 'the

---

[39] Perhaps this is why in 3.7f the crowd that comes to Jesus comes from Gentile as well as Jewish areas.

[40] Cf. J. Jeremias, *Jesus' Promise to the Nations* (SBT 24; London, 1958); F. Hahn, op. cit., pp. 26–46; D. Bosch, *Die Heidenmission in der Zukunftsschau Jesu* (AThANT 36; Zürich, 1959); Kästing, *Die Anfänge der urchristlichen Mission* (Munich, 1969), pp. 124–6; Wilson, op. cit., pp. 1–28.

[41] Op. cit., pp. 55ff.

call to Israel and subsequently the redemptive incorporation of the Gentiles in the Kingdom of God'.[42] It was then to be expected that the early Christians would first preach to Jews alone, but later as they came to believe they were living in the times of the end, in a self-realizing eschatology, they would take care to ensure that the Gentiles should begin to stream to Zion.

(2) While some of the teaching of Jesus is clearly set in the context of the Law, even though it may modify or correct the Law (e.g. the antitheses of Matt. 5.3–12; Mark 7.1–23), other parts of his teaching bear no relation to the Law. Sayings such as the original logion underlying Mark 8.35 and its parallels ('whoever would save himself shall lose himself; whoever will lose himself shall save himself') or Mark 2.17 ('I did not come to call the righteous but sinners') are true no matter whether addressed to Jews or Gentiles and can quite easily be extracted from their Jewish context. The kernel of Jesus' teaching about discipleship bears no limitation to Israel and is universally applicable. The widening of the definition of 'neighbour' from fellow-Israelite to all men points in the same direction. But again the universal applicability of such parts of Jesus' teaching will not have been seen at once.

If the concept of a streaming of the Gentiles to Jerusalem in eschatological times was a part of the teaching of Jesus preserved in the Gospels we must ask whether the evangelists saw it as taking place in their own time. Did they regard it as an eschatological expectation in process of realization or did they view it as still future? We have seen how Matthew and Luke eliminate from Mark many of the passages which view the Gentile mission as part of the earthly activity of Jesus; they do nothing to indicate that these passages refer to a post-resurrection period. On the other hand many of the passages to which Jeremias drew attention as referring to this future coming of the Gentiles to Zion are still set in a future eschatological context in the Gospels. So Matt. 8.11 is not viewed as already in process of realization. Matt 5.14 does not lay any task of evangelism on the church; in its context with v. 15, where 'in the house' suggests

---

[42] Op. cit., p. 71.

Israel, and with v. 16, which needs only to be fulfilled at the end, there is no reference to a pre-end-time coming of the Gentiles to Zion. The passages referring to Gentile participation in a future messianic feast or in the judgment (Matt 25) still remain future. Indeed, did these and many other passages to which Jeremias alludes not still contain their future eschatological significance, it would have been impossible for him to have argued so easily that they had this significance for Jesus. We note further that 'in all the world' (Matt. 26.13) may have geographical connotation without referring to the Gentiles. Mark's reference to the Gentiles (using Isa. 56.7) at the cleansing of the temple is omitted by both Matthew and Luke.

Luke comes nearer to what Jeremias supposes took place, in that, when he is relating events which precede the ministry of Jesus, he uses many of the passages to which Jeremias drew attention: 1.78f. (Isa. 40.1f.); 2.30–31 (Isa. 40.5; 52.10); 2.32 (Isa. 49.6); 3.4–6 (Isa. 40.5). Of these, the first, because of the use of the first person plural (cf. v. 77), has nothing to do with the Gentiles, and the other three are natural references to the mission to the Gentiles in an evangelist whose second book shows his great interest in that mission. We should also note that in Luke 24.45f; Acts 10.43; 26.23, where reference is made to the Old Testament in regard to the Gentile mission, no texts are quoted. Acts 26.18 cites Isaiah but does not relate it only to Gentiles, as the theory of Jeremias would require, but to both Jews and Gentiles.

Finally, it should be pointed out that Matthew and the other evangelists would not have needed to provide commissions instructing the disciples to go to the Gentiles if they had been able to deduce these easily and clearly from the earlier material in their Gospels. It would appear that the evangelists themselves were not aware that the teaching of Jesus that the Gentiles would stream to Zion at the end could be readjusted to show that they should now be evangelized. In other words, the evidence which Jeremias supplies is not used by the evangelists themselves to justify a mission to the Gentiles.

We now need to return to Acts, where there is not only the commission of 1.8 but also specific instructions to Peter and

Paul in respect of the Gentiles. It is not surprising that Luke does not bring in the commission of 1.8 when he deals with Paul's mission to the Gentiles, for Paul was not present when 1.8 was spoken; but why was it not raised when Peter, who did allegedly hear it, was sent to Cornelius? Within the sequence of Acts we take it that Cornelius was the first Gentile Christian.[43] Luke gives extensive coverage to his conversion, more than to that of any other person, not excluding Paul.[44] He tells the story twice (10, 11) and reverts to it at the Jerusalem council (15.7–9). The historicity of the conversion of Cornelius has been much discussed[45] but does not concern us. Nor do we need to settle whether Peter's vision originally related to table-fellowship with Gentiles or to their admission into the church (the two are not unrelated[46]); in its Lucan setting it clearly answers the question about admission and may be understood parabolically.[47] The vision is only one of a number of super-natural interventions in the story. Cornelius also has a vision (10.3–7) in which an angel appears to him and the presence of the angel is stressed by repeated mention (10.3, 7, 30; 11.13).[48] Peter explains his visit to Cornelius as a response to his vision and to a word from the Spirit (11.12). When Peter had finished speaking, the Spirit fell on his hearers, who spoke with tongues and praised God (10.44–46). Conversion of the first Gentile is

[43] Originally the Ethiopian eunuch may have been a Gentile but Luke did not so regard him.

[44] There are over 140 lines of the UBS text devoted to Cornelius; the three accounts of Paul's conversion amount to less than 130 lines. On Luke's emphasis cf. J. Dupont, 'Le Salut des gentils et la signification théologique du livre des Actes', *NTS* 6 (1959/60), pp. 132–5.

[45] See the commentaries on Acts, in particular, E. Haenchen, *The Acts of the Apostles* (ET Oxford, 1971), H. Conzelmann, *Die Apostelgeschichte* (Tübingen, 1963), O. Bauernfeind, *Kommentar und Studien zur Apostelgeschichte* (WUNT 22, Tübingen, 1980), G. Stählin, *Die Apostelgeschichte* (Göttingen, 1970), J. Roloff, *Die Apostelgeschichte* (Göttingen, 1981), and M. Dibelius, *Studies in the Acts of the Apostles* (New York, 1956), pp. 109–22; S. G. Wilson, op. cit., pp. 171–95; M. Hengel, *Acts and the History of Earliest Christianity* (London, 1979), pp. 92–8; W. Dietrich, *Das Petrusbild der lukanischen Schriften* (BWANT 94; Stuttgart, 1972), pp. 256ff; K. Löning, 'Die Korneliustradition', *BZ* 18 (1974), pp. 1–19.

[46] Conzelmann, op. cit., p. 61, thinks Luke found it in another connection and applied it here. Löning, art. cit., regards it as integral to the narrative and therefore as pre-Lucan.

[47] Wilson, op. cit., p. 174; Stählin, op. cit., p. 152.

[48] Haenchen, op. cit., p. 357.

thus seen to have been engineered not by Peter but by God,[49] and Peter's action may be regarded as a response to a divine commission.[50] Cornelius' significance as the first Gentile convert, emphasized by divine intervention, is driven home by the immediately succeeding pericope (11.19ff),[51] which tells how the Gospel was preached to Gentiles at Antioch and how a great number became Christians. Though 10.35 might suggest that only God-fearers could become Christians (the piety of Cornelius is stressed also at 10.2, 22),[52] 10.45, 15.7–9 in its context, and 11.20–21 following so quickly after the Cornelius incident, indicate that this is not so; *everyone* who believes in Christ becomes a Christian (10.43); 11.1–19, especially verse 19, turns an individual conversion into a universal principle.[53] What then is the relation of this story to 1.8? Behind the Cornelius account there is almost certainly some genuine traditional core in which a Gentile was converted, and with which some act of seemingly divine intervention was associated, probably the glossolalia of Cornelius and his friends[54] or possibly the vision of Peter.[55] Its result was Cornelius' acceptance by the Jerusalem church; its leaders, however, may have regarded themselves as doing no more than receiving into their fellowship the occasional God-fearer. Only in Acts is the revolutionary nature of their action brought out. If Luke had been asked to reconcile the conversion of Cornelius with 1.8 he could well have answered that while it is one thing to be given a general instruction as in 1.8, a particular instruction, as in this narrative, is necessary to initiate the full process of the general instruction. The command about

---

[49] Cf. Bauernfeind, p. 141.

[50] Cf. B. J. Hubbard, 'The Role of Commissioning Accounts in Acts', in *Perspectives on Luke–Acts* (ed. C. H. Talbert; Edinburgh, 1978), pp. 187–98.

[51] Dibelius, op. cit., pp. 117f.

[52] W. Dietrich, op. cit., pp. 277f, raises the question whether, because of this, universality is really intended.

[53] Cf. Wilson, op. cit., pp. 173f; Conzelmann, op. cit., p. 62.

[54] Hengel, op. cit., p. 94, thinks rather of the associated outpouring of the Spirit as original.

[55] So Löning, art. cit. Haenchen, op. cit., is over-sceptical about the whole story.

the Gentile mission (1.8) is thus seen to be carried out by one of those, and in Luke's eyes the chief of those, to whom it was given.[56]

It is noticeable that in ch. 15, where the final decision about the Gentiles is made, Paul and Barnabas play a very small role. Does Luke then see the Gentile mission as proceeding in the first instance from Peter? It is only after Peter's action that Paul is shown to be involved in the Gentile mission (11.19ff); 9.27–29, the only earlier reference to his missionary activity, apparently confines his preaching to Jews.

Paul's position is different from Peter's since he could not have been expected to know about the commission of 1.8. At or just after his experience on the road to Damascus, Acts records that Paul received a commission. This commission was made known to him by Ananias in 9.10ff and 22.12ff and in a vision in the temple in 22.17–21. Although in ch. 26 the commission coincides with the experience they were probably originally separate events.[57] The accounts diverge in detail, and it is difficult to believe that they all come directly from Paul. We do not need to solve the problem of their interrelationship and divergences except in so far as these relate to Paul's commissioning; equally we do not need to determine the nature of the original events. In so far, also, as they are to be regarded as accounts both of Paul's conversion and of his commissioning, we are not concerned with the former aspect, least of all with describing either Paul's psychological condition at the time or what Luke took that condition to be. We can proceed most satisfactorily by taking the three accounts in turn and examining the 'commission' and/or 'revelation'.

In the first account the crucial verses are 9.15f.[58] σκεῦος ἐκλογῆς, whatever the meaning of σκεῦος ('tool', 'vessel'), indicates God's selection of Paul to βαστάσαι[59] the name of

---

[56] Wilson, op. cit., p. 177. Luke 5.1–11 and John 21.15–19 may reflect the tradition of a special revelation to Peter (so Kästing, op. cit., pp. 47ff) but it is difficult to see much in common in them and in Acts 10.

[57] So O. Bauernfeind, op. cit., ad loc.

[58] ὅ τι σε δεῖ ποιεῖν (v. 6) has only an immediate reference.

[59] See Burchard, op. cit., pp. 100–3, for discussion of the meaning of the word.

Christ. Before whom is Paul to do this? Before (τῶν)[60] ἐθνῶν τε καὶ βασιλέων υἱῶν τε Ἰσραήλ. Clearly the Jews are included. This is not then in Luke's eyes a commission (whether 'to preach' or 'to be a confessor') to Paul as apostle to the Gentiles; Paul is related to both Jews and Gentiles.

The second account varies the picture. In 22.14f Paul is again God's choice[61] to be a witness to all men. Witnessing is not here confined to the idea of suffering for the faith, but has the more general reference which we find in Acts from 1.8 onwards. Paul is to witness to what he has seen and heard (the verbs are in the past tense) and this must be what he has seen and heard in the Damascus-road experience; he is not appointed to witness to some doctrine ('the Gospel is for the Gentiles') but to his encounter with Christ. This witness is for all men (πάντας ἀνθρώπους). The next incident (22.17–21) finds him in Jerusalem, and we shall return to examine it. In the third account (26.12–18) Paul is again sent as witness not only of what he has seen[62] but also of what God will show to him (26.16). The content of what God will show to Paul is not clear; the reference may be to future visions (e.g. 16.9f; 18.9f) or to God's protecting power as seen in the way he delivers Paul from danger; the latter is unlikely. Since Paul does not testify to his future[63] visions apart from the one in the temple (22.17–21), probably this is in mind. Paul is sent to the λαός (i.e. Israel) and the ἔθνη (i.e. the Gentiles) from whom God has rescued him. His task is outlined in verse 18. It is phrased partly in terms reminiscent of the work of the servant of Yahweh[64] (cf. Isa. 42.7, 16) and partly in terms drawn from other sections of Luke ('forgiveness of sins', cf. 2.38). The final phrase (καὶ κλῆρον ...) recalls 20.31, where it was addressed to Gentiles,[65] and it is certainly more suitable for them than for Jews. This is true of most of the phrases, in

---

[60] It is doubtful if τῶν should read; its retention or omission does not affect the meaning.

[61] προχειρίζειν does not contain any necessary idea of a pre-temporal election.

[62] The text is again uncertain.

[63] Burchard, op. cit., pp. 111f.

[64] Surprisingly (verse 16) Luke introduces ὑπηρέτης and not παῖς or δοῦλος. It is introduced in addition to μάρτυς, which is his usual description.

[65] Probably drawn from Hellenistic Judaism; so Burchard, op. cit., pp. 117 n. 261; cf. H. Schlier, *Der Brief an die Epheser* (1971), p. 84 n. 1.

particular of the first two. Hellenistic Judaism would have used them in relation to conversion from idolatry. Yet it is possible to see how Luke could consider them as addressed to Jews as well as Gentiles. The tradition behind the verse may have referred only to Gentiles; Luke's context requires it to be seen as relating to both Jews and Gentiles.

That Luke, on each of the three occasions he records the commissioning of Paul, views him as sent to both Jews and Gentiles accords with the way he depicts Paul as going in each town first to the Jews and only turning to the Gentiles after the Jews have rejected him. (As we shall see, Paul's letters reveal he did not ignore Jews). The one exception to this unanimous picture in Acts is found in Paul's temple vision (22.17–21). This incident is distinct from the Damascus-road experience; it takes place after Paul has returned to Jerusalem. In a vision Jesus appears to Paul and tells him 'Go' (which must mean at least from Jerusalem, but probably in Luke's eyes refers to the missionary journeys), for Jesus will send (future tense) him afar εἰς ἔθνη. This appears to be a commissioning of Paul as a preacher to the Gentiles alone, which he never is in Acts; he always goes both to Jews and Gentiles. Can we therefore take εἰς ἔθνη here as 'to the world outside Palestine including the Jews in those areas', which Burchard[66] suggests is the meaning of ἔθνη in Acts? The evidence for the use of the word in the plural in Luke and Acts, whether with or without the article, does not support this view, and there is no reason to make an exception to the general usage. There appears to be an inconsistency. Since this goes against what we have found elsewhere for Luke, it is probably best to assume that he is here employing a piece of tradition which originally referred to Paul's commissioning as one to the Gentiles only. We note also that whereas in the narratives of Acts Paul turns to the Gentiles because the Jews persecute him or hinder his preaching, he does so here because of a vision; can this then be described as 'by revelation', δι' ἀποκαλύψεως (Gal. 1.12), the way Paul himself describes it? Have we here a different definition of Paul's commission? If so we return to the more general view of Acts in ch. 26.

---

[66] Op. cit., p. 166. On the one occasion (2.5) when it has this possible meaning the context makes this clear.

Whether or not the Temple vision gives us access to the underlying tradition there is no doubt that there was a pre-Lucan tradition. We do not need to work out what this was for the whole of Paul's Damascus-road experience. For our particular concern we note that the phrase ἐνώπιον ἐθνῶν τε καὶ βασιλέων υἱῶν τε Ἰσραήλ (11.15) suggests adapted tradition.[67] Either the first two substantives[68] or the first and the third are compatible but all three do not go easily together. In the first case all mankind is summarized as 'peoples and kings' (witness has to be given occasionally and officially before the authorities and also regularly before ordinary people) and in the second case as 'Gentiles and Jews'. Whichever way we take it the conclusion is the same: Paul's commission is directed towards all men. We do not need to decide whether in the underlying tradition the main emphasis lay on 'apostolic suffering'[69] or on the persecutor turned persecuted[70] or on witness before men in the sense of preaching; suffering is of course appropriate in a context of defence in court or before neighbours. In any case, if Paul suffers before men, this can only be consequent upon his witness for Christ to them. Löning[71] argues that in the very earliest form of the tradition verses 15f were lacking; in that tradition Paul was set out as the persecutor who had been transformed into the persecuted.[72]

Finally, we note that there does not appear to have been any direct contact between the developing tradition in and behind Acts and the story Paul himself relates about his conversion and calling in Gal. 1.[73]

We now turn to this and to the other passages in which Paul writes about his own relationship to the Gentiles. His earliest detailed reference is found in Gal. 1.12, 15, 16 and 2.1–10. In ch. 1 he emphasizes that he did not receive his Gospel from

---

[67] For other indications see K. Löning, *Die Saulustradition in der Apostelgeschichte* (Münster, 1973), pp. 113–15.

[68] So Löning, op. cit., pp. 37ff.

[69] Cf. W. Schmithals, *The Office of Apostle in the Early Church* (London, 1971), p. 46.

[70] Cf. Burchard, op. cit., pp. 102f.

[71] Op. cit., p. 61.

[72] Ibid., pp. 97f.

[73] Löning, op. cit., pp. 54ff.

those who had been in the church before him; he received it δι' ἀποκαλύψεως;[74] the anarthrous noun probably lays stress on the method by which he received the gospel rather than indicating an actual act of revelation, though all the aorist tenses in the passage suggest that this is what it was. The way in which Paul received this gospel is contrasted with the ways men normally receive information from one another. The content of the revelation is probably 'Christ',[75] and therefore 'call' and conversion are regarded as simultaneous,[76] for in verse 16 Christ is revealed (ἀποκαλύψαι) 'in Paul' and the result is that he preaches 'Christ' to the Gentiles; it was part of the revelation that he should preach to them; a revelation would hardly have been necessary to evangelize Jews. The nature of Paul's experience is indicated by ἐν ἐμοί: Betz[77] correctly criticizes the modern tendency to differentiate between visionary[78] and verbal experiences; ἐν ἐμοί may indeed be a phrase used to suggest their unity. In one sense the experience on the road to Damascus was external to Paul; he saw the risen Christ (1 Cor. 9.1; 15.8f). In another sense it was internal, because no one else saw the vision, and because he knew how to verbalize the experience as 'Jesus is God's son' and understood it as an instruction to preach the gospel. Paul's conversion to Christianity and his commission to preach the gospel to the Gentiles are the results of one experience, whether or not the commission was immediately understood or obeyed.[79] The whole of Gal. 1 would imply that his call to be an apostle was also part of the same experience.[80]

[74] κατὰ ἀποκάλυψιν in 2.2 probably refers to a charismatic experience as in 1 Cor. 14.6, 26; cf. D. Lührmann, *Das Offenbarungsverständnis bei Paulus und in paulinischen Gemeinden* (WMANT 16, Neukirchen-Vluyen, 1965), pp. 39–44.

[75] We take Ιησοῦ Χριστοῦ in verse 12 as a genitive of the object.

[76] E.g., Schmithals, op. cit., p. 30.

[77] H. D. Betz, *Galatians* (Hermeneia, Philadelphia, 1979) ad loc.

[78] Lührmann, op. cit., pp. 39ff, 73ff strongly contests the view ἀποκάλυψις implies a vision.

[79] E. P. Blair, 'Paul's call to the Gentile Mission', *Biblical Research* 10 (1965), pp. 19–33, argues strongly that it was later events (e.g. the refusal of the Jews to accept Christianity) which led Paul to understand his position as apostle of the Gentiles.

[80] The texts underlying Gal. 1.15, drawn from Isa. 49.1–6 and Jer 1.4f, refer to a mission to the Gentiles; cf. J. Munck, *Paul and the Salvation of Mankind* (London, 1959), pp. 25f.

Paul does not deny that others beside himself are apostles and have been commissioned to preach the gospel, but he does not say so in so many words;[81] he implies it in 1 Cor. 15.11; in Gal. 2.7–9 he allows that Peter has a commission to preach to the circumcision. He does not say how Peter received this commission, whether by revelation, whether through the authority of the earthly or risen Jesus. Perhaps Paul would not have made this distinction. He has no need in this context to discuss how Peter (and others?) received their commission. Was Peter the only one to be commissioned to go to the circumcision or, more probably, is Peter mentioned alone because of his importance or pre-eminence among the apostles? Peter's commission, and perhaps revelation (and presumably the commission and perhaps revelation to others of the Jerusalem group), differed in content from Paul's; Peter is not sent to the Gentiles – or at least Paul does not appear to view Peter as sent to the Gentiles.

We assume here with many commentators that εἰς τὰ ἔθνη and εἰς τὴν περιτομήν in 2.9 are intended racially and not geographically.[82] τὰ ἔθνη in Paul generally means the Gentiles in contrast to the Jews, or Gentile Christians in contrast to Jewish Christians. In Rom. 4.17f the reference may be to all peoples including Jews, but if this is so it is because the Old Testament is being quoted (at Gal. 3.8 this may also be the case, but τὰ ἔθνη may here be Gentile Christians). Within the context of Galatians, where the discussion relates to Gentile Christians, it is difficult to view it in 2.8 as meaning anything other than 'to the Gentiles'.[83] When we examine Paul's actual practice

---

[81] The attempt of H. Schlier, *Der Brief an die Galater* (KEK; Göttingen, 1949) to infer this from οὐδὲ γὰρ ἐγώ (1.12) reads more into the phrase than is there; Paul here contrasts himself, if he does contrast himself, with the Galatians who did receive the gospel from men, i.e. from himself and Barnabas. Probably Paul indicates by the phrase no more than that he is about to speak of himself (so A. Oepke, *Der Brief des Paulus an die Galater* (THNT 9, Berlin, 1957); cf. G. S. Duncan, *Galatians* (Moffatt; London, 1941), 'with regard to myself'.

[82] So Betz, op. cit.; see p. 100 n. 414 for further references.

[83] E. de W. Burton, *Galatians* (ICC; Edinburgh, 1921) argues that if Paul had intended 'the Gentiles' he would have used the simple dative τὸις ἔθνεσιν (assuming a governing verb like 'preach') or πρός with the accusative (assuming a governing verb like 'go'). Those, however, who support the geographical reference have not produced evidence that τὰ ἔθνη can mean 'the lands of the Gentiles'. In 2.8 the contrast is with the apostleship of Peter to ἡ περιτομή which

according to Acts we find that he normally went first to the Jews
in a town and only after they had repelled him did he turn to
the Gentiles; his letters also show that he had continued
contacts with Jews (1 Cor. 9.20; 2 Cor 11.24; Rom. 11.14; 1
Thess. 2.16). According to Rom. 9–11 his ultimate purpose was
the conversion of the Jews. His contacts with Jews, however, may
have been part of his strategy to reach Gentiles, and he may not
have considered that the Jews were a direct target for his
missionary work. As for Peter, he worked in Antioch outside the
Jewish geographical area (Gal. 2.11–14), moved around suffi-
ciently for Christians in Corinth to know about his travelling
habits (1 Cor. 9.5) and died, if tradition is correct, in Rome; we
must assume that his travels were connected with his mission to
the Jews. He did not, then, regard himself as geographically
confined. Peter, however, did preach to Cornelius and we shall
return to this. If he wrote 1 Peter or saw to its writing, then he
had considerable dealings with Gentiles.

If then the division was made on racial grounds,[84] that does
not of itself imply that the Jerusalem apostles had not received a
general revelation that the gospel was intended for all men; they
may have accepted Paul's mission to the Gentiles on the
grounds that they had known of its success (2.7 ἰδόντες; 2.9
γνόντες) and that Paul had told them of the revelation he had
received. They therefore left that mission to him. It would be
incorrect to deduce from this that Paul and Peter preached

can hardly be 'the land of Israel'. Thus in 2.8 τὰ ἔθνη must be the 'Gentiles'.
While words can change their meaning from sentence to sentence τὰ ἔθνη is
again opposed to ἡ πτεριτομή in verse 9. Instances of the use of εἰς to denote
the recipients of messages are also found; in particular we have εὐαγγελίζεσθαι
εἰς in 1 Pet. 1.25. More interesting is Mark 1.39 if we read the UBS text, where
εἰς ὅλην τὴν Γαλιλαίαν goes with ἦλθεν and εἰς τὰς συναγωγὰς αὐτῶν with
κηρύσσειν; some of the sense of movement in ἦλθεν (the strong v. 1 is ἦν)
perhaps produces the εἰς; but may there not be something similar in Gal. 2.9?
Paul and Barnabas have come up to Jerusalem and are going away again. We
find similarly, but unusually, εἰς τὰ ἔθνη after λειτουργός in Rom. 15.16, where
there may again be a latent idea of movement (cf. v. 19, 20). We see no reason,
then, to accept the geographical or territorial view of τὰ ἔθνη.

[84] Neither Munck's attempt, op. cit., pp. 119–22, to get the best of both worlds
by arguing that the division was made on both geographical and racial grounds,
nor that of F. Hahn, op. cit., p. 81, who refers to 'main emphasis and purpose',
can be sustained.

different gospels, only that their commissions were differently directed. However, as we have been beginning to see, there are other grounds for thinking that the Jerusalem apostles had not received at an early period a commission to go to the Gentiles.

If, as is improbable, the division was made on a geographical basis, then Peter would have been dealing with Gentiles in Jewish areas, and it must be assumed either – and this is the more likely in the light of the Cornelius incident – that he had received a revelation to this effect, or that he accepted the revelation Paul had received and applied it to himself.

Before we leave this problem, it is wise to remember that after an important meeting where a policy is hammered out without the production of an agreed document, those who have made and accepted the decision often leave the meeting with quite different ideas of what has been agreed and therefore execute the policy in unexpected ways, unexpected that is to the other party to the agreement. Even where there is an agreed written document it often contains latent, and sometimes deliberate, ambiguities, which later lead to differing policies being carried through. Moreover, changing circumstances with the passage of time lead participants to see that modifications must be produced in the agreement and they make these modifications without a further conference, justifying it to themselves on the grounds of the changed circumstances. An agreed policy may also turn out to be impractical: it is impossible to carry on a mission to Gentiles and ignore Jews, and vice versa. This was probably soon realized and a rigid division of those to be approached was in effect given up; Paul may have justified it to himself by saying that he has to start in each synagogue with Jews in order to reach the Gentiles so that he may once again attract the Jews back through jealousy about the conversion of the Gentiles (Rom 11). Paul never abandons his interest in the Jews.

Other references by Paul show that he saw a special relationship between his own ministry and the Gentiles. His awareness of his apostleship to the Gentiles appears most clearly in Romans (1.5,13;[85] 11.13). He holds this apostleship as a 'grace

---

[85] This must refer to the Gentiles, and not Israel together with the Gentiles (as is argued by T. Zahn, *Der Brief des Paulus an die Römer* (Leipzig, 1910), pp. 46ff).

gift' (Rom. 1.5). In 15.15–18 the terms are varied and Paul speaks of himself as a λειτουργός of Jesus Christ, which because of its context should probably be given a sacerdotal flavour. As such he offers τὰ ἔθνη to God. Does this mean that he offers the Gentile Church as such[86] or the Gentiles whom he himself has converted?[87] Probably the former. There is a problem related to this (15.16) with another similarly formed phrase which he uses: εἰμι ἐγὼ ἐθνῶν ἀπόστολος (11.13). Do these phrases mean that he is *an* apostle (minister) to the Gentiles, i.e. one among a number of such apostles (ministers) or do they mean he is *the* apostle (minister) to the Gentiles?[88] The absence of the articles in the phrase does not necessarily imply that Paul is suggesting he is *an* apostle (minister). The context alone can decide the meaning. As to the context, it is only necessary to point out how often commentators translate '*an* apostle' in 11.13, but go on afterwards in their notes to speak of '*the* apostle of the Gentiles' or of Paul 'as apostle of the Gentiles'; the latter phrase may be strictly non-committal but as they use it it implies a sense of uniqueness. Their comments correctly represent the form of the argument of the passage.[89] It is clear that, just as Paul would never have argued that Peter and James were the sole missionaries to the Jews, so he would never have denied that there were other missionaries to the Gentiles; Barnabas was one ('apostle' does not necessarily mean the same as 'missionary'). But were there other apostles in the full sense?[90] It would appear to be more in keeping with Gal. 2 and the division of responsibility between Paul on the one hand, and Peter and James on the other, if Paul is regarded as believing he has a special relationship to the Gentiles which no one else has, and which is expressed in the word 'apostle'.

[86] So W. Sanday and A. C. Headlam, *Romans* (ICC, Edinburgh, 1895), ad loc.

[87] So C. K. Barrett, *Romans* (BNTC; London, 1957), p. 275.

[88] E.g. J. H. Moulton and N. Turner, *A Grammar of New Testament Greek*, vol. iii (Edinburgh, 1963), pp. 179f. Cf. 1 Cor. 12.27; 3.9, 16; Rom. 1.20, 2.5; Phil. 2.16; 4.3; 1 Thess. 5.8. We note that ἔθνη is often used without the article where we would expect it; Rom. 3.29; 9.24; 11.12; 15.18; 1 Cor. 1.23; 2 Cor. 11.26; Gal. 2.15.

[89] On Paul's uniqueness cf. E. Käsemann, *Commentary on Romans* (London, 1980), pp. 306f, 393.

[90] 'Apostle' is used in a number of ways. By 'full sense' we mean the sense which Paul used in claiming equality with Peter.

When we speak of Paul giving himself a special position in regard to the Gentiles, we cannot ignore 1 Cor. 15.8, though it does not mention the Gentiles. Here Paul equates his Damascus-road experience with the appearance of the risen Jesus to Peter, the Twelve, etc. We can leave aside the question whether Paul regarded this experience as a post-ascension event as Luke would have done, for Paul never indicates his knowledge of the ascension as a datable event. The most striking feature of the reference is Paul's claim that the risen Christ appeared last to him. Within the sequence 'then, then, then' ἔσχατον can only imply that there will never be another appearance of the risen Christ to anyone. Thus the event which either included or led to Paul's commission to go to the Gentiles cannot be repeated. The belief that, some considerable time after the resurrection-appearances were finished, he, Paul, was granted a special appearance, and that there would never be any more appearances, must in any case have produced in Paul an intense feeling about his own unique position.

Just as we asked whether the evangelists had seen the significance of Jesus' teaching about the eschatological streaming of the Gentiles to Zion, we must ask the same in respect of Paul. The problem is not simple. Paul knew his Old Testament thoroughly; he rarely makes explicit reference to the teaching of Jesus. If he did know and use the teaching of Jesus in this respect, his use would be masked by his knowledge and use of the Old Testament. We may then reformulate the question: did Paul, in arguing for the place of the Gentiles in the people of God, make use of the concept of the eschatological streaming of the Gentiles to Zion, seeing it as already in process of accomplishment in his own time and through his own ministry?[91] Since negatives are always difficult to prove, it is impossible to argue he was unaware of the idea. However, when we examine the Old Testament texts which he quotes in respect of the admission of the Gentiles, few of them contain it. Jeremias[92] provides a very comprehensive list of those in the Old Testament which do imply it. From this list Paul uses only one passage, Isa. 11.10 at Rom 15.12. The vast majority of the

---

[91] Jeremias, op. cit., pp. 36ff.
[92] Op. cit., pp. 57ff.

passages he employs seem to have been chosen for other reasons. He uses Hos. 1.10 (at Rom. 9.26); 2.23 (at Rom. 9.25); Isa. 28.16 (at Rom. 10.11); 52.7 (= Nahum 1.15 at Rom. 10.15); 52.15 (at Rom. 15.21); 53.1 (at Rom. 10.16); 65.1, 2 (at Rom. 10.21f); Joel 2.32 (at Rom. 10.13); Deut. 32.11 (at Rom. 10.19); 32.43 (at Rom. 15.10); 9.4; 30.12–14 (at Rom. 10.6–8); Ps. 19.4 (at Rom. 10.18); 18.49 (at Rom. 15.9); 117.1 (at Rom. 15.11). These passages are often ones which originally referred only to the Jews and have been universalized by Paul, or are passages which contain a mention of the Gentiles but without any reference to their coming to Zion. Paul has adapted them all to his own purposes. He has used them in the same way as the passages he uses in Rom. 3.4 to prove the universality of sin and man's need of grace. The use of Isa. 11.10 may therefore be due to chance and not because it referred to the Gentiles coming to Zion. Of the two passages which may be reflected in Gal. 1.15 the one, Jer. 1.5, speaks of Jeremiah as a prophet to the ἔθνη but no idea of the evangelism of the Gentiles or their coming to Zion is involved; the other, Isa. 49.1, does go on in 49.6 to use this theme, but had Paul this in mind when his words play only on 49.1? The pre-Pauline hymn of Phil. 2.6–11 makes use of Isa. 45.23 and this could certainly refer to the conversion of the Gentiles, but it is not given an eschatological orientation in Isaiah; in Philippians the event is still future, something which takes place at the end. Paul's desire to incorporate the Gentiles will not, then, necessarily have arisen out of his knowledge of the Old Testament; its primary source was his experience on the road to Damascus. His study of the Old Testament was a secondary influence in clarifying and sustaining a view obtained elsewhere. If before his conversion Paul had been a Jewish missionary seeking to win Gentiles to Judaism,[93] his conversion would have made it reasonably easy for him to understand the need to win them to Christ. Since his activity as a Jewish missionary would have been based on the Old Testament without recourse to the argument for an eschatological coming of the Gentiles to Zion (with no Messiah the situation would not have been eschatological), he would have gone

---

[93] For the existence of such a mission see Jeremias, op. cit., pp. 11ff; Hahn, op. cit., pp. 21ff.

ahead as a Christian missionary without appealing primarily to
these eschatological texts.

In consequence of our conclusion in regard to Paul's use of
the Old Testament, we cannot argue that in its light he gave his
own position eschatological significance. This also entails the
rejection of the view that the collection which Paul raised to
bring to Jerusalem was the eschatological tribute of the Gentiles
to Zion.[94] Paul brings the offering from only a few areas, and he
cannot have been ignorant of the Gentiles who lived in North
Africa, in Europe west of Italy, and in the countries to the east of
Syria.[95] He is certainly aware of Spain and the fact that it has not
been evangelized (Rom. 15.24), and plans to go there after the
collection has been taken to Jerusalem (15.25)! It may be that
he looked upon himself as bringing some of the tribute of the
Gentiles to Zion, but there was more to come from other areas
brought by others and perhaps even later by himself. This gives
him a position no more important than that of the initiator of
the collection, more or less the same as the position he had in
respect of the mission to the Gentiles. It is as the initiator of a
continuing process that he offers the Gentiles to God (Rom.
15.16). The grounds are insufficient for the view that in 2 Thess.
2.7 Paul viewed himself as the κατέχων and linchpin in the
eschatological process.[96]

In passing, we may note that, taken all in all, there is much
less evidence in the New Testament than is sometimes supposed
for the view that the idea of the Gentiles as streaming in
eschatological times to Zion had become a present reality and
was actually taking place in the early church.[97]

As to the second area in which we saw preparation in the
teaching of Jesus for the admission of the Gentiles, i.e. its

---

[94] Cf. Hahn, op. cit., pp. 108f; Munck, op. cit., pp. 282ff; D. Georgi, *Die
Geschichte der Kollekte des Paulus für Jerusalem* (Hamburg-Bergstedt, 1965); K. F.
Nickle, *The Collection* (SBT 48; London, 1966).

[95] Cf. C. E. B. Cranfield, *Romans* (ICC; Edinburgh, 1979), vol. ii, pp. 766f.

[96] For the view see Munck, op. cit., pp. 37f, and for reasons for its rejection see
Best, *1 and 2 Thessalonians* (BNTC; London, 1979) and the references given
there.

[97] Rom. 16.25–27 seems unaware of the idea. The exegesis of this post-Pauline
passage is difficult; probably we should take verses 25–26 as a three-member
series, χρόνοις αἰωνίοις σεσιγημένου, φανερωθέντος δὲ νῦν, διά τε ...
γνωρισθέντος (cf. Cranfield, op. cit., pp. 811f). The prophetic writings are

universalist core, we cannot point to any direct link between that and Paul. Certainly Paul's teaching on man's inability to put himself right with God and his dependence on God's grace is in line with passages like Mark 2.17 and the saying behind Mark 8.35, but there is no direct connection.

We now move to the post-Pauline tradition[98] as we find it first in Colossians. Col. 1.26f (the passage parallel to Eph. 3.2f) speaks of revelation; the content of the revelation is 'Christ in the Gentiles' and refers probably not so much to Christ as indwelling the individual Gentile as to Christ among the Gentiles;[99] the hope of glory now belongs to the Gentiles as much as it did and does to the Jews. This is a mystery hidden from the beginning of time[100] but now made known τοῖς ἁγίοις αὐτοῦ. Despite the unusual addition of αὐτοῦ to οἱ ἅγιοι[101] there seems no real reason for understanding this in any way other than as a reference to all Christians.[102] To say that the mystery has been revealed to the church does not imply that at some moment all the church was gathered together and a voice spoke from heaven, but that the church now knows the content of the mystery; nothing is said, however, about how it received this revelation or who among its members were the channels of reception. It could be one person (e.g. Paul) or a group (the apostles). Because of the prominence given to Paul's personal position in the passage, he is probably to be regarded as the

those of the Old Testament prophets; they are properly understood in the light of the gospel as the gospel itself is only properly understood in the light of the Old Testament. This would not suggest that the 'prophetic writings' by themselves would have given a clear lead on the question of the gospel as intended for the Gentiles.

[98] On the post-Pauline understanding of Paul see above all A. Lindemann, *Paulus im ältesten Christentum* (BHT 58; Tübingen, 1979) *passim*.

[99] So C. F. D. Moule, *The Epistles to the Colossians and to Philemon* (CGT; Cambridge, 1957), p. 83; E. Lohse, *Colossians and Philemon* (Hermenia; Philadelphia, 1971), p. 73; E. Schweizer, *Der Brief an die Kolosser* (EKK; Neukirchen-Vluyn, 1976), p. 88; J. Gnilka, *Der Kolosserbrief* (Herder; Freiburg-Basle-Vienna, 1980), p. 102.

[100] Taking αἰώνων and γενεῶν as temporal.

[101] So E. Lohmeyer, *Der Brief an die Kolosser* (KEK IX, Göttingen, 1929), p. 82.

[102] Lohmeyer, op. cit., p. 82, and W. Bieder, *Brief an die Kolosser* (Zürich, 1943), p. 94 suggest angels. E. Käsemann, *Leib und Leib Christi* (Tübingen, 1933), p. 146 n. 5 suggests charismatics.

recipient. Note that in verse 24 he does not say, 'I fill up my portion of what is lacking of sufferings for the Colossian church' but 'I fill up what is lacking of sufferings for the Body (i.e. the universal church)': a unique position.[103] The same is also probably true of 4.3f; this begins in the first person plural; the Colossians are to pray that 'we' (Paul and his helpers) may have an open door to preach the Gospel. It then changes to the first person singlular 'that I may reveal the mystery'. φανεϱοῦν is probably undertranslated as 'make clear'; it is used for revelation.[104] In any case the signular gives Paul a unique position.

In Ephesians[105] the special position of Paul is again brought out. In Eph. 3.8 no greater claim may be made than that Paul preached the gospel to Gentiles (the greater claim can only be made if πάντας is read). In 3.1, however, what Paul is, he is said to be in respect of the Gentiles, not some Gentiles or a particular congregation of Gentiles but *the* Gentiles, and in 3.3 we have the wider claim made that Paul was given κατὰ ἀποκάλυψιν an understanding of the mystery; if, as is highly probable, 'mystery' in verse 3 is the same mystery as 'the mystery of Christ' in verse 4,[106] then it implies that it was made known to Paul by revelation that the Gentiles were to be included in the people of God. In Galatians it might be argued that Paul is no more than the apostle to some Gentiles;[107] in Ephesians he is related to all the Gentiles; he has been given the revelation about their admission and he is in some sense 'their apostle'.

---

[103] Cf. T. Holtz, 'Zum Selbstverständnis des Apostels Paulus', *TIZ* 91 (1966) pp. 321–30. It is interesting that NEB translates 'This is my way of *helping* to complete'; cf. GNB, 'I am *helping* to complete'. There is no word for helping in the Greek. These translations are pure theological paraphrase in order to remove the offence of Paul's uniqueness.

[104] Cf. Gnilka, *Kolosserbrief,* ad loc.; Schweizer, op. cit., ad loc.; Lohse, op. cit., ad loc.

[105] We assume that the author of Ephesians knew Colossians and belonged to a Pauline school. His knowledge of the tradition about Paul was not, therefore, limited to Colossians. For a discussion of some of the problems related to the origin of Ephesians see my article 'Recipients and Title of the Letter to the Ephesians', *ANRW* II 25.4, pp. 3247–79.

[106] So the vast majority of commentators. 'Mystery' in 1.9f is more comprehensive; Paul makes no claim as a special representative in respect of that revelation.

[107] So C. K. Barrett, 'Pauline Controversies in the Post-Pauline Period', *NTS* 20 (1973/4), pp. 229–45 at p. 239.

The anarthrous noun in κατὰ ἀποκάλυψιν may refer to *a* particular act of revelation, but more probably distinguishes how Paul believed or, more correctly, how the writer of Ephesians believed – that Paul came to his view from other possible ways of doing so (cf. Gal. 1.12); he was not told by others, the veil was not lifted from his eyes as he read the Old Testament, he did not deduce it by human reason from general principles, e.g. that all men are equal in the sight of God. These things, of course, may have influenced Paul without him realizing it. What is said is that he obtained the knowlege by a direct and personal communication from God. We do not need to discuss how this took place. The aorist ἐγνωρίσθη suggests an event in the past but gives no indication as to its duration or date. The author of the letter presumably associated it with the experience on the road to Damascus.

In this very same passage in Ephesians we also find the idea that a group of 'officials' within the church received the revelation:[108] it was made known to the holy apostles[109] and prophets[110] (verse 5). It is highly probable that this means a revelation to the group as a group rather than to individuals within it, who would have received it at varying times and places. Without identifying when the group received the revelation, the strong implication is that we are in touch here with the same tradition as we found in the concluding section of each of the gospels and at the beginning of Acts. There are two important variations in Ephesians: (1) The introduction of the 'prophets'. Prophets and apostles also comprise a group in 2.20. where together they form the foundation of the church. This may imply that the author to the Ephesians sees the command to go to the Gentiles as part of the foundation of the church; if so he

---

[108] We do not know whether the author of Colossians was aware of this tradition or not. If he was, he may simply have seen no need to use it. Since one of the main themes of Ephesians is the church, the author is obliged to give some position to the founders of the church (2.20).

[109] There are no good grounds for omitting 'apostles'.

[110] We take these to be New Testament prophets. We do not, however, take the whole phrase 'holy apostles and prophets' as the author's reproduction of τοῖς ἁγίοις αὐτοῦ of Col. 1.26. It is not that he has limited the wide group of Col. 1.26 to a narrower group of leaders, as C. L. Mitton, *The Epistle to the Ephesians* (Oxford, 1951), p. 89, supposes. He is using the other strand of the tradition which we have already found in the Gospels and Acts.

agrees with Matthew, Luke, and John. In 2.20 the apostles and prophets appear to be a continuing body, perhaps regarded as linking Christ to the remainder of the church. Paul as an apostle would obviously be included. In 3.5 Paul can hardly have been included if this represents the same tradition as Matt. 28.16–20, though he appears as we have seen in 3.3. Probably the author of Ephesians had not thought this problem through. He simply picks up and uses in 3.2f, 5 two very different strands of the tradition about the revelation that the gospel is for the Gentiles. (2) The reference to the Spirit ἐν πνεύματι is probably to be connected to ἀπεκαλύφθη. Does it mean that the Spirit imparted the revelation to the apostles and prophets ('by or through the Spirit')? If so it may indicate an earlier stage of the tradition, which later hardened into the view that the apostles alone were the recipients of the tradition.[111]

Paul's unique position is continued in the Pastoral Epistles, though nothing is said about the apostles[112] or any other group as recipients of the revelation about the Gentiles or the commission to go to them.

In 1 Tim. 2.7 it is said that God[113] appointed Paul as herald and apostle and teacher of the Gentiles. His position is affirmed strongly by the parenthetical asseveration 'I speak the truth, I am not lying'. This probably refers backwards to 'apostle'[114] rather than forwards to 'teacher of the Gentiles',[115] though even then Paul's apostleship and his relation to the Gentiles cannot be separated[116] since herald, apostle, and teacher do not represent three different functions but three different aspects of the one mission to the Gentiles.[117] Note that we have here the same

---

[111] The assertion in 3.5 that the revelation was not previously known to the sons of men implies that the author did not find it in the Old Testament; he cannot therefore, have been likely to be one who accepted the present reality of the eschatological streaming of the Gentiles to Zion.

[112] Though no apostle other than Paul is mentioned in these letters it goes too far to say with M. C. de Boer, 'Images of Paul in the Post-Apostolic Period', *CBQ* 42 (1980), pp. 359–80, that he is the only apostle recognized by them. If the author is laying special stress on Paul, there is no need for him to mention other apostles.

[113] God is the real agent of the passive.

[114] So most commentators.

[115] So J. N. D. Kelly, *The Pastoral Epistles* (BNTC; London, 1963) ad loc.

[116] Cf. D. Guthrie, *The Pastoral Epistles* (Tyndale; London, 1969).

[117] C. Spicq, *Les Épîtres pastorales* (Paris, 1969), ad loc.

problem of anarthrous substantives which we found in Rom. 11.13; 15.16. Is Paul the only apostle to the Gentiles or one of a number of such apostles? In a second passage, 2 Tim. 4.17, the uniqueness of Paul's Gentile apostolate is made clear.

Commentators are divided about the background to this passage. Some envisage it as representing Paul's acquittal in Rome and the continuance of his mission to the Gentiles, probably in Spain.[118] Others see in it a reference to Paul's actual trial in Rome without any implication about a future mission; in his defence of himself the gospel was proclaimed to 'all the Gentiles', for the whole world could be viewed as representatively present in Rome and in the courtroom;[119] the πάντα of 'all the Gentiles' can be taken either metaphorically or hyperbolically. What the Gentiles hear is not Paul but the kerygma from Paul;[120] Paul is only the instrument. When, however, we take into account πληροφορηθῇ we realize that Paul is a unique instrument, for the word carries a sense of completeness. In Rome the kerygma to the Gentiles is brought to fruition; Paul's special position as their apostle is complete. Others may continue to preach to them, but none can continue Paul's unique apostleship. It would appear that here we go back through the tradition of Eph. 3.2f and Col. 1.24–29 to the passages in Romans and Galatians where Paul is apostle to the Gentiles. Since many have preached and will preach to Gentiles, his uniqueness lies in the revelation given to him of their place in the church rather than in the preaching itself.

We have discovered at least two main strands of tradition: one describes the recipients of the commission and/or revelation as the apostles, the other as Paul. Both are continued in the non-canonical literature. In the second century the Apostles are regularly described as sent to all the world, and often the Gentiles are explicitly mentioned as the object of their

[118] E.g. W. Lock, *The Pastoral Epistles* (ICC; Edinburgh, 1924), ad loc.; E. F. Scott, *The Pastoral Epistles* (MNTC; London, 1941), ad loc.

[119] E.g. Kelly, op. cit.,; E. K. Simpson, *The Pastoral Epistles* (London, 1954), ad loc.; D. Guthrie, op. cit., ad loc.; C. K. Barrett, *The Pastoral Epistles* (NCB; Oxford, 1963), ad loc.

[120] G. Holtz, *Die Pastoralbriefe* (THNT; Berlin, 1972), ad loc.

preaching (*Preaching of Peter* 4, as quoted in Clem. Alex. *Strom.*
6.48.1;[121] *Hermas*, Sim. 9.17.1f; *Ep. Diog.* 11.1; Justin M. *Apol.*
1.39.3; 1 Clem. 42.3; Polyc. *Phil.* 6.3; *Ep. Barnabas* v. 9; *Ep. Apost.*
30 (41);[122] *Asc. Isa.* 3.17f; the longer ending at Mark 16.15[123] and
the shorter, etc). This sending and preaching is often explicitly
related to a word or action of the risen Jesus (e.g. 1 Clem. 42.3)
and it may be assumed to contain implicitly the command to go
to the Gentiles. There were of course certain parts of heretical
Jewish Christianity which held that the apostles were sent only
to Jews. The other strand of the tradition, which relates it
specifically to Paul, is less frequent. He is regularly recognized
in orthodox Christian writing as an apostle[124] (1 Clem. s.5; 47.1,
4; Ign. *Rom.* 4.3; cf. Polyc. *Phil.* 3.2; 11.2; *Apoc. Paul* (Nag
Hammadi, v. 2) 21.29); this, of course, does not exclude the
existence of other apostles. Ignatius often uses the word in the
plural, and there is no reason to suppose he excludes Paul from
it.[125] Paul is not excluded in 1 Clem. 42.1–5, where it is said the
apostles received the gospel from Christ after the resurrection;
he is thus brought within the first strand of the tradition. He is
also regularly depicted as a missionary (1 Clem. 5.6f; cf. 42.1–5).
This is true even in Jewish-Christians writing; in the *Kerygmata
Petrou* H 2.16[126] he (= Simon) is described as being a missionary
to the Gentiles earlier than Peter but as one who brought to
them darkness rather than light.

Finally, in *Ep. Apost.* 31[127] his special mission to the Gentiles,
stemming from the time of his conversion, is recognized. It is in
this writing, as in Eph. 3, that we have subjoined again the two
strands, for in the preceding paragraph of *Ep. Apost.*, as we have
seen, the twelve apostles were given their commission by the
risen Jesus to go and preach to all the world, to Jews and
Gentiles. Yet here Paul does not receive his commission as

---

[121] See E. Hennecke and W. Schneemelcher, *New Testament Apocrypha* (ET by
R. McL. Wilson, etc., London, 1963–5), vol. ii, p. 101.

[122] Op. cit., vol. i, p. 212.

[123] For the discussion see most recently, J. Hug, *La Finale de l'évangile de Marc*
(Paris, 1978), pp. 81ff, 153ff, 169f.

[124] Of course he is rejected as such in heterodox Jewish-Christian writing.

[125] Cf. Lindemann, op. cit., pp. 86f.

[126] Hennecke, op. cit., vol. ii, pp. 121f.

[127] Hennecke, op. cit., vol. i, p. 213.

apostle to the Gentiles directly from God but through the Twelve.[128] The elimination of any unique position for Paul is continued in Irenaeus.[129]

If we look back at the evidence we can see that, on the one hand, there was a widespread tradition (the gospels, Acts, Ephesians) that the revelation that the gospel was intended for all men was given to the group of apostles (disciples, the Twelve, the Eleven) by a supernatural revelation from the risen Christ (gospels, Acts) or through the Spirit to the group of apostles and prophets (Ephesians); on the other hand, Paul and the Pauline tradition believed that a revelation with similar content came to Paul and was associated in some way with his experience on the road to Damascus. It was probably only a revelation about the place of the Gentiles, for Paul would naturally have assumed that Jews were to be included in his mission. As we have seen, he had many contacts with Jews. In addition, though no trace of it can be found outside Acts, Peter was led by signs from heaven to baptize the centurion Cornelius. To all this we have to add the fact of the Gentile mission, which could well have begun spontaneously quite apart from any revelation or supernatural sign and quite apart from both the apostles and Paul.

The tradition that the revelation about the Gentile mission was given to the apostles can hardly be original. It is not referred to in the Peter-and-Cornelius incident or in the council of Acts 15, and presumably its origin postdates these events. Equally we should have expected some reference to it in the discussions of Gal. 2.1–10 if it was then in existence. It is also very doubtful if there was a generally recognized post-resurrection revelation to the Twelve to evangelize Jews. Their evangelization would have been carried out on the basis of what Jesus had said to the Twelve before his death. If there had been such a formal revelation, the division of responsibility recorded in Gal. 2.1–10 would not have been between Paul on the one side and Peter and James on the other but between Paul and the

---

[128] Cf. 3 Cor. 3.4 from *Acts of Paul* (Hennecke, op. cit., vol. ii, p. 375) for Paul's dependence on the Twelve.

[129] E.g. *Adv. Haer.* iii. 13.1.

Twelve.[130] In view of the structure of Mark and the way in which
he argues that the gospel is intended for the Gentiles, it is
unlikely that he knew the tradition of the revelation to disciples
to go to all the world. If Ephesians is by Paul, then 3.5 shows that
when he wrote that letter he was aware of the tradition, and
must therefore have learnt it after the incident of Gal. 2.1–10. If
Ephesians is not by Paul 3.5 is of no help in dating the origin of
the tradition. All this means that we cannot put a precise date
on its appearance.

If we cannot say with any accuracy when the tradition of a
revelation to the Twelve appeared, can we say how or why it did
so? The Gentile mission was thoroughly established before we
learn of its existence; by that time there was no need of a
revelation to the church to include the Gentiles in its mission
activity. In any case the apostles can hardly have been gathered
together as a group to receive such a revelation at any period
later than the first few years, and this is too early for its
appearance. We must regard it therefore as an imaginary
construction read back into the early period as a *post factum*
justification of an existing practice. The variety of forms in
which the tradition is found reinforces the view that it was a
conclusion drawn from the fact of the mission rather than from
an actual event, for then the words of the revelation would have
been more or less fixed. If we were able to regard the Ephesian
form of the tradition as the most primitive we might be able to
go a little further. The reference in 3.5 to the prophets and the
Spirit may suggest that in its first stage it was believed that the
revelation was given to the apostles through prophetic inspira-
tion. Later (Matthew, Luke–Acts, John) it was understood to be
a revelation to the apostles without reference to the prophets.
The factors which led us to the writing of the Gospels, which
include some desire to root everything in history, may have led
to the reading-back of the revelation to the time of the risen
Lord. Given that Christians believed they had a supernatural

---

[130] Hubbard's attempt to see a two-stage development, beginning with a
commission to preach to Israel, founders on the division of responsibility
indicated in Gal. 2. After the agreement of Gal. 2 there would have been no
reason for a commission to appear which was limited to Israel alone; cf. Kästing,
op. cit., p. 45.

instruction for what took place, but had no details of its exact form, each of the evangelists would have been able to clothe the instruction in his own language and concepts. There is another possibility. Eph. 3.5 may suggest its origin lay with a Christian prophet. We can either regard the prophet as an inspired charismatic like Agabus or as a preacher who proclaimed the Word. The former would be highly unlikely in view of the lateness of the appearance of the tradition. A preacher, however, might have drawn the implication from his knowledge that Jesus sent out his disciples two by two in his own lifetime calling them to be fishers of men, and from his awareness of the existence of the missionary activity of the church in his own time; he might also have associated these with the known revelations to, and commissionings of, Peter and Paul. He would have proclaimed his conclusion as the word of God; later this was transferred to the lips of the risen Lord. Any suggestions, however, about the origin of this form of the tradition must be very speculative.

The tradition of Paul as the recipient of the revelation that the Gospel was intended for Gentiles also has its difficulties. In the letters it is seen as a revelation and commission in respect of the Gentiles; in Acts Paul is sent to both Jews and Gentiles. Clearly no revelation would be necessary to send a Jewish Christian to Jews though a commission might be. Acts (22.21) however also contains traces of an underlying tradition which tied Paul more closely to Gentiles alone.[131] We cannot doubt that he believed he received this revelation, but we can doubt whether he was right in seeing himself as a unique instrument of God in this respect. Peter preached to, and baptized Cornelius into the church without knowledge of the revelation given to Paul. The Gospel was apparently preached to Gentiles at Antioch (Acts 11.19–26) before Paul came there. Though the language, the style, and many of the ideas of this passage (e.g. the preaching to Jews prior to Gentiles, vv. 19f) are Lucan, he apparently uses in verse 20 a piece of good tradition.[132] The new step at Antioch may have been spontaneous, or it may have been the result of information received about Peter and Cornelius

[131] See above, p. 119.
[132] Cf. Roloff, op. cit., p. 177.

(the positioning of the incident is probably Lucan, and there-fore there is no necessary original relation between the two events)[133] or of knowledge of Paul's preaching to Gentiles elsewhere. The latter seems more probable. Why else in a situation in which Gentiles were being evangelized should Paul be summoned (11.25f), unless it was known that he would be favourable to this activity? However, the connection of Paul with Antioch at this particular moment may be Lucan. If it is reliable, the invitation of the Christians in Antioch could have come about either because they knew of the revelation given to Paul or, much more likely, because they had heard that he was already engaged in a mission to Gentiles. More probable than any of these suggestions is the view that preaching to the Gentiles was a natural development of the position of the group of Hellenists associated with Stephen and Philip[134] who were scattered from Jerusalem after the martyrdom of Stephen. Luke is again probably using good tradition when he attributes all the preaching in Samaria and Antioch and to the Ethiopian eunuch[135] to this group. Some reconciliation between the spontaneous preaching to the Gentiles at Antioch and the view that Paul held about his own position might be offered on the grounds that first in Antioch those who were converted were circumcised but later Paul came and taught that circumcision was unnecessary for Gentiles. He thus could be said to have appreciated more fully than the Hellenist group what preaching to the Gentiles involved. There is however no evidence for this view.

[133] Relative dating of the conversion of Cornelius and the preaching to Gentiles at Antioch is impossible.

[134] This view is widely accepted; cf. most recently, Hengel, op. cit., pp. 99ff; Roloff, op. cit., pp. 178f.

[135] The Ethopian eunuch was probably a Gentile and his conversion that of a Gentile, though Luke does not so regard it.

8

Two Types of Existence

In Ephesians[1] two types of existence, Christian and non-Christian, are outlined and set in opposition. Both types are stated in absolute and relative terms, and this creates problems. The two types are described most clearly in 4.17–21; 4.22–24; 5.8; and 5.15–18. Before examining these passages, we need to note their position in the ongoing argument of the letter. For the purpose of this examination, there is no need to decide whether Ephesians is a genuine letter of Paul, a theological essay, a modified sermon, or an adaptation of a liturgy; for simplicity's sake we shall refer to it as a letter. Nor is there any need to discuss authorship: Ephesians is probably post-Pauline, written by a disciple of Paul and standing within the Pauline tradition. Still, if Paul is the author, little of what is written would need to be altered. As a letter, Ephesians was not addressed to an individual congregation but more widely to an unidentified number as a general letter.

Ephesians begins with a prayer, stressing God's goodness to the readers through what he has done for them in Christ's death, resurrection, and ascension (1.3–23), before going on to draw out their altered position since their conversion. Once Gentiles dead in sin, the readers have now been saved through God's grace and sit with Christ in the heavenly places (2.1–10).

[1] So far as I can detect, Ephesians is one of the few areas of the New Testament that Paul Achtemeier has not illuminated, and so I have not been able to call upon his scholarship to help me.

God's original promise of salvation had been made to the Jews, and the first Christians had all been such. What, then, is the position of the readers *vis-à-vis* Christian Jews? The separating barrier has been broken down and Gentiles are as much members of the church as Jews; no distinction is now to be made (2.11–22). The equal acceptance of Gentile converts came through revelations made to Paul and to the apostles and prophets (3.1–6), which Paul made effective through his ministry (3.7–13). The author ends the first half of his letter with a prayer for these Gentile converts (3.14–21). With this theological foundation thus laid, the author turns to its practical working out, and to this he devotes the remainder of his letter. Emphasizing the need to strive to maintain the unity God has given (4.1–6), the author sketches the nature of the church into which the Gentiles have been admitted; it is the body of Christ of which Christ is head (4.7–16). This basis established, the author turns to the details of how believers should live, and he does so, in part, through the contrasts with which we began. The contrast between pre-Christian and Christian existence is a commonplace in scripture (e.g., Rom. 6.12–14; 8.13; 1 Pet. 1.18; 2.10).

The first passage we mentioned, 4.17–21, commences by describing the reader's previous existence, which is also a description of the culture in which they lived before conversion and in which their non-Christian neighbours and friends have continued to live (4.17–19). In speaking of the past futility of their minds, the author is not suggesting that the readers were unable to reason logically but that their total attitude, their mind-set, was incorrect, resulting in lives empty of real value (v. 17). This included their earlier worship, for it had been the worship of idols and not of the true God. At 2.12, the author had already described the readers as having been without God in the world; naturally, this did not mean they had been atheists, for atheists in our sense were rare in the ancient world; what it does mean is that they had not venerated the true God. In 4.18–19, the author spells out more fully the results of a worthless mind-set: a darkening of the understanding bringing blindness to the truth, and unlike those physically blind, an unawareness of their condition; though perhaps able to prove logically that God existed, they had had no real knowledge of him, for they had been alienated from his life, that is, from the life he gives to his people. This resulted from ignorance and hardness of heart. The author does not specify, as in Romans 1.18–32, that God had caused this condition, but he may well have thought so, for it is a common Old Testament theme (Exod. 4.21; 10.20, 27; Deut. 2.30); yet when in verse 18*b* the author mentions the former ignorance of the readers, it may be to bring out their own responsibility: if so, this would slightly soften the picture. The readers' ignorance and hardness of heart had led to a loss of sensitivity; their conscience did not stab them when they did wrong, and so they gave themselves up to all kinds of sin. The words used indicate that the author had primarily sexual sin in mind, though he may also have been thinking of covetousness (the NRSV relates covetousness to sexual sin, but it is probably better taken separately with the connotation of greed). This is a very stark picture of the past life of the Gentile readers. Converts often paint such pictures of their own past, but here the picture is not just that of the past life of individuals but also of the society out of which they came and the context in which the church still had to live. It is hardly the picture Greco-Roman society would have painted of itself.

In 4.20–21, the author begins to describe the readers' new lives. As Christians, they are different, for they have 'learned Christ'. This is a surprising phrase; one learns subjects, not people. It does not mean simply that the readers had been told the facts about Jesus or given an understanding of his existence, death, and resurrection. Both would certainly have been true, but this peculiar phrase seems to intend something more personal: The readers have been brought into a relation with the living Christ. At first sight, verse 21, too, suggests little more than a knowledge of Christian teaching about Christ; the NRSV's 'heard about him' fails to convey the strangeness of the original Greek, which is, literally, 'you have heard him'. When Christ was preached, the readers heard him in the words of the preacher and were brought into contact with the living Christ. They were also 'taught in him', which is, again, not a normal expression; it seems to be an allusion to the community of knowledge of Christ that comes through membership in his body. The final reference in verse 21 is to truth in Jesus; since Ephesians never stresses the life of the historical Jesus, this is hardly a suggestion that the lives of the readers should resemble that of the earthly Jesus. Yet the use of the name 'Jesus' means that the author is not thinking solely of the exalted Lord; for him the death of the historical Jesus is important (e.g., 1.7; 2.16). The use of Jesus' name is therefore probably intended to anchor the author's discussion in history. In the light of what these verses say, the readers' lives should now be different from what they were. Their past lives have been painted in what can only be described as 'absolute' terms and so also have their new lives, for it is assumed that their relation to Christ is complete.

In 4.22–24, the contrast is between old and new self or old and new person. The idea and the words to convey it are the same as in Colossians 3.9–10; the metaphorical use of the putting on and off of clothing was, however, well known in antiquity; Paul writes of putting on a new person (Rom. 13.14; Gal. 3.27), and thinks of Christ as put on. Some relation must exist between the new self and Christ. The old self was the self of the preconversion life, which was being destroyed by the lusts that characterized it. This places some responsibility on those who are 'old selves' for being so. The new self, however, is the creation of God and is characterized by 'true righteousness and holiness'. Here an absolute is introduced; there is no gradual creation of the new self. The believer is a new self; he or she is not on the way to becoming one. The pre-Christian and the Christian manner of life are thus both described in absolute terms.

This is also true of the description in 5.8 of pre-Christian and Christian existence: 'Once you were darkness, but now in the Lord you are light.' No twilight zone exists, no shades of grey. Light and darkness do not of themselves identify the contrast but emphasize it. They cannot coexist. The context describes something of the nature of 'dark' existence. It involves disobedience to God (5.6); it produces deeds too shameful to mention, though the author has not hesitated to mention them in 5.3–5 (the rejection of their mention is not to be taken literally; it is an attempt to emphasize their wrongness). For its part, light is associated with what is good, right, and true (5.9).

In 5.15–18, the contrast of the two existences is expressed in relative terms. Using wisdom terminology, the author describes believers as wise; but it is not implied that they are absolutely wise, for they are bidden to make the most of every opportunity for good – an unnecessary injunction if they always behaved wisely. Unbelievers are, by implication, unwise; but their failure is not delineated except in so far as it differs from wise behaviour.

The contrasts identified here are put elsewhere in the letter in quite another way without the discussion of actual details of conduct. Unbelievers are dead in sin (2.1, 5) and belong to the sphere of the devil (2.2); they are under the control of 'the powers' (6.12) and subject to the wrath of God (2.3). Believers, however, are 'in Christ', members of his body, built into his temple and belonging to his kingdom (2.19–22; 4.11–16; 5.6); they have been enlightened (1.18) and are already raised with Christ and sit with him in heavenly places (2.6). The approach of Ephesians to moral exhortation is thus consistent with its general theology.

The author is not alone in the way he depicts contemporary culture. It is found in Jewish writers (cf. Jer. 10.14–15; Wis. 13.1; *Sib. Or.* III 36–45; *1 En.* 91.5–7; *Jub.* 22.16–18; 1QS 4.9–14) and in other parts of the New Testament (Matt. 12.39; 16.4; cf. Mark 4.12; John 12.40; Rom. 11.8; 2 Cor. 3.14). Was the ancient Gentile world – the author does not describe the Jewish world, for those to whom he is writing had not previously been Jews but Gentiles – really as bad as he paints it? Jewish authors were not consistent in employing dark colours. In so far as they recognized that God is the God of all peoples, who would in the end be gathered to God, their view of the Gentile world cannot have been entirely negative (Isa. 45.22; 51.5; 56.7; Sir. 1.9–10; *1 En.* 10.21). Josephus, whose own associations in Judaism were with Pharisaism, compares Stoics and Pharisees with no intention of denigrating either (*Vita* 12), and so evaluates Stoicism positively.

When we turn to the way Gentiles described their own world, we do not find it normally painted in black colours. The Stoics commended the four cardinal virtues of prudence, justice, courage, and temperance and attempted to live by them. They also condemned an immoderate desire for pleasure, including sexual indulgence. Epictetus wrote:

> You live in an imperial state; it is your duty to hold office, to judge uprightly, to keep your hands off the property of other people; no woman but your wife ought to look handsome to you, no boy handsome, no silver plate handsome, no gold plate.[2]

> What [does a man lose] by the virtue of unnatural lust? His manhood. And by the agent? Beside a good many other things he also loses his manhood no less than the other. What does the adulterer lose? He loses the man of self-respect that was, the man of self-control, the gentleman, the citizen, the neighbour.[3]

Virgil's *Fourth Eclogue* indicates an aspiration for better things. The satirists (e.g., Juvenal) would have gone unheard and their works would have been lost if there were not already those in society disgusted with what was being satirized. The very existence of the contrast between 'good' and 'bad' in Greek and Roman thought and the employment of all kinds of terms for various virtues and vices implies that some actions were thought to be better than others. Thus, there was an ethical conscience even if, in content, it did not entirely agree with the Christian conscience. The qualities demanded of Christian leaders in the pastorals vary little from those required from leaders in secular society.[4] This shows that pagan life contained many features of which Christians could approve. The pagan moralists condemned activities in a way similar to the condemnations of Ephesians 4.25–27; 5.5 in respect of lying, anger, and covetousness. Of lying, Marcus Aurelius said, 'And the liar too acts impiously.'[5] Concerning anger, Seneca asserts:

> You have importuned me, Novatus, to write on this subject of how anger may be allayed, and it seems to me that you had good reason to fear in an especial degree this, the most hideous and

---

[2] Epictetus iii 7.21. All the quotations from classical authors are taken from the translations of the relevant volumes of the Loeb Classical Library.

[3] Epictetus ii 17–18. He writes very sarcastically, 'Why should we not seduce our neighbour's wife, if we can escape detection?' (iii 7.16). Similar rejections to sexual lust are to be found in M. Aurelius ix 42 and Seneca, *Ep.* 9.3–12; 75.7–18.

[4] See J. Roloff, *Der Erste Brief an Timotheus* (EKK 15, Zürich, 1988), p. 150.

[5] M. Aurelius ix 1.

frenzied of all the emotions. For the other emotions have in them some element of peace and calm, while this one is wholly violent and has its being in an onrush of resentment, raging with a most inhuman lust for weapons, blood, and punishment, giving no thought to itself if only it can hurt another, hurling itself upon the very point of the dagger, and eager for revenge though it may drag down the avenger with it.[6]

And of thieving and covetousness, Epictetus observes:

> For when once you conceive a desire for money ... if you do not apply a remedy, your governing principle does not revert to its previous condition, but, on being aroused again by the corresponding external impression, it bursts into the flame of desire more quickly than it did before. And if this happens over and over again, the next stage is that a callousness results and the infirmity strengthens the avarice.[7]

Many of the areas of behaviour condemned in Ephesians thus came under the purview of the ancient moralists and were likewise rebuked. Musonius Rufus said that philosophy consists in 'thinking out what is man's duty and meditating upon it.'[8] The judgment of Ephesians on society, then, seems unbearably harsh. It may be said, however, that although the moralists taught a morality with a large part of which Christians would have agreed, few, if any, lived by what they taught. Epictetus acknowledges this when he writes that we Stoics 'talk of one thing and do another' (iii 7.17). There would, therefore, have been a difference, but not an abyss, between what the philosophers taught and the way ordinary people lived. Epictetus's admission, however, is one that Christians have continually had to make in the light of their own failures, for they could never claim that they lived wholly in accordance with the moral teaching of scripture.

There are other aspects to consider. The sins of the Gentile world condemned by the author of Ephesians are principally sexual perversions ('licentiousness' in 4.19 should be given this

---

[6] Seneca, *De ira* I 1.1–2; cf. Diogenes Laertes 7.113–14.

[7] Epictetus ii 18.8–10. See also the quotation from Epictetus iii 7.21 previously cited.

[8] Quoted in Wayne Meeks, *The Moral World of the First Christians* (London, 1986), p. 46.

wide sense and not restricted to fornication alone, as in some translations) and covetousness. These are obvious and easy vices to condemn and have regularly been high on the list of sins which preachers feature. By the same token, there were areas of behaviour outside the church that Christians from time to time have commended. Paul wrote highly of Roman justice (Rom. 13.1–7), from which, according to Acts, he benefited on a number of occasions (16.35–39; 18.12–17; 22.24–29; 25.8–12). The realization of the benefits of Roman law and order lay behind the respect shown for rulers (1 Pet. 2.13–17) and the prayers offered for them (1 Tim. 2.2). Moreover, in many areas where we today would fault the Christians of that period, they thought and acted in much the same way as their non-Christian neighbours. They had the same attitude toward slavery and took no official steps to ameliorate the conditions of slaves. Individual Christian slave owners may have acted in kindly fashion towards their slaves, but that was often also the attitude of non-Christians. There is the well-known story of the visit of Augustus Caesar to Vedius Pollio, one of whose slaves broke a crystal dish in the presence of the Emperor. When Vedius ordered the slave to be thrown to man-eating fish, Augustus intervened, forbade the throwing of the slave to the fish and instead ordered all the valuable glass dishes of Vedius to be smashed and the pond itself filled up.[9] The pagan world then was much less deplorable than it appears to have been from Ephesians.

At this point it becomes important to note that Ephesians is not consistent. If its author asserts that believers are now light and not darkness, much that he writes shows that he realized that darkness still existed among them. In a succession of instructions on behaviour, he warns the readers against lying, losing their tempers, thieving, and unhelpful conversation (4.25–30). Sexual sin and covetousness are not mentioned at this juncture, but later the author warns the readers against these, saying that they should not even be named among them (5.3, 5). This cannot be taken literally, for the author himself has just named them, and every time the letter was read aloud in worship, they would have been named. No, the author's

---

[9] See Seneca, *De ira* III 40.2–3.

expression indicates the seriousness of these sins. After all, there would have been no point in the author's warning the readers so strongly against these sins if some believers had not been committing them. Equally, there would have been no need to advise wives and husbands, parents and children, owners and slaves about their behaviour towards one another if their mutual relationships had been perfect (5.22–6.9). The same conclusion follows both from the author's intercession for these groups in prayer (3.16–19) and from his positive exhortations: They are not to grieve God's Spirit by what they do (4.25–31) but rather to be kind to one another (4.32). He can even go so far as to threaten members with exclusion from their inheritance in the kingdom (5.5) and with the wrath of God (5.6). In fact, every instruction the author offers in respect of what he considers true conduct and every warning against sinful conduct is an admission that there are those who have failed in the community. In fact, then, much of what the author writes rejects the position that all is light within the church.

If the author is not consistent in drawing his picture of those within the church, neither is he consistent in his picture of the outside world. Indeed, part of what the author says shows that he recognized the existence of good in the world. When the author writes about behaviour, he often uses ethical terms drawn from contemporary non-Christian ethics. At the outset of his paraenesis, when he indicates the virtues that should typify Christian behaviour within the community, he employs three nouns: humility, gentleness, and patience. Of these, the first would certainly have surprised Gentiles on their initial encounter with it, for the Greek root, ταπειν, normally carried in that language the derogatory meaning of servitude. In biblical and Jewish Greek, by contrast, it had taken on the sense of non-assertiveness, leading to the meaning 'humility'. The other two nouns, however, describe attitudes and conduct of which not only Jews but also Greek and Roman moralists approved. 'Gentleness' is commended by Marcus Aurelius (9.42) and while the term 'patience' (μακροθυμια) was not in regular use, the concept was commended using other terms. The author of Ephesians could not have been unaware of the attitude of society in general to two of his three virtues. When again he sets out to describe briefly in what the life of the new self should consist, he employs a pair of words 'righteousness and holiness' (4.24), which were widely recognized in the ancient world as covering the whole of moral existence.[10] In 5.3–4 the author uses two terms regular in Stoic moral teaching, 'as is proper' (πρεπει) and 'out of place' (ουκ ἀνηκεν), for good and bad behaviour. This means that his image of pagan society and of the actual pre-Christian life of his readers cannot have been as dark as he says. Why, then, does he paint it so darkly?

There is a sense in which our accusations against the author have up to now been superficial. When we examine him more closely, we see that, even on those occasions when he appears to be drawing the contrast between the Christian and the non-Christian life in the most absolute of terms, he allows himself some leeway. When he took over from Colossians 3.9–10 the contrast between the old and the new self, he made a significant alteration. Colossians 3.9–10 describes both the stripping off of the old self and the putting on of the new as actions belonging to the past. In Ephesians 4.22, 24 the references to the putting off of the old and the putting on of the new self may be read as imperatives and therefore as incomplete.[11] Between them there is also an instruction that believers are to be renewed in the spirit of their minds (v. 23). The author therefore recognized that the change from the old to the new is a process. The new self does not immediately take the place of the old. The man who can run a hundred metres in ten seconds does not suddenly discover, when he becomes a new person, that he can run faster or that he has dropped out of contention with those against whom he had previously competed. The woman who writes an award-winning novel does not discover on becoming a new person that she has lost the power to put words together so that others want to read her. When Paul became a Christian, the energy and enthusiasm that he had put into hunting down Christians did not disappear but was diverted into an eagerness

[10] Plato, *Gorgias* 507AB; *Rep.* 10.6B; *Thaetetus* 176B. The combination is also known in Jewish Greek (Josephus, *Ant.* 8.245, 295; Philo, *Sobr.* 10; *Som.* 2.296), but the readers of Ephesians would know it from its non-Jewish use.

[11] It is irrelevant whether the author of Ephesians used Colossians directly or indirectly; the terms probably belonged to the Pauline tradition in which he stood.

to convert Gentiles to Christianity. A continuity thus exists between old and new selves. How extensive is it? If sinful habits have been a part of the old self, do they immediately disappear with the new self, or are they gradually eliminated? Probably Christians, if asked to answer honestly, would admit that they can discern in their new self something of the old. While for obvious reasons we cannot know much of the character of the preconversion Paul, we do see in the converted Paul traces of faults that must have been present in the unconverted Saul. He is sarcastic:

> Already you have all you want! Already you have become rich! Quite apart from us you have become kings! Indeed, I wish that you had become kings, so that we might be kings with you! For I think that God has exhibited us apostles as last of all, as though sentenced to death, because we have become a spectacle to the world, to angels and mortals (1 Cor. 4.8–9; cf. 2 Cor. 11.19; 12.11).

Paul can also speak extremely harshly of others with little of the gentleness of spirit that we might expect from a follower of Jesus or the author of the thirteenth chapter of First Corinthians: 'I wish those who unsettle you would castrate themselves!' (Gal. 5.12; cf. Phil. 3.19; Gal. 1.8–9).[12]

Accordingly, an absolute position in respect either of the Christian life (that it is pure light) or of the world outside the Christian community (that it is pure darkness) is impossible. What, then, led the author into the position where he appears to be making such absolute and impossible assertions? Naturally, there is no need to explain why he adopted at times the relative position, since it was the normal position. Let us, then, examine the two sides of the absolute position, beginning with the author's view of the outside world.

Before we do so, however, there is a general consideration to take into account. One of the main themes of New Testament ethical instruction is the relation of the indicative and the imperative: You are sons of God; therefore behave as his sons should. The author was required, then, to express in absolute

---

[12] For fuller details, see Ernest Best, *Paul and His Converts* (Edinburgh, 1988), pp. 114–23.

terms the position of believers so that he could make that
position into a springboard for his advocacy of good conduct. In
5.8, he carries out this process before our eyes: '. . . in the Lord
you are light. Live [then] as children of light' (i.e., as enlightened people). This kind of argument would be impossible had
the author phrased it: '. . . in the Lord you are twilight. Live
[then] as children of light'. The author's positive statement that
believers are light accords with much of what he says in the
earlier, more theological sections of the letter, for instance, that
they have been adopted (1.3–5). But whereas this shows that
there is a theological justification for the author's absolute
statements in respect of believers, there is no parallel in respect
of unbelievers: 'You are darkness; therefore behave as darkened
people'. The conduct of unbelievers may exhibit dark features,
but no one would argue that it ought to do so. Unbelievers,
despite their unbelief, are still enjoined to behave in a good
manner.

The language and content of the picture of the outside world
in 4.17–19 strongly recalls Romans 1.18–32. There is no reason
to suppose that Ephesians is directly dependent at this point on
Romans. Still, the author of Ephesians, if he were not Paul, was
certainly a disciple of Paul who had imbibed much of Paul's
theological outlook. The contrast of light and darkness is also a
Pauline concept (e.g., Rom. 13.12; 1 Thess. 5.4–5), and the
contrast of the old self and the new was taken, though modified,
either directly from Colossians 3.9–10 or from the Pauline
tradition. Moreover, the presence of some of these ideas in
Ephesians can be traced further back into Jewish thought. Jews
regarded themselves as people who could see, while Gentiles
were blind. God says of the Jews, 'I have given you as a covenant
to the people, a light to the nations, to open the eyes that are
blind' (Isa. 42.6–7; cf. 49.6; 1QSb 4.27; Wis. 18.4). In the
Qumran War Scroll the members of the community are repeatedly described as the sons, or children, of light and their
enemies, the nations, as the sons, or children, of darkness.
Hardness of heart is attributed to the enemies of the Jews. God
says to Moses, 'I will harden Pharaoh's heart, and I will multiply
my signs and wonders in the land of Egypt' (Exod. 7.3; cf. 4.21;
9.12; Jer. 19.15).

Consequently, there was much in the theological atmosphere in which the author of Ephesians was brought up to condition him into making absolute statements about the outside world, for it is highly probable that he was Jewish. But even if he had been a Gentile before conversion, he had obviously thought a great deal about Christianity, and his sources for this would have been the Old Testament as textbook (his use of it shows that he knew it well) and the teaching of his master Paul.

The argument is slightly different when we turn to the author's 'absolute' description of Christian existence. Here we cannot trace his position directly to the Old Testament and only partially to Paul. In one sense the author provides a consistent picture, for in the theological first half of the letter he says that believers are already raised with Christ and sit with him in heavenly places (2.6). Paul never said the latter and, though it is possible to take some of his statements as suggesting that believers have already experienced the resurrection, most scholars do not read Paul in this way. It is clear, however, that Paul could not be read or misread in this way, for in 1 Corinthians 4.8 he condemns those who believed they already reigned as kings, and 2 Timothy 2.18 likewise condemns those who believed that the resurrection is past. In Colossians 2.12; 3.1, a writing to which the author is heavily indebted, the resurrection of believers with Christ is put in the past, and in Colossians 3.3 their lives are now said to be hidden with Christ in God, which might be understood as indicating an immediate presence in heaven. Moreover, the heavenly session could be said to be a logical consequence of resurrection. All this enables us to see how the author of Ephesians could have come to his point of view. If, then, believers have been raised with Christ and sit with him in the heavenly places, must they not be free from sin and able to be described as 'light' and 'new selves'? Furthermore, is this latter notion really any different in substance, though expressed in a very different idiom, from the concept of rebirth that is found in several New Testament writings (John 3.3–5; Tit. 3.5; James 1.18; 1 Pet. 1.3, 23; 1 John 3.9)? When Paul himself describes Christians as new creatures (2 Cor. 5.17), he does not qualify the word 'new' in any way. If, then, they are new, may they not be wholly new? The author of Ephesians could then have provided some theological backing for his absolute position in respect of believers. But not all the writers of the New Testament come to a similar position. Were there other factors that led the author to his characteristic view?

Converts notoriously see their preconversion life in the blackest of colours and, although, as a Jew, the author of Ephesians would probably not have thought of himself as coming from a particularly dark past, he could well have done so. Paul took a very grave view of his own pre-Christian past (1 Cor. 15.9), with the result that within the Pauline tradition he could be described as the foremost of sinners (1 Tim. 1.15). Either Paul himself said, or the author makes him say, that he is 'the very least of all the saints' (3.8). In 2 Corinthians 3.15–16 Paul says that when Jews become Christians, it is as if a veil were taken from their eyes; as Jews they could not see, as Christians they can; this is the contrast of light and darkness, though expressed very differently. Consequently, it is possible that even Jews could look back to their past lives as lived in darkness and their conversion to Christianity as the time when they began to see and became 'light'. But whatever may be said about Jews becoming Christians, the readers of Ephesians were in large part converted Gentiles. When they looked back on their past lives, they saw them as full of sin. Before their conversion they had not thought very much about sin or realized its seriousness in God's eyes. Now, with a wholly new vision, their past became darkened. Some of the terms used by the author to depict the past and present lives of the readers may indeed have come from their baptismal instruction. This is most likely to be true of the light–darkness and the new self–old self contrasts. Another factor in the way the readers looked at their pre-Christian lives may have been the need to explain the failure of others to see the light as they themselves had done. Perhaps it resulted from the sinful and dark culture in which they were enmeshed as well as from their own sinful and dark lives.

So far, our approach has been made in purely individualistic terms, and different converts might have taken different views. What, then, of the church as a whole? Experience of small sects shows that they tend to take a very pessimistic view of what lies outside their group. Intent on drawing firm lines around themselves, they depict in the darkest of colours those who do not belong to them. While Christians restrict the term 'sect' to little groups within the Christian field, sociologists use it more widely of any small group that has a different way of looking at things and a different set of values from society as a whole (probably few non-Christians thought of culture as evil, 5.16). In that sense the early Christians were a sect.[13] The early Christian communities must have seen themselves as very different from those outside them, and those outside them must have regarded these communities as very odd. Christian communities no longer took any part in the civic religions of their area, for that would have involved idolatry. They dropped out of various associations with other people that they felt would compromise them; they tended to marry within their own circles. Though there was at this stage no state persecution, individual Christians and groups would have felt harassment from their neighbours and local ruling authorities because of their separatist position (see, e.g., Acts 17.5–9; Heb. 10.32–33). So not only the common beliefs of Christians but also pressure from outside would have driven them in on themselves and led them to judge the outside world harshly (5.16; 6.13).

Yet, is it right to speak of the early Christians in this way? Did they take an undue interest in themselves? Are there signs of this in Ephesians? The paraenetic section of the letter commences with a discussion of the church as the body of Christ (4.7–16). While often in modern preaching this image is taken to relate to the activity of the church in the world – Christ has no hands but our hands – in Ephesians, and in Paul generally, it is used to teach about the inner life of the community: the relation of members to one another, the special gifts they have that are to be used to help one another, and the closeness of the community to Christ. The image of the church as Christ's body is not applied at all to the church's relation to the world.[14] On turning to the details of the paraenesis, we find the same kind of picture. When in 4.25 the members of the community are told

[13] See Best, 'A First Century Sect', *Irish Biblical Studies* 8 (1986), pp. 115–21. For a discussion of the nature of sectarian communities in general, see B. Wilson, *Sects and Society* (London, 1961).

[14] See Best, *One Body in Christ* (London, 1955), pp. 83–159.

not to lie to their neighbours, this is qualified by the introduction of the image of the body so that 'neighbour' has to be given the sense of 'other member of the community' and not of 'other person' as Jesus used it. When members of the community are told not to steal but to work and earn money (4.28), this is not so that restoration might be made to the person who had suffered the theft (cf. Luke 19.1–10) or that the money earned might be given to the poor in accordance with Jesus' injunction to the man who wanted to become a disciple (Mark 10.21), but so that what was earned might be used to help the community. Members of the community are told to be kind to one another and forgive one another (4.32) without any suggestion that they should also be kind and forgiving to those outside the community. When they are warned against sexual sin (5.3–5), no interest is taken in the person whom they have used for their sin (contrast Epictetus ii 17–18 quoted above) nor when warned against theft (4.28), is there any interest in the person whose goods have been stolen; in neither case was the offended person a member of the community. What is at stake is the purity of the life of the individual member and, through that person, the purity of the community. We may contrast 5.15 with the equivalent injunction of Colossians 4.5 'conduct yourselves wisely towards outsiders'; Ephesians omits 'towards outsiders'. The request for prayer in Colossians 4.3, for what is in effect the spread of the gospel, is omitted in Ephesians; yet it would be wrong to say that Ephesians is uninterested in winning outsiders, for 3.1–13 has set out the revelation that the gospel should be taken to the Gentiles. What we find in Ephesians is similar to what we see in sects: The world outside is evil; men and women must be won into the community from it. Generally speaking, the moral exhortations of the second half of the letter relate to activity within and affecting the community and not to the relation of the community to those outside it. This is not unlike what we find in many of the non-Pauline letters of the New Testament where the command of Jesus to love neighbours, in which he understands neighbours to mean all people, is changed into 'love one another' (1 Pet. 1.22; 4.8; Heb. 13.1; John 13.34–35; 1 John 3.23), so that love is restricted to other members of the community. Paul sometimes takes Jesus' commandment in this way (1 Thess. 4.9–12; Rom. 12.10), but he also at times retains its wider and original reference (1 Thess. 3.12; Rom. 13.8–10; Gal. 5.14). Ephesians, then, evinces a great interest in the life of the community and little in that of the world outside, except to depict it in the darkest of colours. The more darkly the picture is painted, the less likely the members are to fall back into its ways.

Accordingly, it is possible to understand why Epheaians paints in such absolute terms both the outside world and Christian existence. The author, however, was too wise not to know that Christians fail, and so he gives elaborate guidance about their behaviour. Their goodness can then be seen as relative and not absolute or perfect. In this we may compare him with 'conviction' politicians who tend to reject the possibility of faults on their own part and see their opponents and the world outside their own area as under the domination of Satan. While the author of Ephesians may paint the world in absolute colours, there is no hint of the self-righteousness politicians regularly display. He knew that the people to whom he wrote were not perfect and needed to be given guidance so that they might conduct themselves wisely in true righteousness and holiness (4.24).

9

Ministry in Ephesians

Note the title: this is a discussion of ministry and not of *the* ministry in Ephesians, though naturally a good part of the discussion of this essay will be occupied with the latter aspect of the subject. There are at least two possible approaches to the study of ministry; the sociological treats how leadership arises and how it and officials function within the group to which they belong; the theological, the place of ministry in the plan of God for his church. In fact these two approaches can never be wholly separated but attention will be focused on the second, the theological aspect, because this at first sight appears to be the approach of the author of Ephesians. In this essay it is assumed that Ephesians was not written by Paul, but even if he was its author the argument would hardly alter. Attention will however be drawn to the few points where his authorship might make a difference to the conclusions. It is also assumed that the letter was written not to one congregation but to a number, probably lying in Asia Minor.

Fulfilled Ministries

In Ephesians two forms of ministry are set out whose activity is regarded as already complete, though this does not mean their holders are dead. In 2.20 and 3.5 it is implied that the ministry of apostles and prophets is in certain important respects over. In 2.20 they are termed the foundation of the church, and a foundation can only be laid once; in 3.5 they are said to be the recipients of the revelation that the gospel is for Gentiles as well

as Jews; once this truth has been made known and accepted
there is no need for it to be revealed again. In those senses then
the ministry of apostles and prophets belongs to the past.

The word apostle[1] has a wide range of meaning in the NT. In
the Gospels it is limited to the Twelve whom Jesus chose to be
especially close to him. Elsewhere at the other extreme it is used
of the messengers of the churches (2 Cor. 8.23; Phil. 2.25). In
between these extremes it is applied to Paul (Eph. 1.1) who was
not one of the Twelve, and it should be noted that not all
Christians were prepared to grant Paul an equivalence with the
Twelve (2 Cor. 12.11; Rev. 21.12–14 implies there are only
twelve apostles), to some of his associates, Silvanus and Timothy
(2 Thess. 2.6), Barnabas (Acts 14.4, 14), and to Andronicus and
Junia (Rom. 16.7) of whom we know relatively little except that
Junia was a woman. In Eph. 3.5 the reference is clearly to the
Twelve. The revelation that the gospel was intended for all
people is given to them in varying forms as can be seen from the
end of the Gospels and the beginning of Acts. Paul does not
seem to be included in 3.5 for in 3.3 he speaks of a special
revelation of the same truth granted to himself. The definition
of apostle as meaning one of the Twelve probably also underlies
2.20; tradition accords to the Twelve a unique position in
relation to Christ as his first followers; all later disciples depend
on them; they can thus rightly be described as the foundation.

All this is straightforward, but the same cannot be said in
relation to the prophets[2] who in both 2.20 and 3.5 are associated with the apostles. There are many references to prophets
and prophecy as existing in the New Testament church (e.g.

[1] Out of the vast literature on this word it is sufficient to point to W.
Schmithals, *The Office of Apostle in the Early Church* (London, 1969); C. K. Barrett,
The Signs of an Apostle (London, 1970); R. Schnackenburg, 'Apostles Before and
During Paul's Time', in *Apostolic History and the Gospel* (FS F. F. Bruce, ed. W. W.
Gasque and R. P. Martin, Exeter, 1970), pp. 287–303; J. H. Schütz, *Paul and the
Anatomy of Apostolic Authority* (SNTSMS 26, Cambridge, 1975); H. Merklein, *Das
kirchliche Amt nach dem Epheserbrief* (Munich, 1973), pp. 288ff.

[2] On prophets and prophecy see D. Hill, *New Testament Prophecy* (London,
1979); D. E. Aune, *Prophecy in Early Christianity and the Ancient Mediterranean
World* (Grand Rapids, 1983); G. Dautzenberg, *Urchristliche Prophetie. Ihre Erfor-
schung, ihre Voraussetzungen im Judentum und ihre Struktur im ersten Korintherbrief*
(Stuttgart, 1975); U. B. Müller, *Prophetie und Predigt im Neuen Testament,
Formgeschichtliche Untersuchungen zur urchristlichen Prophetie* (Gütersloh, 1975);
Merklein, op. cit., pp. 306ff.

Acts 13.1; 21.9; 1 Cor. 14.1ff) and prophets were certainly honoured by the first Christians; yet a continuing group or a continuing activity can hardly be intended with the references in Ephesians; the foundation has been laid once-for-all and will not go on being laid. For this reason some commentators have identified the prophets here with those of the Old Testament. Of these, at least in Christian eyes, there can be no more; they are a past group; but of course what they said and wrote was influential in the church and might be regarded as foundational. If however the OT prophets were intended the order 'prophets and apostles' would have been expected. The books of the prophets are moreover not the only books of the OT; 'The Law and the Prophets' would have been the proper phrase to denote OT revelation. In any case the OT prophets were hardly the recipients of the revelation to evangelize the Gentiles.

If the OT prophets have to be ruled out of consideration who then were the prophets who could be regarded both as the foundation of the church and as the recipients of the revelation that the gospel was not for Jews alone but for all? Is there any way in which we can see prophets as associated with this revelation? We should first note that there was a recognized class of prophets (Acts 13.1; 1 Cor. 12.28) and prophets were not necessarily just believers who from time to time were inspired by the Spirit. Since prophets were normally regarded as offering directions for the way in which the church should move (Acts 13.1–3 shows them as involved in the sending out of missionaries to preach to Gentiles, thus shaping its existence and future nature) they may have been more widely involved in the movement towards the Gentiles than is sometimes thought. Matt. 28.16–20; Luke 24.47–49; Acts 1.8; John 20.21b all offer the revelation but in verbally different forms. Since no heed seems to have been paid to this revelation until much later when the Gospel began to be preached to the Gentiles at Antioch (Acts 11.19f) the verbalization of the commission may have been later than the end of the earthly life of the risen Jesus;[3] in this case prophets, receiving the word of the exalted

---

[3] See E. Best, 'The Revelation to Evangelize the Gentiles', *JTS* 35 (1984), pp. 1–30, and *supra*, pp. 103–38.

Christ, spoke it to believers, and later the commission was associated with the earthly Christ. Prophets might then have been identified with the revelation in some strands of tradition and Eph. 3.5 may represent such a strand. There is another way in which we may see how believers may have seen them as related to the beginning of the church. Revelation describes itself as a prophecy (Rev. 1.3; 22.7, 10, 18, 19) suggesting that prophets have a role in relation to the forecasting of the nature of the End. That this is so is confirmed by the references to them in the Markan Apocalypse (13.22). If 1 Thess. 4.15–16, or some part of it, comes not from the incarnate Christ but represents a prophetic saying, we have again a connection between prophets and the End. May it not be that a part of the foundation of the church is the certainty that it has an end in the purpose of God and that that end is carefully planned? A planned end for a group will always shape the course of its life from its beginning.

Continuing Ministries

In 4.11 five different ministries or leadership roles are named: apostles, prophets, evangelists, shepherds and teachers. We have already looked at the first two of these and seen that they were not ministries designed to continue for all time, though there may be still those in the church who were termed apostles and those who prophesied. 2.20 and 3.5 imply strongly that those called apostles and prophets filled foundational roles and were not contemporary with the author and his readers. Even if Paul is the author the apostolic role in view is not that of a general government of the church but of something that happened at the beginning and only then. We do not need therefore to consider the apostles and prophets again but can turn our attention to the remaining three 'officials' (it is difficult to know what title to give them; it could be leaders, ministers, officials, office-bearers; we shall use all these from time to time) whose work was certainly a present reality for the author of Ephesians and his readers.

Before considering the remaining names in the list we need to set the list in its context. In 4.7 the author said that grace had

been given to every church member by Christ; this is very similar
to what is said about charismatic gifts in 1 Corinthians 12.1ff. 4.7
is then justified with a quotation in 4.8; the quotation depends
in some way on Ps. 68.18, though it does not use the exact words
of the Psalm. Verses 9, 10 then expand the quotation. Now at v.
11 the author appears to return to what he had said in 4.7 but
with a significant variation. The gifts are no longer universal
and intended for all believers; Christ instead is said to give
certain people to the church; the gifts are not the ability to
perform various functions as in 1 Corinthians 12 but are the
people themselves (apostles, prophets, etc.); the church is not
explicitly mentioned but the succeeding verses show that it is it
which is the recipient of the gifts. There is another significant
variation from 1 Corinthians; there it was God who was said to
appoint the leaders of the church (12.28); here it is Christ.
Although no mention is made of a grace being bestowed on
those Christ has chosen it may be assumed that the charisma
appropriate to the role which each is to play will have been
given (cf. Calvin). The change of emphasis from v. 7 in relation
to people as gifts rather than 'graces' was however already
foreshadowed in 1 Cor. 12.4–30 which began by enumerating
the various charismata with which different members of the
community might be endowed but ended in vv. 28f by enumerating identifiable leaders, apostles, prophets, teachers; after
listing these first three Paul apparently ran out of 'titles' and
went on by listing functions. Since none of the 'titles' is
explained we may assume that Paul's Corinthian readers were
familiar with them. The same must be true of the leaders
mentioned in our verse in respect of the readers of Ephesians.

There is no need then for our purpose to ask whether the
author of Ephesians saw the leaders he identifies as present in
the church from the beginning, or to attempt to trace out the
origin of each title in its earlier history. The author is dealing
with his current situation; it is sufficient to realize they were
titles known to him and his readers. There is also no need for us
to cross-identify his titles with those in other parts of the NT
(e.g. with bishops, deacons and elders). In the first century the
situation in respect of ministry was fluid; it was only after the
time of Ephesians that titles and the functions attached to them

began to harden. It is sufficient to note that the titles are not mutually exclusive; Paul is termed both apostle and teacher in 1 Tim. 2.7 (cf. Acts 15.35). Indeed Ephesians does nothing to distinguish between the functions of those that are listed; they are considered as a group and not in respect of their individual contributions.[4] Our author's list is limited to five names, three of which are those mentioned in 1 Cor. 12.28, though there is no reason to suppose that he was directly dependent thereon; they appear in other parts of the NT.

The list is enumerated and distinguished by means of μέν ... δέ ... δέ ... δέ[5] ... An article is associated with each title; it is probably not to be understood in the sense 'he gave some to be ...' but rather 'he gave those who are ...'. Does the initial μέν serve to contrast the apostles with the others in the list (so Schnackenburg)?[6] It does not do so in the enumerations of Matt. 13.4–7; 13.8; 16.14; 21.35. Had AE intended this contrast he would have chosen a stronger particle to distinguish the first name from the rest or a fresh μέ with following δέ ... δε ... to differentiate the other names from one another. Moreover in 2.20; 3.5 apostles and prophets are held together as a group.

Apostles and prophets in 2.20 and 3.5 are, as we have seen, figures of the past, though the aorist ἔδωκεν cannot be used to support this, otherwise the evangelists, shepherds and teachers would also be confined to the past. As we have seen the term apostle was not limited to the Twelve and there were still people so named at the beginning of the second century (cf. *Didache* 11.3–12); prophets appear regularly as active in the NT period. May apostles and prophets in v. 11 then, unlike 2.20 and 3.5, not be seen as a continuing gift to the church? May the missionary who took the gospel to a fresh area not be regarded as its initiating or founding apostle (William Carey has been termed the apostle to India)? There is a possible ambiguity here. If Paul wrote the letter he is still alive and if another author wrote in

[4] E. D. Roels, *God's Mission* (Franeker, 1962), p. 185.

[5] Cf. Blass, Debrunner, Rehkopf, *Grammatik des neutestamentlichen Griechisch* (Göttingen, 1976), §250; Moulton, Howard, Turner, *Grammar of New Testament Greek* (Edinburgh, 1963), pp. 36f; A. T. Robertson, *A Grammar of the Greek New Testament in the Light of Historical Research* (New York, 1919), pp. 1152f.

[6] So R. Schnackenburg, *The Epistle to the Ephesians* (ET, Edinburgh, 1991), ad loc.

Paul's name he has to sustain the view that Paul is still alive. So no simple distinction can be drawn between apostles and the other ministers listed; the last three certainly still exist and if apostles still do they are not the apostles of 2.20 and 3.5.

In 1 Cor. 12.28 others were named in addition to apostles and prophets; AE also extends the list beyond them. The first additional category is that of the evangelist.[7] If this term is understood to refer to the authors of the Gospels then certainly it would represent a ministry like that of apostle and prophet which belonged to the past. It was however apparently first used with this sense by Hippolytus, *De Antichristo* 56 and Tertullian *Adv. Praxean* 23. It is hardly likely that Gospels were in existence in sufficient number by the time of Ephesians for this under-standing of the word to have appeared. Today the word is regularly applied to those who conduct missions in existing Christian countries. It was previously used widely of those who travelled as missionaries taking the gospel into fresh areas, and in this sense many commentators regard the evangelists as successors to the apostles. If we were to accept this latter idea there is no reason to go further with Klauck[8] and suppose that shepherds and teachers have taken over the work of prophets. But to see the evangelist as missionary to unbelievers does not fit the context of Ephesians which continues in v. 12 to signify the ministry of all those that it names as directed towards the saints. The term needs therefore some further investigation.

The word evangelist appears only twice in the NT. Acts 21.8 applies it to Philip whose work as a travelling missionary is recorded in Acts 8.4ff, yet at the time when he is termed evangelist in 21.8 he has an established home and his family are living with him in it; he is then no longer a travelling missionary. In 2 Tim. 4.5 Timothy is told to do the work of an evangelist and this appears to be equated with fulfilling his ministry and not be the title of an office.[9] When we look at 1 and 2 Timothy to see what roles Timothy was to fulfil we find he is expected to remain at Ephesus (1 Tim. 1.3), i.e. not to travel, to correct false

---

[7] For the word see G. Friedrich, *TDNT* II, pp. 736f.

[8] H.-J. Klauck, 'Das Amt in der Kirche nach Eph 4,1–16', *Wissenschaft und Weisheit* 36 (1973), pp. 81–110.

[9] Cf. Merklein, op. cit., p. 346.

doctrine (1 Tim. 1.3f; 4.1f; 2 Tim. 2.23; 3.1ff), to see to the
appointment of suitable people as bishops and deacons (1 Tim.
3.1ff; 2 Tim. 2.2), which suggests the oversight of individual
congregations in an area rather than travelling into new areas
where the gospel was not yet known; he is also to set an example
to others through his conduct (1 Tim. 4.12), to take charge of
preaching and teaching and to be particularly diligent in
respect of his own (1 Tim. 4.11–16); and he is to give moral
teaching to various groups and to believers generally (1 Tim.
5.1ff; 2 Tim. 2.14ff). He is never instructed to seek the conversion of unbelievers. His ministry is accordingly related entirely
to those who are already within the church (2 Tim. 4.2 offers a
good summary) and it is within the church that he does the
work of an evangelist.

The use of the word 'evangelist' in the NT provides then no
direct evidence that it denotes travelling missionaries. The non-
Christian evidence is too slender to provide any clue to its
meaning. Apart from coming later to denote the writers of the
Gospels the word almost disappears from the Christian vocabu-
lary. Eusebius applies it to Pantaenus who in imitation of the
apostles was a missionary in India (*EH* V 10.1ff; cf. III 37.1ff). If
then we are to seek out what being an evangelist signifies we
need to go to the root from which it is derived, gospel,
εὐαγγέλιον. That this regularly denotes the content of what is
proclaimed to unbelievers needs no proof; it is however also
used in relation to what goes on within a believing community
(Rom. 1.15; 1 Cor. 9.14; 2 Cor. 11.7; Gal. 2.14; Phil. 1.27); Mark
uses the word to describe his Gospel (1.1) and that Gospel is
addressed to believers; Mark also says that Jesus went about
preaching the gospel (1.14) yet he continually refers to what
Jesus does as teaching; he also uses the word in his appeal for
more dedicated lives from believers (8.35). Paul is still preaching the cross to believers (1 Corinthians 1–4); in 2 Cor. 8.9 he
proclaims the gospel to overcome a worsening financial situation within the church (it may not be the way we would state the
gospel but it is a way of putting it relevant to the situation).
Other statements of the gospel are used in exhorting in various
ways those who are Christians (Phil. 2.6–11; 1 Cor. 15.3–5; 1
Tim. 3.16). On the other hand as if to mock our careful

differentiation between the roles fulfilled by different ministers Paul's evangelizing of Sergius Paulus is described as teaching (Acts 13.12). Any division between ministries to the world and to the church breaks down again in 2 Cor. 5.20 where Christians are assumed to stand in need of reconciliation.

The gospel then speaks as much to believers as to unbelievers; they continually need to be reminded of it as Kate Hankey's hymn 'Tell me the old old story ...' drives home. There is no point in their lives at which believers no longer need to go back to gospel fundamentals. Ephesians itself provides a good example of this for in 5.2 its readers are brought back to the gospel when God's claim on their lives is set before them. There is then no reason to suppose that evangelists are regarded in Ephesians as directing all their activity towards unbelievers, still less to suppose that they are mentioned because the communities to which the letter was written had come into being through their activity,[10] though that is not to say that this was not the way they came into being. It would of course be wrong to exclude evangelists from work directed towards unbelievers; as preachers they go both to the unconverted and the converted.[11] Paul the apostle exercised that same dual role and in that sense evangelists might be regarded as successors to the apostle.

There is moreover some confirmatory evidence from the early church that evangelists worked within the Christian community as well as outside it. The term is used in the *Apostolic Church Order* or *Apostolic Canons* 19 in relation to the office of reader in the early church; he is told to bear in mind that he takes the place of an evangelist, εἰδὼς ὅτι εὐαγγελιστοῦ τόπον ἐργάζεται. Harnack believes that the reference to the reader belongs to one of the second century sources of the *Church Order*.[12] In the *Apostolic Constitutions* VIII 22 (cf. 28) when the reader is set apart the prayer requests for him a prophetic spirit, which would hardly be necessary if all that was required from him was a clear voice (cf. Cyprian, *Ep.* 39.5; 29). When Origen

---

[10] So H. Schlier, *Der Brief an die Epheser* (Düsseldorf, 1971), ad loc; A. T. Lincoln, *Ephesians* (Word Biblical Commentary, Dallas, 1990), ad loc.

[11] So J. E. Belser, *Der Epheserbrief des Apostels Paulus* (Freiburg, 1908), ad loc.

[12] A. Harnack, 'Die Quellen der sogennanten apostolischen Kirchenordnung', *TU* II.2 (1886); cf. A. J. Maclean, 'The Ancient Church Order', *JTS* 3 (1901), pp. 61–73.

expands Eph. 4.11 in his Johannine commentary (I.5; see *GCS* 10.7.8ff) he clearly regards the evangelist as operating within the church; in his commentary on Eph. 4.11 in relation to the evangelist he alludes to Isa. 52.7 where the good news is brought to Zion and not to non-Israelites.[13] We can thus conclude that at least part of the work of the evangelist lay within the congregation.

The remaining two names in the list, shepherds and teachers, are closely linked through a single article and ϰαί. Have we then two groups of people each fulfilling a separate and distinct role or one group exercising two roles? This question must be left until we have identified the roles indicated by each word. Since the role of the teacher is easier to envisage we begin with it.

Teachers[14] follow apostles and prophets in the list of 1 Cor. 12.28 (cf. 14.26) and their work appears among the charismata listed in Rom. 12.7. The existence of 'specialist' teachers is confirmed by Gal. 6.6; Jas. 3.1; Barnabas 1.8; 4.9; Hermas *Sim.* ix 15.4. The activity of teaching is referred to frequently in the Pastorals and is an important part of the work of Timothy and Titus (1 Tim. 2.12; 4.6, 11, 13, 16; 5.17; 6.2; 2 Tim. 2.2; 4.3; Tit. 1.9; 2.1, 7). The writer of our letter was presumably himself fulfilling the role of a teacher when he wrote.[15] Teachers will have passed on tradition which they deduced from the OT (2 Tim. 3.16) or received from earlier Christians (cf. Rom. 6.17; 1 Cor. 4.17; Col. 2.7; 2 Thess. 2.15) and then related it to their contemporary situation; they will also have looked deeply into that tradition and drawn lessons from it for the new areas of life with their new problems which believers were constantly facing. The task of teachers cannot however be confined to imparting information or opening up new ways of thought but will always have included exhortation that their hearers should live by what they taught (Eph. 4.20f). In that sense they will have been leaders in their congregations. Gentiles will necessarily have had much to learn when they became Christians; in 4.20 they are depicted as 'learning' Christ. Apart from designated

---

[13] See J. A. F. Gregg, *JTS* 3 (1902), pp. 413f.

[14] See A. F. Zimmermann, *Die urchristlichen Lehrer* (WUNT 2.Reihe 12, Tübingen, 1984), especially pp. 92–118.

[15] Merklein, op. cit., p. 350.

teachers every Christian was expected to be a teacher (Heb. 5.12; Col. 3.16).

This seems relatively clear but clarity disappears once we turn to the term linked with teachers, ποιμένες. It is better to translate this as 'shepherds' rather than the normal rendering 'pastors'; in this way we retain the original underlying image and avoid all the overtones surrounding the modern use of 'pastor'. However in using 'shepherd' we need to recognize that the image which it evokes in a modern Westerner differs in one important respect from the original: in the West shepherds generally drive their sheep; in the East they lead them. The shepherd image appears to have entered Jewish thought from its use in the Near East of rulers who led their people.[16] It was also used in this way in Greco-Roman culture though not as widely; it is in fact so obvious a metaphor that the readers of the letter would have had no difficulty in picking up its nuance, especially in the light of its frequent appearance in the OT which was now their main religious book. There the image was applied to God (Gen. 49.24; Ps. 23.1; 80.1; Isa. 40.11), though the word shepherd itself was not always used (Jer. 50.19; Isa. 49.10). It denoted the way he cared for and protected his people (cf. 1 Sam. 17.34ff). In the NT the image was transferred and applied to Christ rather than God (1 Pet. 2.25; Heb. 13.20; John 10.1–10; Mark 6.34; 14.27; Matt, 25.32). Either in parallel to its non-Jewish use in the Near East or as a result of its application to God it was also applied in the OT to the activity of leaders in Israel (2 Sam. 5.2; Ps. 78.71; Jer. 2.8; 3.15; Ezek. 34.2), and then in the NT applied to church leaders (John 21.16; Acts 20.28; 1 Pet. 5.2); the church itself is described as a flock of sheep (John 10.2ff; 21.16; Acts 20.28; 1 Pet. 5.2; cf. Jer. 23.2f; 50.6, 17). Eph. 4.11 is however the only place in the NT where the noun is used of church officials. The image is vague; its OT and pre-OT usage would suggest that primary emphasis would lie on shepherds as those who led, provided for and protected

---

[16] Cf. J. Jeremias, *TDNT* VI, pp. 485–502; R. Schnackenburg, 'Episcopos und Hirtenamt: Zu Apg 20.28' in his *Schriften zum Neuen Testament* (München, 1971), pp. 247–67; K. Kertelge, 'Offene Fragen zum Thema "Geistliches Am" und das neutestamentliche Verständnis von der "Repraesentatio Christi" ' in *Die Kirche des Anfangs* (FS Heinz Schürmann ed. R. Schnackenburg, J. Ernst, J. Wanke, Freiberg, Basel, Wien, 1978), pp. 583–605.

those in their care. Yet when carrying out these duties shepherds in the church would have had to preach and teach, that is fulfil the functions of evangelists and teachers. In order to differentiate them in some way from the latter it is probably right to stress either the element of leadership or that of general oversight (Acts 20.28; 1 Pet. 5.2; yet John 21.16 hardly relates to leadership or oversight). Perhaps it is wrong to attempt to draw rigid distinctions between the three groups, evangelists, shepherds, teachers; in the modern church most priests and ministers exercise all these roles from time to time. This suggests we see evangelizing, shepherding and teaching as three essential ministerial functions. Some distinction exists between evangelizing on the one hand and shepherding and teaching on the other in that the second and third functions are exercised entirely within the community but the first both inside and outside it.

This perhaps offers a clue to a question raised earlier but left aside: Are shepherds and teachers one group or two (the idea that only one group is described goes back as far as Jerome)? Shepherding and teaching are different functions yet the same people could exercise both from time to time. Leadership involves truth, i.e. correct teaching, for the leader has to say in what direction he wishes to lead, and teaching involves leadership for the teacher must be seen to be leading others in the way he or she advocates; teachers are more than academics providing information! Such an explanation is preferable to that which regards pastors and teachers as local officials whereas evangelists operate in a wider area (the latter explanation goes back to Chrysostom and Theodoret; see their commentaries on Ephesians). It is true that one article governs both teachers and shepherds; of itself this does not prove they are one group for one article also governs apostles and prophets in 2.20 and there we have two groups. If then we accept the idea that two groups are envisaged we should not think of a rigid separation between them. In new movements leadership in its various aspects, and teaching and exhortation must be included among these, is flexible and only hardens into fixed categories with the passage of time. The later church certainly shows the development of more specialized ministerial roles, but for our purposes there is no need to trace out their appearance. It is sufficient to say that Ephesians offers no template for today's ministry.

There is then in v. 11 a list involving both the names of officials and describing their functions. Does this mean that our author believes he has set out an exclusive list of officials and functions? He does not mention presbyters, deacons and bishops. When he wishes to he can make clear that his lists are non-exclusive (see 1.21 and 6.12 where we have two lists each ending with a generalizing term). He probably intends then that the list should be taken as exclusive. Yet it would be wrong to accept the conclusion of Fischer,[17] that our author's omission of bishops was a deliberate attempt to preserve the Pauline conception of ministry, for there is little else in the letter to support such an idea.

If the list is exclusive we need to go further and ask if preaching, ruling and teaching were the only ministries within the church of that time in the group of congregations to which the letter is addressed? Certainly these three appear to be ministries, or functions, whichever we term them, which the church has always retained; their nature is permanent if the titles identifying them are not. All three appear at first sight to be ministries possessing a primary verbal orientation, yet there are other verbal ministries, e.g. prophecy. Prophets continued in the church at least to the end of the first century (*Didache* 13.1f; 15.1f). Perhaps our author having mentioned prophets as part of the foundation of the church did not wish to mention them again lest there would be confusion. But were there not also important non-verbal ministries? Before we turn to examine this question it is interesting to observe that none of those listed in v. 11 is specifically described as a leader, though in other letters words are used indicating leadership (1 Thess. 5.12; 1 Cor. 12.28; Rom. 12.8; Heb. 13.7, 17). Leadership in the narrow sense of what is required to hold a community together and direct it in the way it should go may then have belonged to all three of evangelists, teachers and shepherds; we can exclude apostles and prophets as no longer active; if they had been they too would have shared in leadership. The same would have

[17] K. M. Fischer, *Tendenz und Absicht des Epheserbriefes* (FRLANT 111, Göttingen, 1973), pp. 15f, 21f, 38f.

been true of 'rulers' if they had been explicitly mentioned. Interestingly the letter does not suggest that ruling lay within the ambit of apostles; they are 'foundations' and receive revelations (2.20; 3.5). Perhaps the writer of the letter was not worried about the exercise of authority by some Christians over others.

1 Pet. 4.11 distinguishes between charismata relating to speech and to practical service. The latter area of activity also appears in Rom. 12.7f; 1 Cor. 12.9f, 28. It may be summed up in the phrase 'loving service' for which the key word is often taken to be διακονία. Loving service is advocated for all believers in the paraenetic section of Ephesians (e.g. in 4.28, 32; 6.18) and is of course what should be taking place in the various areas which the *Haustafel* (5.22–6.9) treats; but it is apparently not seen as belonging to the duty of particular officials as it was in Acts 6.1–6. Grotius in his commentary noting the omission of workers of miracles justified this on the grounds that their work did nothing to equip or prepare the saints. Yet even if we allow this in respect of those who heal or speak in tongues (and not all would allow this) it cannot be extended to cover all forms of loving care. Schnackenburg[18] suggests that the teaching and shepherding ministries are mentioned because of the danger of false belief (cf. v. 14), yet 'caring' ministries by their love can also preserve others from straying into false ways, especially if those false ways relate to matters of conduct rather than doctrine; it is indeed probable that the disturbance which appears to threaten the church (4.14) comes from false ethical teaching rather than erroneous doctrine; the danger from false doctrine never looms large in this letter. Verses 12–16 suggest that one reason for the existence of ministers is the need to build up the community and draw the members together in unity; loving service will do this as effectively as teaching and shepherding. Worship may do the same; its conduct is not however linked to a limited number of 'officials'; 5.19 is the only place where it is mentioned and there it appears to be something for all believers. Prayer is also a ministry open to all (6.18f).

The eucharist which many modern theologians would regard

---

[18] *Ephesians*, pp. 190f.

as the principal means of expressing and sustaining church unity is nowhere mentioned in the letter, least of all in connection with the officials, but this may possibly be because the list primarily denotes functions rather than people. We do not know enough about who presided over the eucharist in this period to say whether this lay within the sphere of teacher or shepherd, or even if it was held to be important that some particular person should officiate. In his instructions on the conduct of the eucharist Paul does not say who should preside (1 Cor. 11.22ff); it may well have been the householder in whose house the church met. In the *Didache* (9.1–10.7), while instructions are given about the conduct of the eucharist, nothing is said that would suggest there was an appointed official to preside, except that there is an implication in 10.7 that a prophet if present should do this. The way also in which the prayers to be used at the eucharist are presented as if it was open to all readers to pray suggests that anyone might preside. This also applies to baptism. Ignatius seems to accept bishops, whether as individuals or as pre-eminent among a group of elders, as important and it may be that they would have presided at the eucharist. Certainly by the time of Justin Martyr there was a definite president (*Apol.* 1.67). The centralization of power is a common phenomenon in groups as they grow and develop. So far as baptism goes Paul does not appear to have been concerned about who should officiate for in Corinth after his initial baptism of the first few believers he left the administration of the rite to others without laying down rules about who should do it (1 Cor. 1.14–16). All this implies the impossibility of drawing up guide lines for the modern ministry from Ephesians. In keeping with this is the absence of any reference to the choice and appointment of shepherds, evangelists and teachers; there is no reason to doubt that some method or methods did exist (cf. Acts 13.1–3; 1 Tim. 4.14) but the writer's failure to refer to these matters suggests that he did not think methods of choice and appointment were important.

Evangelists, teachers, shepherds are clearly distinct from those, all believers, who receive charismata to be used for the good of the community (v. 7), and the groups are therefore in the nature of permanent 'officials'. By its introduction of 'officials' Ephesians may be said to have hastened the division between clergy and laity, begun the sacralization of the ministry and at the same time to have supported the idea that ministry of a non-spontaneous nature was necessary for the good estate of the church. It should also be noted that the existence of ministry is assumed without positive argument in its favour which suggests that its existence was not an issue within the communities to which the letter was written. This is in accordance with sociological theory that groups as they grow produce their own leadership and can have no long-term existence without permanent leaders.

Since no mention is made either of the manner of choice of leaders or of a ceremony of appointment all the stress lies on their selection by Christ. It was important for their own encouragement that evangelists, shepherds and teachers should know that they had been selected and given to the church by Christ. Dependence on Christ would enable them to hold steady when things were difficult. Knowledge that Christ had selected them would also help their communities to accept and respect them even if their words and actions were at times disliked.

It is impossible to tell whether the author thinks only of men as holding these appointments. διδάσκολος[19] is of common gender; there is apparently no regular separate feminine noun denoting shepherdesses[20] and yet there must have been shepherdesses in the rural economy of the ancient world; εὐαγγελιστής is too rare a word for any deduction to be drawn. The communities certainly contained women as the instruction on marriage shows (5.22–33), yet the community can be addressed as if all were males (6.23). The author may not have been worried about the sexual orientation of the officials he mentions.

Granted the existence of these officials what does the writer of Ephesians envisage as their function? Since he does not distinguish between their roles we can only ask after their function as a group. His answer comes in v. 12 where there are three prepositional phrases each indicating purpose; the first is introduced with πρός and the other two with εἰς. Controversy

[19] See Liddell, Scott, Jones, *Greek-English Lexicon*, s.v.
[20] Ibid. s.v.

has centred on the relation of these phrases to one another as may be seen from the renderings of KJV and NRSV; the former regards them as parallel and thus makes all three relate to the function of the leaders; the latter, in accordance with the variation of preposition, makes only the first relate to the 'ministers' and the second and third to the saints who are mentioned in the first. Verse 13 certainly refers to the life of the whole community. Somewhere therefore within v. 12 or at its conclusion there must be a movement from 'ministers' to 'saints'. Even if we assume that all three phrases relate to the role of the officials there is however no reason to distinguish between the phrases and attach each one to a different official. For our purposes it is unnecessary to follow out the controversy as to the place where the change takes place; it is sufficient to note that the role of the leaders relates to the saints and to see what the first clause means; indeed even if the other phrases also relate to the officials little is added to what the first phrase tells us. Its meaning centres on καταρτισμός. This is the noun's only occurrence in the NT though the cognate verb is found fairly regularly. Noun and verb have several related meanings:[21] 'repairing' (Matt. 4.19; Mark 1.19), 'setting broken bones', 'equipping, preparing', 'training, disciplining'. Only the last two groups of senses are appropriate to 4.12. Of these the final sense would apply strictly only to the teachers of v. 11; it is therefore best to choose the sense of equipping or preparing which can be associated with any of the roles of the leaders. Their function is then to enable the saints to carry out their ministry. The ministry of the officials does not find its fulfilment in their own existence but only in the activity of preparing others to minister.

The ministry of the saints

In very general terms this may be described as a building up of the whole body of the church in love (4.12, 16). Its purpose is presented both positively (v. 13) and negatively (v. 14) and the source of strength to achieve this end comes in vv. 15f. The

---

[21] See Liddell, Scott, Jones, s.v.

strength is from Christ who supplies both grace to the members of his body for their various activities (v. 7) and everything they require so that all may grow in love (vv. 15f). No description is however given here of the way the saints are to exercise their ministry; this needs to be gleaned from other parts of the letter.

In 5.19 they are instructed to address one another with psalms, hymns and various other spiritual songs. It should be noted that their singing is described here as addressed to one another and not, as we might expect, to God and although antiphonal singing was well known[22] in the ancient world this is not what is envisaged here; had our author intended it he would have made himself clearer. It is probably impossible to distinguish satisfactorily between the three song types which he names; they are probably intended to cover all the singing in public worship which was addressed to other believers. Fixed forms may have been used (5.14 is part of a Christian hymn) and there may have also been spontaneous or charismatic singing. The songs will have been directed at others to encourage them in their contests with evil and to instruct them in the gospel; in a sense those who used them will have been fulfilling the roles of the leaders of 4.11. As well however as addressing one another believers in some of their songs will have praised God (5.20). Nothing is said about the role of the leaders in the directing of such thanksgiving or worship in general. What is described is a ministry of the laity. In their thanksgiving believers would remember among other things, their election by God, their redemption through the blood of Christ, their resurrection with Christ into the heavenly places, indeed all the themes of salvation that are mentioned in the first three chapters.

A further item in the ministry of all believers is presented in 5.21. This verse is difficult to set in its context; it leads on to the *Haustafel* of 5.22–6.9 but is also governed by the same principal verb as vv. 19f. It must in part at least be taken with vv. 19f and indicate a mutual relationship which is wider than that found within the household; the latter is treated in the *Haustafel*. The

---

[22] Cf. Ezra 3.11; Philo, *De Vita Contempletiva* 84; Pliny, *Epistles* X 96.

concept of mutuality between believers is a common NT theme; its best known expression is the Johannine form of the love commandment (John 13.34f). Ephesians shows it as involving mutual forbearance, meekness and lowliness (4.2) and the willingness to forgive one another (4.32). In 5.21 a strong verb, ὑποτάσσω, signifying subordination, is used to denote it. Subordination implies a sense of order in society and in our context will of course be voluntary. Its best illustration is provided by the way Jesus washed the feet of his disciples (John 13.1ff). It is not an easy attitude to attain and it is important therefore to note that our verse is still controlled by the reference to the Holy Spirit in v. 18; it is impossible without the assistance of the Spirit.

The ministry of believers is not however restricted to mutual forbearance; it has a more active side. Believers should not slander one another nor titillate each other with smutty talk (4.29, 31); they should not lose their tempers with one another and should speak the truth at all times to one another (4.25–27); they should contribute in practical ways to the physical needs of one another (4.28).[23] All this covers a wide range of activity which was not even glanced at in the discussion of the roles of their leaders.

The ministry of Paul

Paul fulfilled all the five functions or ministries listed in 4.11. He was an apostle (1.1); he prophesied (1 Corinthians 14); he was an evangelist, preaching the gospel as a missionary to unbelievers (see Acts) and to believers (in all his letters he bases what he has to say on the essentials of the gospel); he wrote letters and visited the communities which he had founded to shepherd and teach their members. This is seen particularly in this letter in 4.1 where he encourages them to Christian behaviour and where he prays for them in 1.15ff; 3.14ff. He was also the recipient of divine revelation (3.3) and had a special place in the preaching of the gospel to the Gentiles (3.7–9). He thus appears to allocate to himself a unique place in salvation

---

[23] See Best, 'Ephesians 4.28: Thieves in the Church', *IrishBS* 14 (1992), pp. 2–9, and *infra*, pp. 179–88.

history. This is not out of accord with some of what he says about his ministry elsewhere. He identifies himself as the last in the line of those to whom the risen Jesus appeared (1 Cor. 15.8); he says the gospel came to him through revelation (Gal. 1.12); unlike other preachers he calls on his converts to imitate him (1 Cor. 4.16; 11.1; Phil. 3.17).

If the author of Ephesians was not Paul then he certainly conceived of Paul's ministry in the way we have just seen the letter depicts it. But how then did our author conceive his own ministry? He would probably not have described himself as an apostle if that term is taken to imply someone of a rank equal to that of the Twelve, though he might have thought of himself as an apostle on a lower scale. There is nothing 'prophetic' about his writing in the sense of the way he uses the term in 2.20 or the way many envisage prophecy as a foretelling of the future. But he does proclaim the essentials of the gospel to his readers, teaches them about the OT, and expounds and reapplies earlier tradition. We do not know enough about what he meant by shepherd to decide whether he thought he was shepherding his readers, but probably he did. He would then have fulfilled in his own way the three continuing ministries of 4.11.

Clergy and laity

We have suggested that Ephesians contains the beginnings of the distinction between 'officials' and ordinary believers, yet it is not easy to determine precisely how that distinction is envisaged. There does not appear to be any area of ministry carefully marked out (e.g. presiding at the eucharist) into which non-ministerial believers might not enter. When they address one another in song they are presumably doing much the same as leaders who teach and shepherd and who drive home the meaning of the Gospel. They have a prayer ministry just as much as had Paul (6.18–20). They are joined with their leaders in the building up of the body of Christ (note the 'we all' at the beginning of 4.13). Nothing is ever said about the need for them to approach those outside the church but then that part of the activity of evangelists is not featured in the letter. It may be that if we knew more about the roles of teachers, shepherds and evangelists we would see a distinction between them and all believers. But the author of Ephesians has not spelt out the roles of these ministers; he may not have needed to because everyone was aware what these roles were or because he was writing a letter to a number of churches and roles would have varied from congregation to congregation or because they just did what everyone else did but devoted more time and energy to it. Teachers and shepherds were terms drawn from the secular world where they had already been applied to leaders. If leaders were just those who devoted more time and energy to teaching and shepherding than others in the church then it may be that our initial assertion that the author conceived of ministry primarily in a theological manner and not in a sociological may not be wholly correct. He may have thought he was making theological statements in 2.20; 3.5; 4.11 but in fact have been responding to the pressures which appear in every new and growing group and these pressures include a veneration of founders. Leaders then were not people who had special tasks within the whole but people who exercised the roles which were open to all but in a special way. It should be noted finally that in Ephesians ministerial roles were not directly linked to varying functions in the body as in Rom. 3.3ff; 1 Cor. 12.12ff.

10

Ephesians 4.28: Thieves in the Church

It is first necessary to set this text within the ongoing argument of the epistle. After the initial address (1.1f) the author (he was probably not Paul, though if he was this would make no difference to the understanding of this text) in a eulogistic prayer (1.3–14) shows God's intention toward the world of his making; he is redeeming it through what he has done in Jesus Christ. The readers have been enlightened to understand this and Christ has been elevated to God's right hand (1.15–23). Previously the readers had been dead in sin; now saved by God's grace they sit with Christ in heaven (2.1–10). God's Jewish people would never have expected this to happen to the readers since the readers had not previously been Jews but Gentiles; now however they belong with Jewish Christians in the one church, God's temple, in which his Spirit dwells (2.11–22). In bringing this about Paul had had a double role as recipient of the instructions that Gentiles were to be received and as chief instrument in the carrying out of that instruction (3.1–13). The recognition of God's goodness in this leads the author to a final paean of praise (3.14–21).

Now that he has outlined the plan of God's salvation and shown his readers' place within it the author turns to the way they should live in the community God has created for them, and this occupies him to the end of the letter (4.1–6.20). Prior to turning to the details of behaviour he sketches the nature of the community of which they are members (4.1–16). It is the body

179

of Christ, of which Christ is head. Its members have received spiritual gifts for the good of the community and they should use them to build up their fellow members. It is important to note that the author does not describe these gifts in terms of how they might be used to win others to the community or to ameliorate social conditions in the world outside. The body of Christ is looked at in terms of its inward life rather than as a body with a duty to those not belonging to it.

Before taking up the details of conduct the author again reminds his readers of the life they have left; once they lived in a world that was alienated from God; now they are new people (4.17–24) with a new type of existence. Outlining this new existence occupies him until almost at the close of the letter he reminds them of the spiritual help they may receive in what is essentially a contest with evil spiritual powers (6.10–18).

We return now to the beginning of the discussion of the details of conduct. In 4.25–29 the author sets down four parallel injunctions on speaking the truth, on not being angry, on not stealing and on speaking to others in such a way as build up the community. Each injunction starts with a negative statement followed by one on the type of conduct required and ends with a motivation. The first injunction sets the limits of the discussion. Believers are members of the same body, not humanity as a whole but the church, and so they should speak the truth to one another. We might have expected him to instruct believers to tell the truth whether they were dealing with non-Christians or Christians but what he writes is in line with what he said in discussing the nature of the church; his concern is with the inner relationship of its members rather than with their relation to the outside world. It is not that he advocates the abandonment of truth telling when dealing with non-Christians; for some reason of his own which he does not disclose he is not interested in detailing conduct toward unbelievers. This we shall see holds true also for the verse which is our main concern.

In v. 28 the subject changes abruptly (there is no connecting particle) from not being angry to theft, though of course remaining within the area of obvious moral error. The plural of the preceding verses also changes to the masculine singular. In the previous exhortations the plural, though masculine, is to be taken as covering both sexes; here the singular cannot, and the masculine is appropriate since the exhortation goes on to argue that those who have stolen should instead earn money. This was something which women in most parts of the ancient world could not do.

While it is probable that lying (v. 25) and anger (vv. 26, 27) were connected in some Jewish paraenesis (*Testament of Daniel* 1.3; 2.1; 3.5f; 4.6f; 5.1; 6.8) there is no reason to suppose that theft was also joined with them; its presence here may then either have been due to a connection with them in early Christian catechetical instruction or, more probably, our author for his own reasons has introduced the new subject. It would be certainly wrong to suppose a connection in thought between v. 26 and v. 28 as if the anger mentioned in v. 26 came from Christians who were infuriated at fellow-members who had been stealing and did not support the community.[1] Theft however appears in two of the lists of vices given in the NT (1 Cor. 6.10; 1 Pet. 4.15; cf. *Didache* 3.5), and may have been more common than we would expect. While the lying of members (v. 25) and their anger against one another (v. 26f) would disturb communal living it is not implied that those who are accused of stealing stole from fellow members. On the other hand the new conduct required from thieves would bring positive benefit to the community, and it is this which may have served to tie in our verse with vv. 25–27. As a sin theft differs from lying and anger in that probably only a few members of the community would have committed it. Occasionally commentators (e.g. Hodge) express surprise at its inclusion as a sin to which Christians were open. Yet in some societies theft is endemic ('it fell off the back of a lorry', 'everyone does it'); indeed the sexual sins in which some of the Corinthian Christians indulged are in a way equally surprising for church members. The inclusion of theft as a possible sin in the exhortation gives us some information as to the kind of people who became Christians in the first century and reminds us how difficult they found it to break away from the ethical norms of the society from which they had been converted. Theft of course had

---

[1] As G. Agnell, *Work, Toil and Sustenance* (Lund, 1976), p. 128, supposes.

been recognized in Judaism from the time of the Decalogue as a major sin (Isa. 1.23; Jer. 7.9; Lev. 19.11; *Pseudo-Phocylides* 153ff; cf. Strack-Billerbeck I, pp. 810–13) and was also widely condemned in the Gentile world. This is probably why our author does not need to explain that stealing is wrong. Since our letter is a general letter directed not to one church but to a number it may for that reason give us a better insight into the kind of people who became Christians in the early days.

The present participle κλέπτων with the article is best taken as equivalent to a substantive, 'the thief', as denoting the person who becomes involved in stealing. It is not that these Christians were once thieves and have now given up the practice; if that were so the injunction would have been unnecessary. But thieving would have been a part of the life of some Christians before conversion and while it might go too far to say that then or now they lived by stealing it still formed a part of the way they lived. Slaves are hardly in view here (*pace* Hendriksen, Masson, Caird in their commentaries on Ephesians) for though they could steal, as Onesimus may have taken some of the property of Philemon with him when he ran away, they were not in a position to make this a common practice. Our author again is not thinking of theft as equivalent to careless work or slacking in a master's time; if he meant this he would have said so. Slaves moreover if they had been stealing were not in a position to give it up so as to devote their labour to earning and thereby to contribute to the welfare of the community. Their work was allotted to them by their owners who would have reaped whatever reward there was in it. The way slaves are to work is dealt with in 6.5–9. What is in view here are day labourers and men with some skill in a trade, perhaps even shopkeepers; all these could have mixed stealing with their normal occupations.[2] There were many day labourers whose work would have been in part seasonal because related to the market gardens which lay around cities and provided produce for them; others would have had to depend in other ways on the availability of work, e.g. when ships were being unloaded in the docks or when

---

[2] Cf. M. I. Finley, *The Ancient Economy* (2nd edn. London, 1985), pp. 73–5, 107, 185f; C. Hezser, *Lohnmetaphorik und Arbeitswelt im Mt 20, 1–16* (Freiburg and Göttingen, 1990), pp. 64–6.

master builders required additional labour for heavy and unskilled tasks (without much machinery there would be bursts of activity when many labourers would be needed); the work of skilled tradesmen could for similar reasons also have been seasonal. There were many ways in which shopkeepers could have stolen from their customers by cheating them (e.g. with false weights) though if this was what was in mind we would expect it to have been made clearer. When there was no work for day labourers and skilled tradesmen there was no money; there may have been public relief for the distressed in Rome but not for those in other parts of the Empire[3] and Ephesians was not written to Roman Christians but to those in Asia Minor. Wages also were too low for capital to be built up as a reserve to cover periods of unemployment. Those without regular work may have been forced during periods of unemployment to steal to maintain themselves and their families.

Those who have been and are stealing are bidden instead to seek work. Work was highly valued among Jews as a normal human activity (Exod. 20.9; Ps. 104.23; Prov. 6.6; 28.19; Ecclus. 7.15; *T.Issach* 5.3; Josephus, *c.Ap.* 2.291; the idle rich are denounced in passages like Amos 6.4–6). Jesus had a trade and teachers of the Law were generally expected to support themselves (*m.Abot* 2.2). Work was also highly valued in the Greco-Roman world (Epict. 1.16.16f; 3.26.27f; 8.26.2f; Dio, *Orat* 7.112f; 123f) though there in contrast to Judaism manual labour was often, but not invariably, regarded as inferior to work with the mind.[4] That our author envisages those who stole with their hands rather than those engaged in financial swindling is indicated by the following exhortation which instructs them to work with their hands to relieve the needy. The energy and ingenuity devoted to theft would be better used in honest work. There is then an inner logic in the movement from theft to work. Our author does not mention restitution of what has been stolen, let alone the fourfold restoration offered by Zacchaeus to those he had cheated (cf. Lk. 19.1–10), nor does he demand repentance or threaten with eternal punishment those who

---

[3] Finley, op. cit., p. 40.
[4] Cf. R. F. Hock, *The Social Context of Paul's Ministry* (Philadelphia, 1980), pp. 38ff, 44, 45, 48.

disobey what he says. Here as with the other injunctions of 4.25–29 his attention is focused solely on the welfare of the community. Paul had made a point of working to support himself during his missionary activity, presumably for the benefit of that activity (1 Thess. 2.9; 1 Cor. 4.12), and so indirectly for the benefit of the churches he founded. The words of v. 28 are very similar to those of Paul in 1 Cor. 4.12; that passage may have been known to our author, or, more probably, since the contexts of the two passages are very different, the words may have been regarded as the true pattern for the behaviour of a missionary and then simply carried over to apply to ordinary life.

Although referring to work our verse provides no 'theology' of work for only the case of 'reformed' thieves is considered. The purpose of work has been evaluated in many different ways: it gives self-satisfaction through the act of creation, it enables people to get on in the world (the profit motive), it prevents revolution, those who work can remain independent of others (1 Thess. 2.9), a motive very like the Stoic idea of self-sufficiency (cf. Phil. 4.11), or gain respect from the outside world (1 Thess. 4.11f), or cease to be a burden on the community (2 Thess. 3.6ff). Some of these reasons would be more true of the modern than the ancient world for in the latter most work was dull and repetitive; it also required real effort and application as the word for working, κοπιᾶν, implies (Paul uses the root of his own work in 1 Cor. 4.12; 2 Cor. 6.5; 11.23, 27; Gal. 4.11; Phil. 2.16). Many of these reasons for work (whether they are good or bad reasons is irrelevant) would hold true as much for unbelievers as for believers (4.22–24). A fresh motive has however been introduced here to apply to believers: the good of the community. In many ways it is a motive similar to the link Jews made between work and alms-giving (Agnell, op. cit., p. 128; cf. *T.Issach* 5.3; 7.5; *T.Zeb* 6.5f; *Pseudo-Phocylides* 22ff). In seeing the purpose of work as directed to benefiting (χρεία is used of physical need in Mk. 2.25; Jn. 13.29; Acts 2.45; 4.35; 20.34; Rom. 12.13; Phil. 2.25; 4.16) the community our author reflects the emphasis on the sharing of goods which we find among the early Jerusalem Christians (Acts 2.45; 4.32–5.11; 6.1ff) and which led to the collection made among Gentile churches for them (Rom. 15.26f; Gal. 2.10; 2 Cor. 8.1ff; 9.1ff). Yet he does not lay the duty of sharing on the community as a whole but only on thieves within it. Sharing however probably forms the background to his injunction; it comes to the surface here because having begun by mentioning a vice, theft, he wishes to supply a good motivation for his readers; having started from theft as a way of life he needs to put something positive in its place.

While the total meaning is clear, the good of the community, τὸ ἀγαθόν,[5] has been understood in different ways. (a) The word may have been deliberately chosen to draw out the difference in moral value between what the thief could do now and what he has been doing, and should be taken adverbially, 'working honestly'. (b) It could be taken as the direct object of ἐργαζόμενος and refer to the product of the work (Agnell, op. cit., p. 129); the carpenter, for example, if making a chair should make a good chair. (c) It could denote the objective of the work (cf. Gal. 6.10), 'doing what is good with one's own hands'. (b) reads too much into the word and at the same time is rather narrow (cf. Lincoln in his commentary on Ephesians in the Word series); (c) is in the end very little different from (a), but (a) is to be preferred because of the contrast with the person's previous way of life.[6]

Among those whom our author envisages as his audience a few will have been wealthy and well-educated; he apparently does not look on them as potential thieves, though that gives us no reason to suppose that such people do not at times cheat others in their commercial and financial activities; even small shopkeepers may do so. Yet to tell these people not to thieve but to work would not in fact help the needy since their cheating enabled them to make money; if they stopped cheating they would only have less to give to others! Ephesians refers to those who were not slaves and yet worked in one way or another with their hands, e.g. day labourers (see above). If they work they

---

[5] The order of the words of this final clause varies in the manuscripts but the meaning is not basically affected whatever order is chosen.

[6] W. D. Morris, 'Ephesians 4.28', *ExpT* 41 (1929/30), p. 237, supposes a primitive corruption of the text which originally read τὸν ἄρτον; as with almost all 'primitive corruptions' there is little to be said for this.

may bring in some income which can be used for the good of the less well off in the community; the general poverty of the ancient world meant that there were always some who were in real need. It could be argued that our author should have overlooked the sin of theft since those who gained money in this way might still have contributed to the poor; he knows however that theft is basically wrong and so cannot encourage among his readers a 'Robin Hood' attitude (stealing from the rich to benefit the poor).

More generally poverty was endemic in the ancient world; in an economy of scarcity anyone who does not work becomes a burden on others (2 Thess. 3.6ff). There was then a great need for all to share together and be liberal to one another (Rom. 12.13; 1 Tim 6.18; *Didache* 4.6–8) and we can see the first Christians active in this respect (Acts 2.44; 4.32ff; Gal. 2.10; Phil. 2.14–20; 2 Cor. 8.1–5; 9.1–5; Rom. 15.25–27; 1 Cor. 16.1–3). The practical question of what was to happen to the thief and his family if he was no longer able to thieve to support them and could not obtain work is not discussed; the thief and his family instead of contributing to the financial needs of the community would then have been a drain on its resources.

When reading this injunction in Ephesians we have to imagine a situation very different from that of today's western world where there will almost always be some form of welfare relief for those without work. The wealth of the western world is such that there is no need for everyone to be in fulltime work and earning money in order for society as a whole to be prosperous; a considerable number of unemployed can be supported without causing an undue burden to fall on the remainder who are working. Again our author limits what he says to those who stole physically; theft cannot really be restricted in this way either in the ancient world or in ours; financial manipulation or the underpayment of employees can equally be forms of theft. We do not know the views of our author on these sins or on those who having made money in dishonest and/or wrong ways then give vast sums to charitable or religious causes. Consequently the simple statement of v. 28 gives little guidance for today's complex financial and industrial set-up.

The most disturbing feature of v. 28 however is not its failure to cover different forms of theft, but its limitation to criticism of conduct directed only towards fellow believers. In this limitation it is in line with the sharing of the early Jerusalemite Christians which was equally restricted to the community; Barnabas sold his farm and gave the money to the community (Acts 4.32–37; cf. 5.1–6). Yet when the rich man came to Jesus to ask him what he should do to inherit eternal life Jesus told him to sell his possessions and give the proceeds to the poor; he did not tell him to bring the proceeds with him into the community of the disciples to be shared among them. In the light of this it is necessary to ask why our author is not interested in seeing the wider distribution of the money raised by those who ceased thieving and began to work. The problem here applies equally to his limitation of truth telling to fellow disciples (4.25) and it is his general attitude throughout all his discussion of behaviour. Believers are told to be kind and to forgive one another i.e. fellow believers, and not told to be kind and forgiving to all (4.32). Fornication is not to be named among them because it might cause a scandal to outsiders but because it is not fitting to mention it among the saints. Whereas in 1 Pet. 2.18–25 slaves are instructed how to behave when attacked by non-Christian masters, both the masters and slaves of 6.5–9 appear to be Christians and so their relationship is an inner community affair.

If we explore why Ephesians restricts itself to inner community behaviour we might answer that it is a general letter whose author probably did not know what was going on in each of the churches which his letter would eventually reach; it is then more difficult for him to speak of how Christians should behave towards outsiders for in this respect their circumstances would be very different while the inner life of their communities would be much the same. Yet one would still have expected him to indicate that lying was as grave an offence when non-Christians were deceived as when Christians were. He could also have suggested as does Paul (1 Thess. 4.12) that it is important for Christians to be seen to live quiet and orderly lives and so gain the respect of outsiders. It is however probably true that the community felt pressures from outside because its members were different (they did not worship idols, they had only one

God and not many) and this drove them in on one another for mutual support; as a result their conduct towards one another became all important.

Our author could have written a different letter in which he set out clearly all the ways in which Christians should interact with non-Christians but he did not choose to do so and we cannot guess at what he would have written if this had been his objective. It is impossible for us to discover with any degree of completeness his reasons for the restricted view of conduct he adopts; we have to interpret the letter he has written and not another we might have liked him to write. Yet as we do so in the light of what we read elsewhere in the New Testament, and especially what we learn from the example of Jesus, we need to widen what he says so that those we teach do not think there is a different attitude for Christians to take up to non-Christians from that to other Christians.

11

The Haustafel in Ephesians
(Eph. 5.22–6.9)

There is no intention in this paper of exploring in detail the moral teaching of the Ephesian Haustafel. By and large its ethic does not differ greatly from Jewish and pagan contemporary teaching where Jewish and pagan husbands expected obedience from their wives, from their children and from their slaves; we find the same in the Haustafel in Ephesians. The main difference from pagan and Jewish teaching lies in the Christian motivation. We shall not then be examining the ethical teaching in detail but instead looking at the place of the Haustafel in the whole argument of the letter, at the relevance of its teaching to the Christian households of the ancient world and at whether it existed prior to its use in Ephesians. In recent years the Haustafel form has been the object of considerable attention and listed at the end of the paper are some of the more important books and articles on the subject.

The Haustafel in Ephesians consists of three sections referring respectively to the relationships between wives and husbands, children and parents, slaves and masters. A normal ancient household would have contained at least all these three sets of relationships; the husband, the father and the master would have been normally the same person. Even what we would describe today as middle-class households probably contained at least one slave; small businesses would have had one or more who would have lived in the household of the owner. In each section of the Haustafel the duty of the 'inferior' in the

189

relationship is put first. Sometimes commentators describe the relationships as mutual or reciprocal, but this is incorrect. A mutual or reciprocal relationship is one in which each side has exactly the same relation to the other as the other has to it. A typical mutual or reciprocal relationship lies in the summons to 'love one another'. There is an example of it in 5.21. But the relationship of husband to wife in the Haustafel is not the same as that of wife to husband. What we have are three paired relationships.

Before proceeding further it is necessary to say something about Ephesians itself. As the textual evidence in relation to 1.1 shows it was not written to the church in Ephesus and probably not indeed to any particular congregation. It was originally sent to a group of congregations in Asia Minor or to Christians generally who lived in that area.

Colossians has a similar Haustafel (3.18–4.1) and, more generally, most scholars accept the existence of some kind of relation between this letter and Ephesians. There are five possible solutions to the nature of this relationship: both letters were written by Paul, both letters were written by someone other than Paul, Paul wrote Colossians and the author of Ephesians used it, Paul wrote Ephesians and the author of Colossians used it, Paul wrote neither letter and the two letters were written by two different people. It is unnecessary at this point to decide between these though later it may be possible to suggest which are less probable.

While the Haustafel in Ephesians is similar to that in Colossians there are also considerable differences between them, most noticeably in respect of the amount of attention given to each of the paired relationships. Ephesians devotes twelve verses to the wife–husband relation and develops it into a discussion of Christ and the church; Colossians has only two verses, one relating to the husband and one to the wife and does not mention the church. Ephesians has four verses on the child–parent relation, three given over to the conduct of children and one to that of the parent; Colossians has again just one verse for each group in the pair. Both letters take five verses to cover the slave–master relation with four going in each case to the conduct of the slave and only one to that of the owner or master.

The most significant feature about the Haustafel in each letter is that it covers only households where all of the members are believers. We should not be misled by the word children; nothing is said about their age; in both the Greco-Roman and Jewish worlds children were expected to be obedient to their parents into adulthood; thus believing children, young adults, as distinct from babes in arms are included. Neither Haustafel then covers the situation of mixed households where some believe and others do not. This, that the households which are considered consist only of believers, is surprising and requires fuller examination. Had the author of Ephesians been considering mixed households he would not have been able to parallel the relation of husbands and wives with that of Christ and the church as he does in 5.22–33.

1 Peter also contains a Haustafel (2.13–3.7). Some doubt exists as to whether 1 Pet. 2.13–3.7 should be termed a Haustafel since it contains a section (2.13–17) on the relation of believers to the state, and the state is of course, outside the household. It has however been customary to apply the term also to it, though it might be better to describe as a 'social code' what we find in Colossians, Ephesians and 1 Peter; however since it has become customary to apply the word Haustafel (the term goes back to Martin Luther) to the equivalent sections in these three letters and to material also in some of the other New Testament letters, we shall, for simplicity's sake, continue to use it, though recognizing its inadequacy. The Haustafel in 1 Peter again covers three areas of conduct but they are not the same as those of Colossians and Ephesians.

In 1 Peter the first area, 2.13–17, relates to the behaviour of citizens towards the state. No possibility existed then of a paired relation in this area. While today church leaders may address governments and tell them how to behave the first Christians were in no position to do so and even if they did no government would have listened.

The second area in 1 Peter, 2.18–25, that of slaves and masters, is again different from the equivalent sections in Ephesians and Colossians for in 1 Peter it is only slaves who are addressed, nothing being said to masters. Thus again there is no paired relationship. Peter does not address the masters because he was toadying up to the wealthy in the congregations to which he was writing but because the masters being unbelievers were not present in the congregation to be addressed. The content of what is said to the slaves indicates that they were slaves who had domineering masters. There may have been masters who were Christians but since they would naturally treat their Christian slaves as brothers in Christ they are not in special need of counsel. Thus so far as slaves are concerned 1 Peter treats only those in mixed households. There must have been many such households and slaves in them were often in difficult situations and much more in need of advice than those in Christian households.

In the section, 3.1–7, in 1 Peter relating to husbands and wives only one verse touches on the behaviour of husbands but six are given over to the conduct of wives. It is at once clear that the husband is envisaged as an unbeliever for the wife is instructed to win him to the faith through her quiet and submissive conduct. Thus again mixed households are principally in mind.

There is no section in 1 Peter on the behaviour of children, though young men are addressed in 5.5.

It is not surprising that 1 Peter should deal with the situation of Christians in mixed households for their position when they were the 'inferiors' must have been very difficult. Plutarch in his advice to the married and those about to marry writes 'Wherefore it is becoming for a wife to worship and to know only the gods that her husband believes in, and to shut the front door tight upon all queer rituals and outlandish superstitions' (*Coniugelia Praecepta*, Mor 140D; ET as in LCL). To many honourable men in the ancient world Christianity would have seemed an outlandish superstition and to include queer rituals. From the Christian side the strain which could arise within a mixed household is seen in Justin Martyr's *Second Apology* 2. The position of a believing wife with an unbelieving husband must therefore at times have been intolerable. Not less would be the position of a believing slave who might be required to make preparations for and to take part in the worship of the household gods.

It is impossible to make any estimate of the proportion of

unmixed and mixed households in the early church but other parts of the New Testament provide evidence as to the existence of the latter. 1 Cor. 7.12–16 refers to unbelieving spouses; if the believing spouse encounters trouble he or she is advised not to break up the marriage but to continue in the marital home so that the unbeliever may eventually be won for Christ. In 1 Cor. 7.39 Paul counsels widows to marry 'in the Lord', i.e. within the church; this instruction would have been unnecessary if some widows had not been marrying outside it. In 1 Tim. 3.1ff those eligible to be chosen as bishops should be those who manage their households properly, which seems to mean those who have believing households; but if this has to be set down as a condition in the selection of bishops there must have been many households which were mixed (cf. 1 Tim. 3.12). In 1 Tim. 6.1f slaves are told to be obedient to their masters, especially to non-believing masters. Even if it is impossible to estimate the number of mixed households it is inherently probable that there were many. Although Acts records a number of baptisms of whole households where the (male) head was converted there is no reason to suppose this always happened, and it was unlikely to have done so where the wife was converted and the husband was not. The Gospels show Jesus as teaching that individuals responding to the gospel might be forced to leave their homes and families (Mark 8.34–36; 10.21, 29); the result would be the break up of homes. Even if passages like these do not go back to Jesus but are church formations they represent the experience of the church; mixed households were a normal result of Christian evangelization.

If we accept that there were many mixed households in the early church and if Ephesians deals only with unmixed households what consequences follow?

1. In the light of the evidence from 1 Cor. chap. 7 and Paul's knowledge of the lives of converts it is hardly likely that he compiled the Haustafel in Ephesians. If he received it in the tradition, whether that was Christian, Jewish or pagan in origin, it is also hardly likely that he would have used it. He had a more realistic view of the kind of people the church contained. The presence then of this Haustafel in Ephesians is a strong argument against Pauline authorship.

2. It appears that the author of Ephesians, whoever he was, did not know very much about the membership of the churches to which he was writing. If he had been intending to write only to believers living in unmixed households he would surely have made this clear somewhere in the letter.

3. It is probable then that the author of Ephesians did not himself compile the Haustafel but received it as tradition and incorporated it into his writing.

4. If he did encounter it as a piece of tradition, and took it over, this does not say much for his pastoral insight. Its use shows a singular lack of imagination and contrasts strongly with the Haustafel in 1 Peter which deals with the more difficult cases of wives married to non-Christian husbands and slaves owned by non-Christian masters. That is not to say that the author of Ephesians gives bad advice but that his advice applies only to a fraction of those to whom he writes; many would have been left untouched by his counselling.

5. The content of the Haustafel shows the danger of mirror reading the text; mirror reading consists in the deduction of information about the recipients of a letter from its content. If applied to the Haustafel it would imply that all the intended recipients of Ephesians lived in unmixed households and this is extremely unlikely. That is not to say that the technique of mirror reading cannot be used, but that it must be practised with great care. Using it, it is fair to deduce from Ephesians that Greek was understood by at least some of those to whom the letter was sent, though we cannot deduce that all of them knew Greek for those who did might have translated it into the native tongue of those who did not. The nature of the injunctions in the second part of the letter make it reasonable to assume that there were some who were thieves (4.28), some who were not always truthful (4.25), some who lost their tempers (4.26f), some men who resorted for their sexual pleasure to others than their wives (5.3). Those kind of deductions from the text are admissible.

6. A close relationship exists between Colossians and Ephesians and the Haustafel in Ephesians is in many respects similar to that in Colossians in covering the same three paired relationships, wife–husband, child–parent, slave–master. Did then the

author of Ephesians derive his Haustafel from Colossians and expand it in the case of the first two pairs? Since of the three sets of relationships we find the greatest similarity in that of slaves and masters it is useful to compare them to see if, in effect, the author of Ephesians used Colossians in the section about masters and slaves. The two sections are almost the same in their first verses (Eph. 6.5; Col. 3.22) and thereafter contain a great many of the same words and phrases, e.g. ἐν ἁπλότητι (τῆς) καρδίας, ὀφθαλμοδουλία, ἀνθρωπάρεσκοι, ὡς τῷ κυρίῳ καὶ οὐκ ἀνθρώποις, yet these words and phrases do not always appear in the same contexts and with the same connections; for example, προσωπολημψία which is in the section on masters in Eph. 6.9 is in that on slaves in Col. 3.25, and κομίσεται is applied differently in the two letters. Although the author of Ephesians is interested in 'inheritance' (1.14, 18; 3.6) he does not pick up the reference to it in Col. 3.24. More significantly in Col. 3.22 slaves are to fear the Lord but in Eph. 6.5 the fear is to be directed towards their masters; it is hardly likely that Ephesians, if copying Colossians, would have downgraded the fear in that way. If the author of Colossians had been copying Ephesians it is also hardly likely that he would have omitted the 'as to Christ' of Eph. 6.5. In the section on children it is difficult to see why the author of Ephesians should change the εὐάρεστον of Col. 3.22 to δίκαιον or that the author of Colossians should carry out the reverse process. It is therefore improbable that either author copied the letter of the other in respect of this section of the Haustafel. These changes between the letters also make it unlikely that both letters had a common author. Presumably the Haustafel existed as a piece of tradition which each used independently. Confirming this is the easy manner in which the Haustafel of Colossians can be detached from its context. The beginning of the Haustafel of Ephesians is grafted into its context through 5.21 but though this verse promises a mutual relation between members of the household, this is not the way in which the Haustafel is developed; 5.21 is therefore a verse constructed to permit the transition from what preceded to the section of tradition.

7. We conclude then that an existing Haustafel was incorporated independently into the two letters. It is fairly easy to make

a guess as to its content. Since Ephesians has developed the first couple of pairs (wife–husband, children–parents) much more than Colossians we base our reconstruction on the form in the latter:

αἱ γυναῖκες, ὑποτάσσεσθε τοῖς ἀνδράσιν ὡς ἀνῆκεν [ἐν κυρίῳ]
οἱ ἄνδρες, ἀγαπᾶτε τὰς γυναῖκας
τὰ τέκνα, ὑπακούετε τοῖς γονεῦσιν
οἱ πατέρες, μὴ ἐρεθίζετε (παροργίζετε) τὰ τέκνα ὑμῶν
οἱ δοῦλοι, ὑπακούετε τοῖς [κατὰ σάρκα] κυρίοις
οἱ κύριοι, τὸ δίκαιον τοῖς δούλοις παρέχεσθε,

Wives, be subject to your husbands as is proper [in the Lord];
Husbands, love your wives.
Children, obey your parents;
Fathers, do not annoy your children.
Slaves, obey your [human] masters;
Masters treat your slaves justly.

As we have seen the third pair (slaves–owners) has been expanded in both letters using the same words but not always in the same way. Since the injunctions in the first two pairs reduce to two couplets it is probable that the third pair originally consisted also in a couplet, though it may have been expanded prior to its use in the two letters. The words in square brackets represent Christian additions, if the form was originally pre-Christian.

Two factors suggest a non-Christian origin for this brief form of the Haustafel. The first is the addition in line 5 of κατὰ σάρκα. κύριος has a special significance for Christians and the injunction to slaves required this qualification so that they should not think that they were simply told to obey Christ; it needed to be made clear that their Christian duty required obedience to their earthly owners. Though κύριος is used at times in Greek to indicate the owner or master of slaves it is not the normal word. This is δεσπότης which is found in Luke 2.29; 1 Tim. 6.1; Tit. 2.9; 1 Pet. 2.18. It is true that κύριος is used frequently in the Gospel parables of the owner or master of slaves but in each case the owner or master, whatever may have been intended in the original parable, is taken to represent God (so for the same reason in John 13.16; 15.15, 20; Matt. 20.24f; Rom. 1.1, 4; 1 Cor. 7.22; Jas. 1.1); moreover δεσπότης was not a usual term for God among Christians (only twice of Jesus in the NT, Jude 4; 2 Pet. 2.1. On the use of the words see H. Rengstorf, *TDNT* II pp. 43–8; W. Foerster, *TDNT* III pp. 1041–6). Had Christians composed the Haustafel they would almost certainly have used δεσπότης and so avoided the ambiguity of κύριος.

A more important indication of the non-Christian origin of the Haustafel is its irrelevance to mixed households. The situation of believing wives married to pagan husbands and Christian slaves belonging to pagan owners could be acute because the wife and the slave were unable as Christians to participate in the pagan worship of their husbands and owners. Pagan husbands and slave owners would have had no objection to their wives and slaves adding another god or goddess to those already worshipped in the household so long as no claim to exclusiveness was made; this was a claim Christians could not escape making (see the quotation above from Plutarch and the reference to Justin Martyr). Probably the writers of Colossians and Ephesians (they may not have been the same) incorporated the Haustafel without realizing that it applied only to a limited group of wholly Christian households. None of the sections in the Haustafel would have been out of accord with Hellenistic ethical thinking. Although no similarly structured Haustafel can be found in the Greco-Roman world, from the time of Aristotle household management was divided into the three areas of master and slave, parent and child, husband and wife (*Politics* 1259A). We find this division continued and developed in Hellenism (Seneca, *Ep.* 94.1–3; Stobaeus [Hense] IV 27.20); Epictetus stresses the second and third areas (e.g. 2.17.3; 3.7.26); he may have omitted the reference to slavery because he had once been a slave.

We also find the same three areas of ethical conduct being treated in Hellenistic Judaism; the clearest example is *Pseudo-Phocylides* 195–227 who deals with each area (see also Josephus, *c.Apionem* 2.189–214; Philo, *Posteritate Caini* 181).

Christians would have been the more inclined to adopt the type of teaching contained in the Haustafel if it had reached them through Judaism and not directly from the pagan world; it is indeed even possible that the form of the Haustafel in Ephesians and Colossians originated in Judaism. But if its origin lay in Hellenism there would have been no difficulty in its being transmitted through Judaism. Jews were expected to marry Jews (see below) so that unmixed households were the normal situation among them. The problems raised by mixed marriages would not then have been as serious for them as they became for Christians. Apart from the emphasis in Jewish teaching on Jews marrying Jews, Jews in the Diaspora tended to live in Jewish communities and would marry within their communities. Christianity however was something new and the Christian groups were small; there was no natural pool of Christian women already in existence from which Christian men could choose their wives or women their husbands. There always had to be a first to be converted out of any existing pagan household and, unless it was the husband who might be able to insist on his family and slaves being baptized, the one who had been converted might remain for a lengthy period, if not for ever, the only Christian in the household.

The emphasis on unmixed households in Judaism goes back at least as far as Ezra who forbade mixed marriages and instructed those who had already entered into them to break them off (9.10ff; 10.1ff; 10.18ff; cf. Tob. 4.12; *T. Levi* 9.9f; Pseudo-Philo, *LAB* 9.5, where incest is regarded as preferable to sexual intercourse with a non-Jew). There were of course Jewish wives, like Esther, who married non-Jews. But in the additions made to her story in the LXX it is said that she had not eaten at Haman's table and had not honoured the king's feast or drunk his wine (4.17[x]; cf. Josephus, *Ant.* xviii.81–84; xx.139); in that way her purity in terms of the law was preserved. In the story of Joseph and Aseneth, Joseph does not have sexual intercourse with Aseneth while she is non-Jewish (8.5) and it is only after her conversion to Judaism that he marries her (18.1ff). Thus attempts were made to preserve the totally Jewish nature of Jewish households and to account for those that were seemingly not so. The Mishnah (*Kidd.* 4.3) carries on the ideal of no mixed marriages; yet at times they must have occurred and *Yeb.* 2.5; 7.5; 8.3 attempt to slay what should happen in these rare cases.

Clearly the case of children would cause no difficulty since children born in a Jewish home would be brought up as Jews.

But what of slaves in a Jewish household? In the Old Testament a distinction is drawn between slaves who were Jewish and those who were not. Only the former could expect to have their freedom granted as of right. Naturally their presence in the household would cause no problems for they would automatically accept Jewish law. But what of non-Jewish slaves? Gen. 17.12f implies they were, if male, to be circumcised; if they refused, then owners were expected to sell them within the year. Such non-Jewish slaves were also bound to keep certain Jewish religious customs, though like women and children they were exempt from others. Through their fulfilment of some of the Jewish law they did not render the household unclean and therefore they could be retained in it and Jewish members of the household could eat the food they prepared.[1]

There would thus be no objection to the origin of the Ephesian and Colossian form of the Haustafel within Judaism, and still less, if its origin lay in the Greco-Roman world, for it to have reached Christianity through Judaism. In favour of the former is the qualification to κύριοι in 6.5; Jews like Christians would probably have avoided this word with its ambiguity.

As we have seen the Haustafel in 1 Pet. 2.13–3.7 differs considerably from those of Ephesians and Colossians. It adds a section on the attitude of the citizens to the state, omits the section on children and parents and treats the mixed household rather than the unmixed; it is therefore unlikely that it is either a development of the form in Ephesians and Colossians or that the form in the two latter epistles was developed from it. Its additional section on the Christian and the civil authorities continues earlier Christian teaching on this subject in Mark 12.13–17 and Rom. 13.1–7, and is in line with the concern that prayers should be offered for rulers (1 Tim. 2.1f). As a whole the Petrine Haustafel resembles Tit. 2.1–10; 3.1,[2] though not strictly parallel in all its sections to the latter. Because the Petrine

---

[1] See G. F. Moore, *Judaism* (Cambridge, Mass., 1932), II, pp. 18f, 135f; R. de Vaux, *Ancient Israel* (London, 1961), pp. 85f; E. Schürer, *The History of the Jewish People in the Age of Jesus Christ* (2nd edn, ed. G. Vermes, F. Miller, M. Black), vol II, Edinburgh, 1979), pp. 420f, 452, 482.

[2] See H. von Lips, 'Die Haustafel als "Topos" im Rahmen der urchristlichen Paränese: Beobachtungen anhand des 1. Petrusbriefes und des Titusbriefes', *NTS* 40 (1994), pp. 261–80.

form treats the mixed household rather than the unmixed it makes a more realistic approach to actual living. The existence of the Petrine form means that two forms of the Haustafel were current in early Christianity and implies its importance in post-baptismal catechetical instruction (none of the conversion stories in Acts shows any sign of pre-baptismal instruction). Traces of the influence of the Haustafel form of instruction are to be found in the Apostolic Fathers, where there may be a mingling of the two forms: 1 Clem. 1.3; 21.6–9; *Didache* 4.9–11; Ignatius, *Polycarp* 4.1–6.1; Polycarp, *Philippians* 4.2–6.1. Other areas of living are introduced in these post-Pauline writings, e.g. widows, bishops. Ministers, though not specifically bishops, had been referred to earlier in 1 Pet. 5.1–5 and this section may originally have been part of the Haustafel used there.

We return finally to the Haustafel of Ephesians in order to draw some conclusions as to its adequacy for Christian instruction. It fulfils its purpose in giving reliable and truthful advice for those who live in wholly Christian households, provided we realize its regulations apply to its own period and not ours. It cannot be seen as other than inadequate, even in its own time, for the pastoral counselling of believers who do not live in wholly Christian homes; these would include those who had obeyed the call of Jesus and left home and kinsfolk to follow him, widows (the care of whom features prominently in other parts of the NT, Acts 6.1–6; 1 Cor. 7.39f; 1 Tim. 5.3–16; Jas. 1.27), divorced people (probably women expelled from their homes because they had adopted the silly superstition of Christianity). It is not a sufficient response to the inadequacy of its counselling to say that the Haustafel in Ephesians presents an ideal for it has no advice to give on how to move from the ideal to the real situation nor does it even suggest that it is necessary so to move. It has moreover no advice for slaves who have been freed and, in accordance with the custom of the time, remained in some kind of relation with their original owner; it must also have left slave wives in the awkward position of not knowing when they should obey their husbands and when their owners if a clash of direction should arise.

All these objections to the inadequacy of the Haustafel in Ephesians apply equally to that in Colossians. The Ephesian form has however one important feature lacking in Colossians: the author of Ephesians receiving it in the tradition realized that he could use it to good effect not only in his moral instruction of believers but also in his other main subject, his teaching about the church. Taking up a theme of the Old Testament, the marriage of Yahweh and Israel, and perhaps also the pagan myth of the holy marriage, he uses his marital instruction to develop his ideas on the church. In doing so he replaces Yahweh with Christ and Israel with the church. It is unnecessary to follow out the details of his teaching but in essence he shows that the church would not have come into being but for the self-sacrificing love of Christ and that its continued existence depends on the care and affection he bestows on it as well as the nurture he provides for it. As far as believers go this enables him to argue for the obedience of the church to Christ. In an odd way this all follows from the fact of the Haustafel's restriction to wholly Christian households. If the husband had been an unbeliever he could not have represented Christ; if the wife had been an unbeliever she could not have represented the church. Generally in the Old Testament the marital imagery is used in respect of a disbelieving and disobedient Israel whom God has wooed and continues to woo. The author of Ephesians seized the opportunity which the picture of the believing household offered him and used it to develop his teaching on the church to which he had earlier devoted a large portion of his letter. Whether he actually realized the ethical inadequacy of the Haustafel is another matter; it looks as if he did not, otherwise he would have modified its two other sections. Those who had earlier introduced the Haustafel into Christian teaching from Judaism, or from paganism, clearly did not see its limitations nor did the author of Colossians. But the author of Ephesians succeeded in turning to good account its restrictive nature in a way he could never have done with the Petrine form of the Haustafel.

Bibliography

M. Dibelius, *An die Kolosser, Epheser, an Philemon* (ed. H. Greeven, Tübingen), pp. 48–50; K. Weidinger, *Die Haustafeln, ein Stück urchristlichen Paraenese* (UNT 14, Leipzig, 1928); E. G. Selwyn, *The First Epistle of Peter* (London, 1947), pp. 419–39; K. H. Rengstorf, 'Die neutestamentliche Mahnungen an die Frau, sich den Manne unterzuordnen', *Verborum Dei in Aeternum* (FS O. Schmitz, ed. W. Foerster, Witten, 1953), pp. 131–45; H. D. Wendland, 'Zur sozialethischen Bedeutung der neutestament-lichen Haustafeln', *Die Leibhaftigkeit des Wortes* (FS A. Koberle, ed. O. Michel and U. Mann, Hamburg, 1958), pp. 34–56; D. Schroeder, *Die Haustafeln des Neuen Testaments* (unpublished dissertation, Hamburg, 1959); O. Merk, *Handeln aus Glauben* (Marburg, 1968), pp. 214–24; J. P. Sampley, *'And the Two Shall Become One Flesh'* (SNTSMS 16, Cambridge, 1971), pp. 17–30; J. E. Crouch, *The Origin and Intention of the Colossian Haustafel* (FRLANT 109, Göttingen, 1972); W. Schrage, 'Zur Ethik der neutestamentlichen Haustafeln', *NTS* 21 (1974/5), pp. 1–22; D. Lührmann, 'Wo man nicht mehr Sklave oder Freier ist', *WD* 13 (1975), pp. 53–83; E. Schweizer, 'Die Weltlichkeit des Neuen Testaments: die Haustafeln', *Beiträge zur Alttestament-liche Theologie* (FS W. Zimmerli, ed. H. Donner, R. Hanhart, R. Smend, Göttingen, 1977), pp. 396–413; L. Goppelt, *Der erste Petrusbrief* (KEK, Göttingen, 1978), pp. 163–79; R. P. Martin, *NIDNTT*, III pp. 928–32; E. Schweizer, 'Traditional ethical patterns in the Pauline and post-Pauline letters and their development', *Text and Interpretation* (FS M. Black, ed. E. Best and R. McL. Wilson, Cambridge, 1979), pp. 195–209; F. Stagg, 'The Domestic Code and Final Appeal in Ephesians 5.21–6.24', *RevExp* 76 (1979), pp. 541–52; D. L. Balch, *Let Wives Be Submissive: The Domestic Code in 1 Peter* (SBLMS 26, Chico, CA, 1981); K. Thaede, 'Zur historischen Hintergrund der "Hausta-feln" des NT', *Pietas* (FS B. Kötting, ed. E. Dassmann and K. S. Frank, JAC Ergänzungsband 8, Münster Westfallen, 1980), pp. 259–68; J. Gnilka, *Der Kolosserbrief* (HTKNT, Freiburg, Basel, Wien, 1980), pp. 205–16; D. Lührmann, 'Neutestamentliche Haustafeln und antike Okonomie', *NTS* 27 (1980/1), pp. 83–97; K. Müller, 'Die Haustafel des Kolosserbriefes und das antike Frauenthema. Eine kritische Rückschau auf alter Ergeb-nisse', *Die Frau im Urchristentum* (ed. G. Dautzenberg, H. Merklein, K. Müller, Freiberg, Basel, Wien, 1982), pp. 263–319; J. H. Elliott, *A Home for the Homeless* (London, 1982), pp.

204–20; G. E. Cannon, *The Use of Traditional Materials in Colossians* (Macon, GA, 1983), pp. 95–131; D. C. Verner, *The Household of God: The Social World of the Pastoral Epistles* (SBLDS 71, Chico, CA, 1983); A. S. di Marco, 'Ef 5,21–6,9', *RivB* 31 (1983), pp. 189–207; K. Berger, *Formgeschichte des Neuen Testaments* (Heidelberg, 1984), pp. 135–41, and *ANRW*, 1984, II 25, pp. 1078–86; P. Fiedler, *RAC*, XIII, pp. 1063–73; L. Hartmann, 'Code and Context: A Few Reflections on the Paraenesis of Col 3.6–4.1'. *Tradition and Interpretation of the New Testament* (FS E. E. Ellis, ed. G. F. Hawthorne and O. Betz, Tübingen, 1987), pp. 237–47; P. Pokorný, *Der Brief des Paulus an die Kolosser* (TKNT, Berlin, 1987), pp. 149–52; B. Witherington, *Women in the Earliest Churches* (SNTSMS 59, Cambridge, 1988), pp. 42–61; M. Y. Macdonald, *The Pauline Churches* (SNTSMS 60, Cambridge, 1988), pp. 102–22; G. Strecker, 'Die neutestamentlichen Haustafeln' (Kol 3,18–4,1 und Eph 5,22–6,9) in *Neues Testament und Ethik* (FS R. Schnackenburg, ed. H. Merklein, 1989), pp. 349–75; S. Moyter, 'The Relationship between Paul's Gospel of "All one in Christ Jesus" (Galatians 3.28) and the "Household Codes"', *VoxEv* 19 (1989), pp. 33–48; H. Gielen, *Tradition und Theologie neutestamentlicher Haustafelethik* (Frankfort am Main, 1990); H. von Lips, 'Die Haustafel als "Topos" im Rahmen der urchristlichen Paränese und des Titusbriefes', *NTS* 40 (1994), pp. 361–80; M. Theobald, 'Heilige Hochzeit', *Metaphorik und Mythos im Neuen Testament* (ed. K. Kertelge, Questiones Disputatae, 126, Herder, Freiburg, Basel, Wien, 1990), pp. 220–54.

Index of Scripture and other Ancient Literature

New Testament

Index of Authors and Names

217

Index of Subjects